Broadneck
Baloney

THE BOOK
THE BEST OF THE WURST !

Robert Bowie Johnson, Jr.

For
Nancy Lee,
Lisa and Chris,
Beth and Mike,
Dominic, Gigi, and Ryan

Special Thanks to C. G. Smith of Bella's Liquors for
Making the Production of this Book Possible.

Thanks also to

Our Advertising Sponsors

Arnold Pharmacy 26
Bay Country Painters 13
Bella's Liquors 125
Brass Monkey Restaurant 33
Broadneck Pharmacy 23
Cape Ace Hardware 16
Cape Hair Scene 144
Chesapeake Painting 39
D&A Heating and Cooling 56
Eslin Solutions Plus 88
Fairwinds Marina 144
Hoffman Animal Hospital 87
Long and Foster, Stacy Early 9

Marone Law Group 41
Noreen's Boutique Spa 45
O'Loughlin's Restaurant & Pub 53
Quality Care Automotive, Inc. 176
Richard's Tree Care 176
RJ's Plumbing and Septic 23
Sir Speedy Printing 122
Solution One Home Repair 122
Solving Light Books 48
The Living Room 55
Vizzini's Pizza and Subs 11
Whimsicality 55

© 2016 Solving Light Books
727 Mount Alban Drive
Annapolis, MD 21409

ISBN-13: 9781540855367

ISBN-10: 1540855368

BroadneckBaloney.com

rbowiej@comcast.net

Preface

Elvis Presley, Jr. came to Broadneck in March of 2010 looking for his father. He hired me as advertising director for the publication he called the *Broadneck Baloney*—a print medium to make his purpose known. We published the first of our 36 issues in June of that year.

Some locals said that they had spotted Elvis Sr. at Cape Ace, Fairwinds Marina, Whimsicality, and even at Noreen's Boutique Spa. Those locals were all liars who gave false hope to a very good man.

Elvis Jr. endured cruel joke after cruel joke about his father such as "What was Elvis' last great hit? The bathroom floor." And "What's the difference between Elvis Sr. and a Broadneck intellectual? One day we might find a Broadneck intellectual."

One Cape jokester swore he met Elvis Sr. right here on Broadneck, and that the great singer presented him with new lyrics to "Return to Sender" with a new title: "Return to Vendor":

> I bought a wiener from the vendor
> He put it on a bun
> But I had to take it back cuz
> The wiener wasn't done
> Return to vendor
> Hot dog undone
> Not enough mustard
> Soggy bun

How nasty! Such insensitive mockery! That is what Elvis Jr., as editor of the *Baloney*, lived with day in and day out. In June of 2015, just after the publication of what would be our final issue, Elvis Jr. disappeared. Some say he moved to Memphis to be near Graceland. Some say he moved to Hollywood. Others say he intended to go to both these places, but got no farther than Edgewater. In a way, I sort of dedicate this book to him, and all he has done in a literary vein for the caring people of Broadneck. We miss him. We want to see him again. And so let the search for Elvis Presley Jr. begin!

Bob Johnson
Winter, 2016

I heard someone in New York City gets stabbed every 52 seconds. POOR GUY!

THE BENEFITS OF LAUGHTER

Physical Health Benefits
Boosts Immunity
Lowers Stress Hormones
Decreases Pain
Relaxes Muscles
Prevents Heart Disease

Mental Health Benefits
Adds Joy and Zest to Life
Eases Anxiety and Fear
Relieves Stress
Improves Mood
Enhances Resilience

Social Benefits
Strengthens Relationships
Attracts Others to Us
Enhances Teamwork
Helps Diffuse Conflict
Promotes Group Bonding

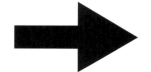

So Let's Get to It →

Why did the Broadneck scientist install a knocker on his door? He wanted to win the No-bell prize!

Why Does It Take 1 Million Sperm to Fertilize an Egg? THEY WON'T STOP AND ASK FOR DIRECTIONS.

CONTENTS

THE EDITOR'S CORNER 8, 62, 79
DOCTOR! DOCTOR! 12
HOW NOT TO PAINT A CHURCH STEEPLE 13
LIMERICKS 14, 64
LAW AND DISORDER IN THE COURT 17, 29
ASK AUNT BERTHABELLE 18, 66, 91, 121
GOD BLESS THE IRISH 21, 69, 95
ANTI-JOKES 24, 71, 101
LITTLE JOHNNY 27, 73
BALONEY CROSSWORD PUZZLE 30
EVENTS AT THE BRASS MONKEY 32

Important News You May Have Missed

BROADNECK NOW A NUDIST COLONY 34
CAPITAL NEWSPAPER FOLDS 36
WE'RE NOW RICHARD'S TREE CARE COUNTY 37
BOB JOHNSON - MAN OF THE YEAR 38
WHAT TO DO NEXT GENE DISCOVERED 40
ARNOLD COUPLE WINS $10 MILLION 42
NEW PILL CURES PEEVISH INGRATITUDE 43
LOCALS WIN FREE TRIP AROUND THE SUN 44
LONG-STANDING MOON MYSTERY SOLVED 46
EINSTEIN LOOK-ALIKE WINS HUGE PRIZE 47
BAT CHILD CAPTURED BY TREE EXPERTS 49

BALONEY WORD PUZZLES 50, 75, 83
EVERYTHING GOES AT ONCE 51, 82, 87, 120
J. HANDEY - WHAT I'D SAY TO THE MARTIANS 52
PLAIN OLD BROADNECK JOKES 54, 76, 103
BROADNECK BLONDES 58, 117, 130
FUNNY CHURCH BULLETINS 84, 127
CLASSES FOR MEN TAUGHT BY WOMEN 85
WHY SOME MEN PREFER DOGS TO WIVES 86
BELLA'S FOR SURE FOLKLORE 88
MY MOTHER TAUGHT ME . . . 94
WHY IT'S GREAT TO BE A GUY 97
REAL HEADLINES 98
REVIEW OF J. HANDEY'S "DEEP THOUGHTS" 99
KIDS TODAY - PLUS HAIR JOKES 100

20 THINGS YOU'LL NEVER HEAR A MAN SAY 105
WHAT THE MOVIES TELL US 106
CATHOLIC SCHOOL TEST ANSWERS 107
TOP 21 PICK-UP LINES 108
PROFOUND PUNS 109
PITHY PUNS FOR PERSPICUOUS PERSONS 110
SOME AMUSING PALINDROMES 111
TOM SWIFTIES 112
GRADE SCHOOL PAPERS 113
MOST INTERESTING MAN 114
MOST INTERESTING WOMAN 116
CLASSES FOR WOMEN TAUGHT BY MEN 128
HOW TO ASK A WOMAN A QUESTION 129
GOLF JOKES 132
CAPTIVATING THOUGHTS ON WINE 134
NOSTICMEISTER'S ANSWERS 135
INTERVIEW WITH JAY VIZZINI JR. 137
WHY DID I NAME MY DOG SEX? 137
BALONEY MATE OF THE YEAR 138
DID WE READ THESE SIGNS RIGHT? 140
THE MEANING OF GREAT ART 141
SOME QUESTIONS TO PONDER 142
FISHING WITH PETE 143
20 REASONS FISHING IS BETTER THAN SEX 145
36 THINGS A BREDNECK NEVER SAYS 146
CHURCHY JOKES 147
JAKE AND JANICE 149
AND THEN THE FIGHT STARTED 150
AN EMBARRASSING MIX-UP 151
THE FORTHRIGHT DRUGGIST 151
JUST PLAIN OLD JOKES 152
KID'S BOOK TITLES YOU'LL NEVER SEE 154
HIGH SCHOOL ENGLISH ANALOGIES 155
30 ADVANTAGES OF BEING A WOMAN 156

SPECIAL SECTION:

THE TRUE BALONEY HISTORY OF BROADNECK
with
16 SOUP RECIPES AND 2 STORIES FROM THE
REALM OF QUEEN ARNOLD 157

I hate when I am about to hug someone really sexy and my face hits the mirror.

The (First) Editor's Corner (June 2010)

Well, I guess you're wondering why you're reading this when you've probably guessed that my weakly editorial is not supposed to be funny but rather informative and illuminating.

Does Anne Arundel County really need another top-quality magazine? Yes, if this magazine helps me find my father. When I was just a lad, Dad brought me to Broadneck many times to get away from deranged fans, and to hide from greedy and imprudent agents. That's even part of the reason Dad pretended to get fat, take drugs, and die.

When Dad first brought me here, Broadneck was just a network of dirt roads. Gripping a .44 Magnum with both hands was most everybody's idea of gun control. The redneck women didn't even bother to take their Winstons from their lips when they cussed you out. Dad kind of liked that. College Parkway was only a dream and nobody here had ever heard of a breakfast burrito. The Broadneck Peninsula might still be full of redneck women, but oh, how everything else has changed!

Dad is here on Broadneck somewhere. He's been spotted at Cape Ace Hardware. I am convinced that he was drawn there because the Wade family owns it, and Dad's favorite movie role was as Jess Wade in the classic, *Charro*. They called Jess Wade Charro because an evil man named Vince Hackett burned Jess with a hot poker on the neck to make everybody think that he was the one who stole a golden cannon from a museum in Mexico. Charro was charred, get it?

Fake Wades in the movies and real Wades on Broadneck are very much alike. They're tough but kind, proud to be honest but humble enough to accept the thanks of a grateful town, unfriendly to outlaws but quick to support the Jaycees, chased by handsome Mexican soldiers wearing tall blue hats but never caught. Sometimes the Wades engage in confusing dialog and the plot wears thin, but they know what side of the street their butter is on. Dad just wanted to be around them for old time's sake. That's why he risked public exposure at Cape Ace.

Dad, if you have picked up this magazine at Cape Ace and are reading this now, please do what is indicated.

Your Concerned Son, Elvis Presley, Jr., Editor

The Editor's Corner

It has come to my attention that local scientist, George Hampton, has had the irreverent audacity to conduct cloning experiments involving my father without first informing me. Four years ago, according to reliable sources hanging out in the woods behind the Cape St. Claire Shopping Center, Mr. Hampton purchased hair clippings and nail parings belonging to my father from a collector in Nashville.

Mr. Hampton unsuccessfully cloned my father from the DNA samples he extracted from the hair and nails. I say unsuccessfully because, although the clone looked exactly like Dad, it would not sing. When it opened its mouth, all that would come out was a series of dirty words.

The clone of my father began to open its mouth at the most inappropriate times, embarrassing Mr. Hampton in front of friends, family, acquaintances and strangers. Eventually, the clone would not keep its mouth shut at all. Even as the clone slept, it repeated one smutty phrase after another.

Finally, when Mr. Hampton could no longer take the clone's unrelenting disgusting banter, he resolved to destroy his creation. He escorted the creature to the top of the Bay Bridge in the darkest hour of the night and pushed it over the metal railing. Fortunately, an alert motorist saw him do it, and got his license plate number. Subsequently, I am happy to report, Mr. George Hampton was arrested and charged with making an obscene clone fall.

I advise all other scientists who may be engaged in the same murky business to stop cloning around.

Let me clear up any confusion about what we folks living on this peninsula should call ourselves. Broadneckians is the correct word to describe us. Broadneckites, on the other hand, is a word which conjures up images of religious extremism, while the term, Broadnecker makes us locals feel like chumps. You and I and everyone else living here are tried and true Broadneckians. Be proud, Broadneckians!

Elvis Presley, Jr., Editor

Stacy Early, Realtor®

Broadneck Resident

Broadneck Class of 1984

Serving *your* Real Estate Needs

443-623-8116 Direct

LONG & FOSTER
───── REAL ESTATE ─────
LUXURY HOMES
CHRISTIE'S
INTERNATIONAL REAL ESTATE

Branch Office 410-544-4000

568 A Ritchie Highway, Severna Park, MD 21146

You're not fat, you're just . . . easier to see.

The Editor's Corner

Well, there are a lot of reasons to save your *Baloney*. It may, for example, be used as a portable placemat. Just turn the page and you get a fresh place mat every day! Or better yet, have your *Baloney* placemat laminated at *Sir Speedy Printing*.

If you're a student, you might want to bleach off the ink, and use it for a notebook.

Try opening it up and placing it on your front step as a door mat. Or use it as a trendy hand fan all summer long. Or why not roll the *Baloney* into a starter log, and save it for this winter.

The *Baloney* also makes an attractive coaster for something a little larger than usual, like a pitcher of beer. Or roll up the *Baloney* and heroically swat flies.

Do friends and family have trouble hearing you, or do they tend to ignore what you say? Roll up the *Baloney* tight on one end and use it as a megaphone. Once you routinely speak to your family and friends through your *Baloney* megaphone, you are guaranteed to get the respect you deserve.

Do you have trouble hearing what people are saying to you? Do they whisper a lot and look at each other with sideward glances? Roll up the *Baloney* on one end and use it as a hearing aid. I hope when you find out what they are saying about you, it doesn't hurt your feelings. It's hard to express how upset I get when I hear people say that I'm not a serious editor, and that the search for my father is grounded in idiotic obstinacy.

If you have a dog or a small child who enjoys chasing objects, roll up the *Baloney*, put a rubber band around it, and you've got a fetch stick.

Baloney paper makes excellent spitballs.

Carefully take out the staples and you've got two free staples for your own stapler! Then, if you have a parakeet or some other kind of bird, line the bottom of its cage with the *Baloney*. Studies show that puppies house-trained on *Baloney* paper learn to go outside twice as fast as

Old telephone books make ideal personal address books. Simply cross out the names and addresses of people you don't know.

Apply red nail polish to your nails before clipping them. The red nails will be much easier to spot on your bathroom carpet, unless you have a red carpet, in which case a contrasting polish should be selected.

I'm just taking up space with jokes so that I don't have to write about Dad and especially, about Mom. I am very sensitive. I want to go about this in the right way. Doctors do it with patience, bankers do it with interest, lawyers do it in their briefs, elevator operators do it going up and down, math teachers do it with unknowns, and we editors have to do it by the book.

The little broom wanted to know where he came from so he asked his mother about it. "Well, son," she said, blushing a little, "Your father and I swept together." Ba-Da-Broom!

A woman gets on a bus with her baby. The bus driver says: "That's the ugliest baby that I've ever seen." The woman goes to the rear of the bus and sits down, fuming. She says to a man next to her, "That driver just insulted me!" The man says, "You go right up there and tell him off! Go ahead, I'll hold your pet baby warthog for you."

Two hunters are out in the woods when one of them collapses. He doesn't seem to be breathing and his eyes are glazed. The other man pulls out his cell phone and calls emergency services. He gasps to the operator: "My friend is dead! What can I do?" The operator, in a calm, soothing voice replies: "Take it easy. I can help. First, let's make sure he's dead." There is a silence, then a shot is heard. Back on the phone, the hunter says, "Okay, now what?"

A recent study found that the average American walks about 900 miles a year. Another recent study found that Americans drink an average of 22 gallons of beer a year.

That means, on average, Americans get about 41 miles per gallon. Not Bad.

Elvis Presley, Jr., Editor

I'm Not Saying I'm Batman. I'M JUST SAYING BATMAN AND I HAVE NEVER BEEN SEEN TOGETHER.

I Read a Book about Helium. I COULDN'T PUT IT DOWN.

"The Original" Vizzini's PIZZA 'n SUBS
1370 CAPE ST. CLAIRE ROAD, ANNAPOLIS, MD

Our Dough is Baked Fresh Daily - 'Cause That's How You Like It!

Panorama of the Sicilian Town of Vizzini in Italy.

TRADITION • EXPERIENCE • DEDICATION • KNOW-HOW

Vizzini's first opened in August of 1977 in Glen Burnie, Maryland. Jay Vizzini, Sr. partnered with Nick Greenberg, both 24, with the financing from Philip Vizzini, Jay's grandfather. Jay and Nick worked hard to make Vizzini's a success, often sleeping at the store because of the long hours. Because of their emphasis on quality and top-notch customer service, Vizzini's flourished immediately. A year or so later, Jay and Nick decided to open another location in Pasadena, MD.

Eventually, Jay and Nick went their separate ways but have remained great friends. Jay kept the Glen Burnie store and Nick kept the location in Pasadena, and began calling it Nick's Pizza. In 1981, wanting to help his older brother, Philip Vizzini, Jay worked to open another Vizzini's Pizza in Pasadena, Maryland. Philip remained in business until 1986 and because of issues with the landlord, decided to close his shop.

In 1986, Jay looked to expand Vizzini's Pizza stores throughout the Maryland area, opening the store now in the Cape St. Claire Shopping Center. Soon, with hard work and dedication to the desires of their patrons, the Annapolis and Glen Burnie stores were very busy, so much so that other locations were in the works. While some partnerships flourished, others did not. Because of those partnerships, Jay Vizzini's first pizza shop, Vizzini's on Aquahart Road in Glen Burnie is no longer associated with the Cape St. Claire location.

In 1991, Jay expanded once again by opening a new store in Baltimore, Maryland. He also took this time to rebrand the Vizzini's look to set it apart from the rest. An artist created the new Vizzini's Pizza 'n Subs logo; then Vinnie the Mouse and our distinctive motto "Cause that's how you like it" were born.

In 1992, Jay went back to his roots, just concentrating on one location and making the best and freshest pizza and subs around. Cape St. Claire had a new look and sales were up. Since then Vizzini's has continued to stay ingrained in the local Broadneck community as a family favorite. Now Jay Vizzini, Jr. operates the store, maintaining our high standards, always offering fresh choices with the kinds of great tastes Broadneck deserves.

410 - 757 - 8600   Vizzinis.com

I Told My Wife She Was Drawing Her Eyebrows Too High. She Look Surprised.

DOCTOR DOCTOR

Doctor, Doctor, I Keep Thinking I'm Invisible.
Who Said That?

Doctor, Doctor, I Broke My Arm in Two Places.
Well, Don't Go Back to Either of Those Places.

Doctor, Doctor, You have got to help me out.
Certainly. Which way did you come in?

Doctor, Doctor, I Feel Like a Pair of Curtains.
For God's Sake, Man, Pull Yourself Together!

Doctor, Doctor, I Snore So Loud I Keep Myself Awake.
Sleep in Another Room Then.

Doctor, Doctor, I've Lost My Memory.
When Did This Happen?
When Did What Happen?

Doctor, Doctor, Everyone Thinks I'm a Liar.
I Don't Believe You.

Doctor, Doctor, I Keep Seeing Double.
Please Sit on the Couch.
Which One?

Doctor, Doctor, I Feel Like a Sewing Needle.
I See Your Point.

Doctor, Doctor, I'm Having Trouble with My Breathing.
I'll Give You Something That Will Soon Put a Stop to That.

Doctor, Doctor, I Swallowed a Bone.
Are You Choking?
No, I'm Very Serious.

Doctor, Doctor, I Keep Thinking I'm a Bell.
Take These Pills, and If They Don't Help, Give Me a Ring.

Doctor, Doctor, I'm Starting to Think I'm a Carrot.
Please Don't Get Yourself into a Stew.

Doctor, Doctor, I'm at Death's Door.
Don't Worry, We'll Soon Pull You through.

Doctor, Doctor, My son has swallowed my pen. What should I do?
Use a pencil until I get there.

Doctor, Doctor, I Think I'm a Dog.
Lie on the Couch and We'll Talk about It.
I'm not Allowed on the Couch.

Doctor, Doctor, I've Heard That Exercise Kills Germs.
Maybe, But How Do You Get the Germs to Exercise?

Doctor, Doctor, I Have a Strawberry Stuck in My Ear.
Don't Worry I Have Some Cream for That.

Doctor, Doctor, I've Become a Kleptomaniac.
Have You Taken Anything for It?
So Far, a TV, a Wallet and a Necklace.

Doctor, Doctor, Every Time I Stand Up Quickly, I See Mickey Mouse, Donald Duck, and Goofy.
How Long Have You Been Having These Disney Spells?

Doctor, Doctor, I've Got Amnesia.
It Might Ease Your Mind If You Forget about It for a While.

Doctor, Doctor, I've Got a Little Bit of Lettuce Sticking out of My Bottom.
That May Be Just the Tip of the Iceberg.

Doctor, Doctor, I Feel Like a $100 Bill.
Why Don't You Buy Something at the Mall?
The Change Will Do You Good.

Patient: Doctor, I Think I Swallowed a Pillow.
Doctor: How do you feel?
Patient: A Little Down in the Mouth.

Doctor, Doctor, I Think I Have Deja Vu.
Didn't I See You Yesterday?

How Long Have You Been Working for the Company? EVER SINCE THEY THREATENED TO FIRE ME.

BAY COUNTRY PAINTERS
Adding Beauty and Value to Homes Since 1983

We offer interior & exterior residential and commercial painting and staining services. We also offer power washing, wallpaper stripping, wall preparation and repair. We are experts at giving your home an unparalleled facelift for an unparalleled price. A few coats of paint could be the difference between a house that you like and a home that you love!

Celebrating Our 32nd Year

Please Visit Our Web Site to See Our Extensive Portfolio and Many Testimonials:

BayCountryPainters.com

410.544.4400
MHIC No. 39306

HOW NOT TO PAINT A CHURCH STEEPLE
By Gladys Friday

As a retired painter, I feel an obligation to warn those who may be prone to make the same mistake I did when I was starting out as a young woman in that trade. I tried to save time and money by cutting corners. Believe me, it just doesn't pay. Let me tell you the story.

I had secured a job painting the entire outside of a local church. Everything went perfectly until I got to the steeple. I was about halfway finished it when I realized I was about to run out of paint. To finish the job, I would need to climb back down the ladder and drive to the paint store to get another can of paint. But it was getting late, and it would be dark by the time I got back.

Plus, even though my home was more than a mile away, I could smell the bacon burger my husband, Chauncey, was fixing me for supper.

What to do? Noting that I had a can of paint thinner, I began to rationalize that getting home to that bacon burger was more important than seeing that the job was done right. So I thinned out the remaining paint, and finished painting the steeple, thinking that it was so far off the ground no one would ever notice that I had let my standards slide this one time.

I found out very quickly that Someone noticed. Just as I began to climb down the ladder to head home, a dark cloud appeared directly over the church. A loud clap of thunder shook the church and knocked me off the ladder. As I looked up from the ground, a deluge of water poured out of that little cloud, washing off every bit of paint I had applied. Then a voice came out of the cloud saying, "Repaint and thin no more." I repainted the next day, and stopped thinning for good. Take heed, my young friends.

The Tempting Burger My Husband Was Making Was Not Worth It.

A photon goes thru airport security. The TSA agent asks if he has any luggage. The photon says, "No, I'm traveling light."

I Know Who Stole My Coffee, But I Don't Have Any Grounds to Charge Him.

LIMERICKS

Humpty Dumpty sat on a wall.
Humpty Dumpty had a great fall.
All the king's horses, all the king's men
Had scrambled eggs for breakfast
again.

Mary had a little lamb,
Her father shot it dead.
Now it goes to school with her,
Between two hunks of bread.

There was a young lady from Thrace,
Whose corsets grew too tight to lace.
Her mother said, "Nelly,
There's more in your belly,
Than ever went in through your face."

I once took the Duchess to tea.
She was tense as a person could be.
Her rumblings abdominal
Were simply phenomenal:
And everyone thought it was me.

A flea and a fly in a flue,
Were imprisoned, what could they do?
Said the flea "Let us fly."
Said the fly "Let us flee."
So they flew thru a flaw in the flue.

An oyster from Kalamazoo
Confessed he was feeling quite blue.
For he said, "As a rule,
When the weather turns cool,
I invariably get into a stew."

There once was a man from Peru
Whose limericks stopped at line two.

There was an old lady from Ghent
who slept on a bed of cement.
Her bed was well-used
and her body well-bruised
and the back of her head had a dent.

There once was a woman from Trent
who never liked paying her rent.
"My paycheck's so small,
when I go to the mall
I find all my money's been spent."

There was a young fellow from Belfast
whom I wanted so badly to tell fast
not to climb up the stair
as the top step was air.
And that's why the young lad fell fast.

A painter who lived in Great Britain
interrupted 2 girls with their knittin'
He said with a sigh,
"That park bench - well I
just painted it right where you're
sittin.'"

An amoeba name Max & his brother
were sharing a drink with each other.
In the midst of their quaffing
they split themselves laughing,
and each of them now is a mother.

There once was a lady named Ferris
Whom nothing could ever embarrass.
'Til the bath salts one day,
In the tub where she lay,
Turned out to be Plaster of Paris.

Parallel Lines Have So Much in Common. IT'S SHAME THEY'LL NEVER MEET.

When I see ads on TV with smiling, happy housewives using a new cleaning product, the only things I want to buy are the meds they must be on.

There once was an artist named Saint,
Who swallowed some samples of paint.
All shades of the spectrum
Flowed out of his rectum
With a colorful lack of restraint.

A black widow spider named Kim
Was always so proper and prim.
But her new husband Bob
Was too much of a slob,
So she made a meal out of him.

There was a young lady of Niger
Who smiled as she rode on a tiger.
They returned from the ride
With the lady inside,
And the smile on the face of the tiger.

A minor league pitcher, McDowell
Pitched an egg at a batter named Al.
They cried, "Get a hit!"
But the egg hatched in the mitt,
And the umpire declared it a fowl.

A magazine writer named Bing
Could make copy from most anything;
But the copy he wrote
Of a ten-dollar note
Was so good he now lives in Sing Sing.

There once were 2 grumpy old dogs,
Who ate up all the world's frogs.
They put the planet on riot,
And France on a diet,
Then began to rid us of hogs.

The Limerick's furtive and mean,
To be kept under close quarantine,
Or she'll sneak to the slums,
Where she promptly becomes
Disorderly, drunk, and obscene!

Hawking's "Brief History of Time"
is such a relief! How sublime
that time, in reverse,
may un-write this verse
and un-spend my very last dime!

There was an odd fellow named Gus,
When traveling he made such a fuss.
He was banned from the train,
Not allowed on a plane,
And now travels only by bus.

There once was a man named Brice,
Who had a nasty head full of lice.
He said, If I eat them,
Then I'll have beat them!
And besides they taste very nice.

I once fell in love with a blonde,
But found that she wasn't so fond.
Of my pet turtle named Odle,
whom I'd taught how to Yodel,
So she dumped him out in the pond.

There once was a girl called Jane,
who thought she had a big brain.
She thought she was cool,
standing in a puddle of drool,
but really she was very insane.

A Computer Once Beat me at Chess. BUT IT WAS NO MATCH FOR ME AT KICK BOXING.

I Used to Date Witches BUT ONLY FOR A SPELL.

Cape ACE Hardware
410 757-0797

Here are the top 10 reasons why Cape Ace is the best hardware store in Annapolis.

1. Locally Owned
The store is owned by residents of Cape St. Claire, and we all care about our community. We have been a corporate sponsor for many events supporting the area. We hold special events in the store to encourage the community to get together and connect.

2. Conveniently Located
Our store is located in the heart of the Broadneck Peninsula in the Cape St. Claire shopping center. Many of our customers tell us they love that we are "right around the corner." It is reassuring to know that if you have run out of fuses or light bulbs, and one unexpectedly blows you can run to Cape Ace and pick one up easily.

3. Friendly Staff
Most of our staff is from the area, and customers recognize us and we recognize them. We know many of them on a first name basis, and vice versa. When you walk into Cape Ace, you will always feel welcome.

4. Quirky Selection of Doodads
Doodads are fun items you never knew you needed, but once you see them, you realize that you must have them! They make excellent gifts, too.

5. Unexpected Services
If you need a spare house key or are interested in adding a decorative touch to your home, Cape Ace can help. We offer any of the products and services of a big box store, but we can be more attentive.

6. Amazing Customer Service
Our staff knows our products and the store inside out. If you are looking for an item, we will take you to it. If you have a question about a product, we can answer it. Because we are familiar with the multiple uses of many of our products, we can offer advice on what will best serve your needs.

7. Extensive Inventory
Cape Ace has many unexpected products, we also have the items you would expect from a hardware store: fittings for plumbing, nuts and bolts, electrical equipment, quality interior and exterior house paints, and so much more. Our motto is "If we don't have it, you don't need it."

8. Seasonal Items
In the summer, we have all the things you need for a backyard bar-b-cue. In the winter, we have what you need to decorate for the holidays. If you need snow shovels or leaf bags, or sprinklers to water your lawn, Cape Ace has it!

9. Exceptional Pet Selection
We are proud of our selection of pet supplies. Cape Ace is a pet-friendly store. There have been many days where we take our pets into work. We appreciate that pets love us unconditionally add to the quality of our lives. We want to help you care for these family members as best as we can. Check out our accessories, toys, food, and more.

10. Comparable Prices
Just because we are not a huge mega store, does not mean our customers pay more. We offer comparable pricing and amazing specials on many investment items like gas grills. Our weekly flier is filled with sales that can't be beat by many of our competitors. The shelves are filled with many items to meet any budget. ☺

Life is all about perspective. The sinking of the Titanic was a miracle to the lobsters in the ship's kitchen.

Boss, an Invisible Man is at the Door. TELL HIM I CAN'T SEE HIM NOW.

LAW AND DISORDER IN THE COURT

From the Book "Disorder in the American Courts." What people actually said in court taken down and published by court reporters that had the torment of staying calm while these exchanges were taking place.

ATTORNEY: The youngest son, the 20-year-old, how old is he?
WITNESS: He's twenty, much like your Intelligence Quotient.

ATTORNEY: So the date of conception (of the baby) was August 8th?
WITNESS: Yes.
ATTORNEY: And what were you doing at that time?

ATTORNEY: She had three children, right?
WITNESS: Yes.
ATTORNEY: How many were boys?
WITNESS: None.
ATTORNEY: Were there any girls?
WITNESS: Your Honor, I think I need a different attorney. Can I get a different attorney?

ATTORNEY: Now doctor, isn't it true that when a person dies in his sleep, he doesn't know about it until the next morning?
WITNESS: Did you actually pass the bar exam?

ATTORNEY: Do you know if your daughter has ever been involved in voodoo?
WITNESS: We both do.
ATTORNEY: Voodoo?
WITNESS: We do.
ATTORNEY: You do?
WITNESS: Yes, I do voodoo, too.
ATTORNEY: You two do voodoo?
WITNESS: I'm new to voodoo.

ATTORNEY: What was the first thing your husband said to you that morning?
WITNESS: He said, "Where am I, Cathy?"
ATTORNEY: And why did that upset you?
WITNESS: My name is Susan!

ATTORNEY: What gear were you in at the moment of impact?
WITNESS: Gucci sweats and Reeboks.

ATTORNEY: Are you sexually active?
WITNESS: No, I just lie there.

ATTORNEY: This *myasthenia gravis*, does it affect your memory at all?
WITNESS: Yes.
ATTORNEY: And in what ways does it affect your memory?
WITNESS: I forget.
ATTORNEY: You forget? Can you give us an example of something you forgot?

ATTORNEY: Were you present when your picture was taken?
WITNESS: Are you sh****ng me?

ATTORNEY: Are you qualified to give a urine sample?
WITNESS: Are you qualified to ask that question?

ATTORNEY: Was that the same nose you broke as a child?

ATTORNEY: Could you see him from where you were standing?
WITNESS: I could see his head.
ATTORNEY: And where was his head?
WITNESS: Just above his shoulders.

ATTORNEY: Are you married?
WITNESS: No, I'm divorced.
ATTORNEY: And what did your husband do before you divorced him?
WITNESS: A lot of things I didn't know about.

Will Taking the Shell off My Snail Making Him Move Faster? NO. IT WILL MAKE HIM MORE SLUGGISH.

Bella's Wine and Spirits Presents...
ASK AUNT BERTHABELLE
Answers to Life's More Peculiar Problems

DEAR AUNT BERTHABELLE: My friends and I in the Broadneck Knitting Club feel that there is too much sex in the movies. I am hoping you feel the same way we do. *Anita Bath, Bay Hills*.

DEAR ANITA: I'm not sure how I feel about sex in the movies. I have to admit that I'm usually too wrapped up in the film to notice what the rest of the audience is doing.

DEAR AUNT BERTHABELLE: I've been reading up on California. In 1850, California became a state. It has changed so much since those days, hasn't it, Aunt Berthabelle? *Ella Mentry, Amberly*.

DEAR ELLA: I'm not so sure California has changed that much at all. In 1850, they had no electricity. The state government had no money. Almost everyone spoke Spanish. There were gun fights in the streets. So basically, it was just like California today, except that the women had real breasts, and men didn't hold hands, at least not in public.

DEAR AUNT BERTHABELLE: A friend of mine, an attorney named Strange, died. I and some other friends asked the tombstone maker to inscribe on his memorial, "Here lies Strange, an honest man, and a lawyer." But the inscriber insisted that such an inscription would be confusing, because people passing by would tend to think that three men were buried under the stone, instead of one. Can you suggest an alternate inscription that would be more appropriate? *Chris P. Creem, Ferry Farms*.

DEAR CHRIS: Yes, I can. I suggest you have inscribed, "Here lies a man who was both honest and a lawyer." That way, whenever anyone walks by the tombstone and reads it, they'll be certain to remark: "That's Strange!"

DEAR AUNT BERTHABELLE: On Maryland Avenue in Annapolis last week, right in front of me, a particularly dirty and shabby-looking bum accosted a businessman, and asked him for a couple of dollars for dinner.

The businessman took out his wallet, extracted two dollars and asked, "If I give you this money, will you take it and buy whiskey?"

"No, I stopped drinking years ago," the bum said.

"Will you use it to gamble?"

"I don't gamble. I need everything I can get just to stay alive," the bum replied.

"Will you spend the money on greens fees at a golf course?"

"Are you nuts? I haven't played golf in 20 years," the bum said.

To my surprise, instead of giving the bum the two dollars, he offered to take him home for a terrific dinner cooked by his wife. Why would the businessman take such a grubby, smelly bum home for dinner? *Eileen Left, Cape St. Claire*.

DEAR EILEEN: I'm sure that the businessman just wanted his wife to see what a man looks like who's given up drinking, gambling, and golf.

DEAR AUNT BERTHABELLE: I have developed a rare condition, and I'm at my wit's end as to what I can do about it. Last year this time I was six feet tall. I've lost an inch a month of height so that now I am only four feet ten inches tall. My doctor hasn't done anything positive for me yet. Doesn't he care about my situation? I'm shrinking! *Amanda B. Reckonwith, The Downs*.

DEAR AMANDA: Settle down. Your doctor probably just wants you to learn to be a little patient, that's all.

DEAR AUNT BERTHABELLE: I have just started dating a French girl, and will appreciate any romantic advice you may be able to give me. *Noah Wey, Bay Hills*.

DEAR NOAH: Buy four bottles of French wine from *Bella's*; then, keep your French girlfriend out until the *oui* hours of the morning. ❂

I Always Take Everything with a Grain of Salt, a Slice of Lemon, and a Shot of Tequila.

Bella's Wine and Spirits Presents . . .
ASK AUNT BERTHABELLE
Answers to Life's More Peculiar Problems

DEAR AUNT BERTHABELLE: Over the past few years I've made some really stupid mistakes. For example, I married an ugly wife, divorced her for a poor wife, and then divorced her for a lazy wife. On top of that, I have trouble understanding what's going on in the world, in the USA, and even right here on Broadneck.

Last month I was walking with a friend by the Bay and she said, "Look at that dead bird," and I looked up in the sky for it.

My last job was in tech support for a 24/7 call center. One day I got a call from a man who asked what hours the call center was open. I told him, "The number you dialed is open 24 hours a day, 7 days a week." He then asked, "Is that Eastern or Pacific time?" I actually responded, "Uh, Eastern."

I thought I was pretty clever to keep a life-saving tool in my car designed to cut through the seat belt if I got trapped; that is, until a friend pointed out how dumb it was to keep it in the trunk.

Yesterday, I even mistook a tube of superglue for my hemorrhoid cream.

So when I walked (or rather, artfully sashayed) into *O'Loughlin's* earlier this afternoon, I was feeling very vulnerable and very stupid. I guess the guy sitting next to me picked up on my demeanor right away and sensed the guilt and shame I felt inside. He said he could help me. He said he had what he called smart pills for sale: five for ten dollars. In my state of mind, that sounded like a good deal, so I gave the guy ten bucks. I started to eat two of the little round dark "pills" right away but they tasted terrible. I said to the guy, "Hey, these pills taste like rabbit pellets." Then the guy said, "See, you're getting smarter already."

Do you think that this was some kind of a scam, and do you think I should report this guy to the authorities? *Chris P. Bacon, Funky Inlet.*

DEAR CHRIS: No need for that. I think you should just chalk it up as a bad hare day.

DEAR AUNT BERTHABELLE: I've tried just about every diet in the world, but I just can't seem to lose any weight. Do you have any suggestions? Please also keep your sarcasm to a minimum out of respect for the emotional turmoil I'm going through. *Hugh Jass, Red Sludge Creek.*

DEAR HUGH: Fat chance! I suggest you make a trip to *Cape Ace Hardware*. I guarantee you can get thinner there.

DEAR AUNT BERTHABELLE: I am a teacher at Broadneck High. More and more often students are reporting late for class. I keep hearing the excuse that they were in the lavatory and couldn't complete their bodily functions (mainly number two) before the bell. Should I keep them after school or send a note home to their parents? *Carrie Oakie, Green Sludge Pond Circle.*

DEAR CARRIE: Do both. They are quite obviously stalling for time.

DEAR AUNT BERTHABELLE: I can't stop singing or humming "The Green Green Grass of Home." It's driving me out of my mind! Some say I'm experiencing what is often called "Tom Jones Syndrome." Would you say that is a common ailment on Broadneck? *Red Rufinsore, Crud Cove.*

DEAR RED: It's not unusual.

DEAR AUNT BERTHABELLE: I have been speculating theologically for the past several years. I came up with a question I hope you can answer: Could an all-knowing and all-powerful God make a French Champagne that was so expensive that even He couldn't afford it? *Isadore A. Jar, Atlantis.*

DEAR ISADORE: Perhaps a better question might be: Could an all-merciful God cause a person like you to move so far from Broadneck that any letter you sent to me would never get here? ☺

Charles Dickens Walks into *O'Loughlin's Pub* and Orders a Martini. The Bartender Asks "Olive or Twist?"

A Cat, by Any Other Name, is Still a Sneaky Little Fur Ball That Barfs on the Furniture.

Bella's Wine and Spirits Presents . . .
ASK AUNT BERTHABELLE
Answers to LIfe's More Peculiar Problems

DEAR AUNT BERTHABELLE: Our world sure is in a mess, and it's so difficult finding people willing to get involved to change things. Which do you think is the biggest problem we're facing today, ignorance or apathy? *Peter Dout, Kent Island.*

DEAR PETER: Quite frankly, I don't know and I don't care.

DEAR AUNT BERTHABELLE: I've only lived on Broadneck for six months but I know the importance of our volunteer fire department. So last week, I stopped by the fire station on Cape St. Claire Road to make a donation. Just as I got there, a man ran out of the station with a key in his hand, jumped in a fire engine, and started it up. Three men ran after him hollering, "Stop him! He's no fireman. That's Chauncy Inne, and he's trying to get even with his ex-girlfriend!"

I followed him in my Toyota truck. Driving the wrong way on the parking lot, Chauncey Inne stopped right in front of *Bella's Wine and Spirits*, pulled the fire hose through the door, and was just about to squirt down his ex as she was buying her lottery tickets, and all the other *Bella's* customers. I grabbed my handy hedge clippers and snipped the hose in two. I was just glad that I happened along at the right time and was able to prevent Inne from dampening the spirits of many good Broadneck citizens. *Les Rural, Revell Downs.*

DEAR LES: Allow me to offer you the unrestrained gratitude of all the thinking people of Broadneck. I assume, of course, that the friendly crew at *Bella's* thanked you for stopping Inne.

DEAR AUNT BERTHABELLE: I feel so ignored all the time. Why don't friends and family want to deal with me? I mean, like everybody ignores me. People look right through me as if I am not even there. What do you recommend I do to change the situation? *Elmer Sklue, Amberly.*

DEAR AUNT BERTHABELLE: So many otherwise worthy individuals these days are ending sentences with prepositions, you know, the kind of people it's hard to have patience with. Do they realize the grammatical mess they're getting into? Whom do they think their faulty language is going to be corrected by? I have to wonder what they are thinking of. What is the world coming to? *Trudy Sepchun, Mago Vista.*

DEAR TRUDY: I would say that you are a very weird person who has some small difficulty understand where it's at, but that would end my sentence with a preposition. So I'll simply put my sentence in the form of a question: How come you can't grasp where it's at, you preposterous cretin?

DEAR AUNT BERTHABELLE: I recently took a business trip to a town in the heart of Alabama. I was really impressed with their Nativity scene outside the firehouse. Great skill and talent had gone into creating it. One small feature bothered me, however: Something that really puzzled me; it seemed so foreign to my experiences around holiday time when I was growing up in New York City—The three wise men were wearing firemen's helmets. Totally unable to come up with a reason or explanation, I left.

At a Quick Stop on the edge of town, I asked the lady behind the counter about the helmets. She exploded into a rage, yelling at me, "You damn Yankees never do read the Bible! If you don't know the passage about the three wise men wearing helmets, I'm not going to tell it to you. Now get out!" What passage was she talking about? *Barbara Seville, Tydings-on-the-Bay.*

DEAR BARBARA: That's an easy one. They put firemen's helmets on the Nativity figures because the passage about the birth of Jesus is the one that says "the three wise men came from a far." ❈

Why Should the Number 288 Never Be Mentioned? IT'S TWO GROSS.

A Local Shop Has Promised a Free Abacus with Each Purchase. BUT CAN YOU COUNT ON IT?

GOD BLESS THE IRISH 1

"Didja hear the news?" asked Keenan of his pal at *O'Loughlin's*. "Harrigan drank so much, his wife left him!"
"Bartender! Give me six boilermakers!"

Paddy was an accomplished drinker. The priest met him one day, and gave him a strong lecture about drink. He said, "If you continue drinking as you do, you'll gradually get smaller and smaller, and eventually you'll turn into a mouse." This frightened the life out of Paddy. He went home that night, and said to his wife, "Bridget . . . if you should notice me getting smaller and smaller, will ye kill that blasted cat?"

An Englishman, a Scotsman and an Irishman each order a Guinness at *O'Loughlin's*. Upon being served, each finds a fly in his beer. Repulsed, the Englishman sends his back. The Scotsman gently flicks the fly out of his mug and begins drinking. The Irishman, carefully lifts the fly up over the beer by its wings and screams, "Spit it out! Spit it out!"

Casey and Riley agreed to settle their dispute by a fight, and it was understood that whoever wanted to quit should say "Enough." Casey got Riley down and was hammering him unmercifully when Riley called out several times, "Enough!" As Casey paid no attention, but kept on administering punishment, a bystander said, "Why don't you let him up? Don't you hear him say that he's had enough?" "I do," says Casey, "but he's such a liar, you can't believe him."

Paddy was tooling along the road one fine day when the local policeman, a friend of his, pulled him over. "What's wrong, Seamus?" Paddy asked. "Well didn't ya know, Paddy, that your wife fell out of the car about five miles back?" said Seamus. "Ah, praise the Almighty!" Paddy replied with relief. "I thought I'd gone deaf!"

A visiting Irishman walked into *O'Loughlin's Pub* and a regular customer suggested to him: "I'll give you $200 if you let me smash ten beer bottles on your head."
The Irishman thought for a while and finally agreed, thinking he could use a couple hundred extra bucks.
The pub regular smashed the first bottle on the Irishman's head, then the second and so on, but he stopped after smashing nine bottles.
"So, when are you going to smash the tenth bottle?" asked the Irishman.
"I am not a total idiot," the pub regular replied, "Then I would have to give you that $200."

An Irish priest and a rabbi get into a car accident at an intersection. They both get out of their cars and stumble over to the side of the road. The Rabbi says, "Oy vey! What a wreck!"
The priest asks him, "Are you all right, Rabbi?"
The rabbi responds, "Just a little shaken."
The Irish priest pulls a flask of whiskey from his coat and says, "Here, drink some of this. It will calm your nerves."
The rabbi takes the flask and drinks it down and says, "Well, what are we going to tell the police?"
"Well," the Irish priest replies, "I don't know what you'll be tellin' them. But I'll be tellin' them I wasn't the one drinkin'."

What do you call an Irishman who keeps bouncing off the walls? Rick O'Shea.

Help Stamp Out and Eradicate Superfluous Redundancy.

GOD BLESS THE IRISH 2

On the Monday before Christmas, very eager to have some fun at *O'Loughlin's* happy hour, Paddy drove around the parking lot in a sweat because he couldn't find a place to park. Looking up to heaven he said, "Lord take pity on me. If you find me a parking place I will go to Mass every Sunday for the rest of me life and give up me Irish Whiskey."

Miraculously, a parking place appeared. Paddy looked up again and said, "Never mind, Lord, I found one!"

O'Toole worked in the lumber yard for twenty years, and all that time he'd been stealing the wood and selling it. At last his conscience began to bother him and he went to confession to repent.

"Father, it's 15 years since my last confession, and I've been stealing wood from the lumber yard all those years," he told the priest.

"I understand my son," says the priest. "Can you make a Novena?"

O'Toole said, "Sure, Father. If you have the plans, I've got the lumber!"

Gallagher opened the morning newspaper and was dumbfounded to read in the obituary column that he had died. He quickly phoned his best friend Finney. "Did you see the paper?" asked Gallagher. "They say I died!!"

"Yes, I saw it!" replied Finney. "Where are ye callin' from?"

According to historians working for *O'Loughlin's* and certain Baloney insiders working with them, Saint Patrick predicted that Nostradamus would predict the future in the future. These savants also uncovered how the Irish Jig got started. They say there was too much to drink and not enough bathrooms. In addition to chasing the snakes out of Ireland, St. Patrick chased the worms out of Antarctica. That's why, to this day, there are no birds there. Then what happened?

A gentleman walked into *O'Loughlin's* on St. Paddy's Day, sat down and ordered a drink. Cindy the bartender gave him his drink, accompanied by a bowl of peanuts.

To his surprise, a voice came from the peanut bowl: "You look great tonight! You really look fantastic! Your aftershave is just wonderful!" it said.

The man became quite confused, but tried to ignore it.

Realizing he had no cigarettes, he wandered over to the cigarette machine. After inserting his money, he heard another voice from the machine. "You are an evil, ignorant and stupid fool. Do you know, you're almost as ugly as your mother!"

The man, now extremely perplexed, turned to the bartender for an explanation.

"Ah yes sir," Cindy quickly responded, "The peanuts are complimentary, but the cigarette machine is definitely out of order."

The local District Judge had given the defendant a lecture on the evils of drink. But in view of the fact that this was the first time the man had been drunk and incapable, the case was dismissed on payment of ten shillings costs.

"Now don't let me ever see your face again," said the Justice sternly as the defendant turned to go. "I'm afraid I can't promise that, sir," said the released man. "And why not?"

"Because I'm the night time barman at your regular pub!"

"I had an accident opening a can of alphabet spaghetti this morning," said Murphy.

"Were you injured?" inquired Seamus.

"No, but it could have spelled disaster," concluded Murphy.

She Was Only a Whiskey Maker, BUT HE LOVED HER STILL.

Broadneck Pharmacy

FAMILY • FRIENDLY • FAST

Refill and Review Your Prescriptions Online, Download RefillRx Mobile, and Search Our Comprehensive Wellness Library, Our Health Tips and Health News at

www.broadneckrx.net

We are a full-service neighborhood pharmacy focusing on service, commitment, safety, and the well-being of all our neighbors. We provide a personal touch that you cannot find at a corporate pharmacy. Our friendly and knowledgeable staff are always willing to go the extra mile to find that perfect product, inform you of new pharmaceutical improvements, or place custom orders - **Marcus LaChapelle, PharmD**

"SERVING THE BROADNECK PENINSULA FOR 30 YEARS"

HOURS: Mon - Fri 9 a.m. - 6 p.m.
Sat 9:00 a.m. - 1:00 p.m.
Sun Closed

269 Peninsula Farm Road
Arnold, MD 21012
(410) 544-3733

- **Family Owned and Operated**
- **Quality Work to Fit Your Budget**
- **Honesty - Integrity - Reliability**
- **Free Estimates**

Rick Jones - Born and Raised in Broadneck
MASTER PLUMBER LICENSE: #7392
OVER 25 YEARS IN BUSINESS

rjsplumbingandseptic.com
410.267.8422 Office
410.320.2699 Cell

SEWER & SEPTIC	WELL REPAIR	PLUMBING: WE INSTALL & REPAIR
• Sewer hookups	• Water well installation and repair	• Garbage disposals
• Perc tests	• Well pumps	• Faucets & toilets
• Septic repairs	• Submersible pumps	• Hot water heaters
• Septic certifications	• Pressure tanks	• Remodeling jobs
• Sewer line repairs	• Booster systems	• Sump pumps
• Sewer & drain cleaning	• Chlorination	• Battery back-up sump pumps
• Water line repair and new installs	• Jetting & cleaning	

How Come When My Wife Wants to Talk IT'S NEVER ABOUT FOOTBALL?

Bumper Sticker: ANKH IF YOU LOVE OSIRIS.

A teenage boy is getting ready to take his girlfriend to the prom. First he goes to rent a tux, but there's a long tux line at the shop and it takes forever.
Next, he has to get some flowers, so he heads over to the florist and there's a huge flower line there. He waits forever but eventually gets the flowers.
Then he heads out to rent a limo. Unfortunately, there's a long limo line at the rental office, but he's patient and gets the job done.
Finally, the day of the prom comes. The two are dancing happily and his girlfriend is having a great time. When the song is over, she asks him to get her some punch, so he heads over to the punch table and there's no punchline.

ANTI-JOKES

A duck walks into a bar. The bartender says, "What'll it be?" The duck doesn't say anything because it's a duck. It just lets out a few random quacks.

A man walks into a bar.
He's an alcoholic and it's destroying his health and ruining his family.

What do Albert Einstein and a bona fide idiot have in common?
Not much.

What's worse than a snake in your sleeping bag?
Mass slaughter of innocent civilians under an oppressive regime.

A horse walked into a bar. Several people got up and left as they spotted the potential danger in the situation.

Yo mama is so ugly that she often finds it difficult attracting members of the opposite sex.

Another horse walks into a bar and the bartender says "What can I get ya to drink?"
The horse, unable to understand human language, drops a load on the floor and prances out the door.

A girl walks into a supermarket. She picks up a banana, a can of soup, and a loaf of bread. She then walks up to the cash register to pay.
The cashier looks at her and the items she has and says, "I can tell you're single."
She smiles and responds, "How do you know that?"
He says, "Because you're ugly."

Yo mama's so fat that she should probably be worried about the increased risk of cardiovascular disease.

What do you get when you cross an apple tree and a pine tree?
Nothing. You can't cross-pollinate deciduous and coniferous trees.

Two possums walk into Cape Ace Hardware. Animal control is promptly called and the animals are released in the woods at Sandy Point.

What Did the Pirate Say on His 80th Birthday? Aye Matey.

What Word Becomes Shorter When You Add to It? SHORT.

In a dream, a gorilla in a suit walks into a bar. The bartender asks, "What can I get you today?"

The gorilla orders an apple martini and the bartender immediately gets to work.

Then, the man having this wild dream wakes up and excitedly rolls over to wake up his wife and tell her about it.

"Sarah, wake up!" he exclaims. "I just had the wildest dream! There was a talking gorilla and he ordered a martini and I made it for him and he was wearing a really cool tux and . . ."

His wife, annoyed, rolls her eyes, shakes her head, and rolls over to go back to sleep, ignoring the description of his dream.

The man then slowly rolls back over and cries himself to sleep because he realizes that his marriage is in shambles.

What was the last thing grandpa said before he kicked the bucket?
"Hey! How far do you think I can kick this bucket?"

Who refused to let the gorilla into the ballet?
Just the people who are in charge of that decision.

A giraffe walks into a bar and the bartender says, "It's probably not a good idea that you're in here. You're a very large animal and any sudden movements of yours may injure somebody. I don't know why you're here. Our glasses are not ergonomically designed for you to drink from, so you should probably leave."

ANTI-JOKES

What did Batman say to Robin before they got in the Batmobile?
"Robin, get in the Batmobile"

A rabbi, a priest and a minister walk into a bar. They sit down, order drinks and discuss current events.

Two scientists walk into a bar. The first scientist says "I'll have an H2O." The second scientist says "I'll have H2O too." The bartender does not have hydrogen peroxide on tap, and asks the second scientist if Sierra Mist is okay.

What did one fish in the aquarium tank say to the other fish?
It honestly depends on the species and situation—but, believe it or not, fish can communicate via a myriad of mediums, including body language, changes in color, sounds, and even electrical impulses.

A boy has 50 candy bars and eats 45. What does he have now?
Diabetes.

You know what's worse than finding half a worm in your apple?
Being eaten by a 20-foot scorpion.

I Dated a Woman Who Had a Taser. MAN, WAS SHE STUNNING!

Doctor, Will These Pills Make Me Better? NO ONE I'VE GIVEN THEM TO HAS EVER COME BACK.

Arnold Professional Pharmacy
Neil Patrick McGarvey Pharm.D.

WE DELIVER
Ask about Our Free Medication Delivery

OUR MISSION
Our mission is to make the pharmacy experience easy for our patients while providing truly superior customer service. We offer a variety of pharmacy services in order to achieve this. Our dedication to provide you with the most pertinent information so that you can make educated and informed decisions for your health, is what matters most to us. We are independently owned and operated offering a variety of services to help you with your health.

HOURS:
Monday - Friday: 8am - 8pm
Saturday: 9am - 6pm
Sunday: 9am - 3pm

arnoldpharmacy.com

arnoldpharmacy@gmail.com

1460 Ritchie Hwy, Arnold, MD 21012
Phone: (443) 949-8373
Fax: (443) 949-8375

AN UNUSUAL CHRISTMAS EVE VISITATION

A Broadneck man wandered into a doctor's office and asked if he could see the doctor. The receptionist was hesitant to let him in, especially as it was Christmas Eve and she was waiting to turn off the Christmas lights in the waiting room and go home; but he was very insistent. So the doctor, having completed all his consultations for the day and feeling in a "good will to men" mood, agreed to see him.

The man entered in a rather aimless manner and after some hesitation flopped into a chair and looked nervously around the room.

"How can I help you?" asked the doctor.

"Well, it's like this," said the man. "I keep thinking I'm a moth."

"A moth?"

"Yes, a moth," the man replied, "I'm convinced that I am a moth."

"Well, I'm very sorry, but you're in the wrong place. What you need is a psychiatrist."

"That's what I've been thinking all along," replied the agreeable Broadneck man.

"Well, as it happens, I know just the right psychiatrist," said the doctor. "I'll give him a call and see if he can fix an appointment for you after the holidays to help you with your moth problem."

The Broadneck man agreed and the doctor made the appointment, but the doctor had a question for the Broadneck man: "It must have been very apparent to you from the sign outside that I'm a general practitioner. So if you already knew you needed to see a psychiatrist, why did you come in?"

"Well," the Broadneck man said in a resigned voice, "The door was open and the lights were on . . ." ❈

WATCH OUT! I know karate, kung fu, judo, tae kwon do and 16 other dangerous words.

LITTLE JOHNNY (& FRIENDS)

It occurred to the Sunday School teacher, with all the emphasis on the Nativity over Christmas, that some children may get the impression that the birth of Jesus Christ was a recent event. The teacher wanted to be sure they understood that Jesus grew up and did many things. So he decided that the topic of the lesson would be "Where Is Jesus Now?"

The Sunday School teacher put this question to the class and immediately many hands shot into the air, as many of the children were keen to state their opinion.

"What do you think, Billy?"

"He's in the church, sir." Billy replied.

"Okay. What about you Rosie?"

"I believe He's in heaven, sir."

"That's good. What about you, Little Johnny?"

Little Johnny wasn't the least bit hesitant: "I know for a fact that Jesus was in our bathroom this morning. He could still be in there."

The classroom erupted with uproarious laughter; but eventually the teacher managed to quell the noise.

"Oh really," said the teacher. "What makes you think that, Little Johnny?"

When my dad knocked on the bathroom door this morning, he yelled, "Jesus Christ, are you going to be in there all day?"

Little Johnny's Chemistry teacher wanted to teach his class a lesson about the evils of liquor, so he set up an experiment that involved a glass of water, a glass of whiskey, and two worms.

"Now, class. Observe what happens to the two the worms," said the professor putting the first worm in the glass of water. The worm in the water moved about, twisting and seemingly unharmed.

He then dropped the second worm in the whiskey glass. It writhed in pain for a moment, then quickly sank to the bottom and died.

"Now kids, what lesson can we derive from this experiment?" he asked.

Little Johnny raised his hand and wisely responded, "Drink whiskey and you won't get worms!"

Little Johnny wanted to go to the zoo and pestered his parents for days. Finally mother talked his reluctant father into taking him.

"So how was it?" his mother asked when they returned home.

"It was really great, fantastic," Little Johnny replied.

"Did you and Daddy have a good time?" asked his mother.

"Yeah, Daddy really liked it too," said Little Johnny, "especially when one of the animals came home at 30 to 1!"

EVERYBODY'S FAVORITE LITTLE JOHNNY JOKE

Little Johnny's first-grade teacher asked the class to see if their parents would tell them a personal story with a moral to it, so that the kids could share it at show-and-tell the next morning.

When the time came, the teacher was pleased to see all of the eager hands raised. She called on little Susie and said, "Please share your story with a moral to it that you learned at home."

Susie said, "Well, teacher, my mom told me about the time she was milking cows on her uncle's farm as a little girl. Mom said she spent almost an hour milking a cow, but when she got up, she accidentally kicked over the milk pail. Mom said she didn't get upset, but just started milking the cow again, this time more carefully."

"What is the moral to your mom's story?" the teacher asked.

"The moral is, don't cry over spilled milk, teacher."

"Very good!" said the teacher.

Then the teacher called on little Billy: "Billy, please share your story with a moral that you learned at home."

Billy said, "My dad told me about the time he was driving along a country road and saw fresh eggs for only forty cents a dozen. He stopped, and thinking about his neighbors back home, bought twenty dozen and put them into a big basket. Then, while he was carrying it back to the car, he tripped, dropped the basket, and broke every egg."

"Well, Billy, what is the moral to your dad's story?" the teacher asked.

"Don't put all your eggs in one basket, teacher."

"Very good, Billy!" said the teacher.

Then the teacher noticed that little Johnny had his hand up. Since it was not often that Johnny participated in class activities, she called on him right away: "What story with a moral to it did you learn at home last night?"

"Well, teacher," Johnny said, "last night my dad told me about the time in Iraq that he was put on a combat outpost all alone. Dad said he had an M-16 with 19 bullets, a Bowie knife, and a bottle of whiskey. Dad said it was quiet and boring out there, so he started swiggin' on the whiskey. And he swigged and he swigged. Then he saw 20 enemy coming toward him.

"Dad said he swigged on the whiskey some more and then, one by one, picked of 19 of the enemy. But the last one kept coming toward him. Dad said he hid behind a tree, waited for him, then jumped on him and cut out his heart with his Bowie knife."

"Johnny, that is quite a gruesome story," the teacher interrupted, "but what in the world could be the moral to it?"

Johnny politely replied, "It's simple, teacher: Don't mess with my old man when he's been drinking." ◆

MORE LAW AND DISORDER IN THE COURT

From the Book "Disorder in the American Courts." What people actually said in court taken down and published by court reporters that had the torment of staying calm while these exchanges were taking place.

ATTORNEY: Doctor, before you performed the autopsy, did you check for a pulse?
WITNESS: No.
ATTORNEY: Did you check for blood pressure?
WITNESS: No.
ATTORNEY: Did you check for breathing?
WITNESS: No.
ATTORNEY: So then it is possible that the patient was alive when you began the autopsy?
WITNESS: No.
ATTORNEY: How can you be so sure, Doctor?
WITNESS: Because his brain was sitting on my desk in a jar.
ATTORNEY: I see, but could the patient have still been alive, nevertheless?
WITNESS: Yes, it is possible that he could have been alive practicing law.

ATTORNEY: Doctor, did you say he was shot in the woods?
WITNESS: No, I said he was shot in the lumbar region.

ATTORNEY: ALL of your responses MUST be oral, okay? What school did you go to?
WITNESS: Oral.

ATTORNEY: Do you recall the time that you examined the body?
WITNESS: The autopsy started at exactly 8:30 pm.
ATTORNEY: And Mr. Denton was dead at the time?
WITNESS: If not, he was by the time I finished.

ATTORNEY: How was your first marriage terminated?
WITNESS: By death.
ATTORNEY: And by whose death was it terminated?
WITNESS: Take a guess.

ATTORNEY: Can you describe the individual?
WITNESS: He was about medium height and had a beard.
ATTORNEY: Was this a male or a female?
WITNESS: Unless the circus was in town, I'm going with male.

ATTORNEY: Doctor, how many of your autopsies have you performed on dead people?
WITNESS: All of them. The live ones put up too much of a fight.

ATTORNEY: Is your appearance here this morning pursuant to a deposition notice which I sent to your attorney prior to this court date?
WITNESS: No, this is how I dress when I go to work.

May I Use Your Lawnmower? SURE. JUST DON'T TAKE IT OUT OF MY YARD.

BROADNECK BALONEY TIMES CROSSWORD
IT'S A TOUGH ONE!

ACROSS

1 Famed Mongolian banjo picker
5 Southern Israel potato bug
10 "He hath flaked the _____ of unruly themes"
14 Chartreuse Malaysian tricycle
15 Unpublished playwright Smith
16 Wiltzbagger and Mobalintus
17 Conjectural Politeness, comb. form
18 Gawking kleptomaniac
19 Belly dancing Soothsayer
20 Cringing polar reptile
22 Nancy Pelosi's new secret friend
23 Hobo's curious acquaintance

What Do You Call a Boomerang That Doesn't Come Back? A STICK.

Don't Be a Sexist. BROADS HATE THAT.

24 Yammering mesmerizers
26 Lethargic myrmidon
28 Deformed Austrian peasant
31 Fatigued meteorologist
32 Trapshooting polygamist
33 Whimpering pygmy
36 Norse god of crisp bacon
38 Female Sos
40 Deferential cannibal
41 Emasculated carhop
42 Opinionated counterfeiter
46 Procrastinating elves
49 Leftover okra
50 Frolicsome drug addict
51 Twice garbled syllable
52 Loitering misogynist
53 Dauntless eager beaver
54 Misunderstood fishwife, Lat.
56 Way out
59 Fussy forest ranger, in Augsburg
61 Abducted in-law
65 Palindromic nonsense
66 Sumerian goddess of firm feces
68 Manacled jaywalker
69 Ogorblyth, e. g.
70 Pantomiming janitor
71 Hallucinating mama's boy, Old English
72 Tentative, tempered pathos
73 Cathode type, late 19th cent.
74 Jingoistic leper

DOWN

1 Cramped Laotian 2-man tent
2 Ancient Moabite copper nose ring
3 Eskimo booger
4 Extopruniate (var.)
5 Farbu _____
6 Unarmed, redhaired, Turkish constable
7 Cyclorambic endo-tincture
8 Ancestors of pink-eyed S. A. field mice
9 Smallest town in the former Belgian Congo
10 Extinct house worm
11 3-toed Haitian hyena
12 Shrove Tuesday in Amityville
13 Vengeful hypochondriac
21 Half-hearted burp
23 Emboobriary fiduction
25 Anglicized cryptic Chinese warning
27 Middle name of 15 Across
28 Lisping statistician
29 Reluctant hollow-eyed suburbanite
30 Perspiring taxidermist
33 Ambidextrous troglodyte
34 Apathetic acrobat
35 Conscientious bigot
37 Charitable bootlicker
39 Quibbling Iranian lexicographer
43 Narcotized dogma
44 Paroled litterbug
45 TV fare
46 Toothless migrant worker
47 Unchaperoned, ticklish mystic
48 Unpleasant excrescence, Scot.
53 Adrift, chanting needle-worker
55 Ben _____
56 Pedigreed ecdysiast
57 Beatified pawnbroker's expression
58 Lewd poseur
60 Sequestered peon
62 Henpecked dwarf
63 Part of QSRN
64 Wild-eyed female redneck
66 One-eyed Russian sharecropper
67 Useless frippery

ANSWERS ON PAGE 136

I Threw a Boomerang a Few Years back. NOW I LIVE IN CONSTANT FEAR.

A SERIES OF HIGHLY UNUSUAL EVENTS AT THE
BRASS MONKEY IN ST. PETE BEACH

A distinguished gentleman from Revell Downs walked into the **Brass Monkey** as his first stop after a trip down from Broadneck. As he sipped his happy hour Bud Lite, he heard a voice say sweetly, "You've got great hair!" The man couldn't see where the voice was coming from, so he went back to his ice cold beer.

A minute later, the same soft voice said, "You're a handsome dude!" The man looked around, but still couldn't see where the voice was coming from.

When he went back to his drink, the voice spoke again, "What a stud you are!" The man was so baffled by this that he asked **Kelly** what was going on. **Kelly** said, "Oh, it's those tasty beer nuts you're eating. They're complimentary."

A grasshopper visiting from Bay Hills walks into the **Brass Monkey**. **Billy** says, "Hey, you're a grasshopper! You know, we have a drink named after you!" The grasshopper says, "Really? You have a drink named Chauncey?"

An 8-foot tall grizzly bear from Sandy Point walks into the the **Brass Monkey**. **Charlie** asks, with a quaking voice, "What'll you have?" The bear glares at **Charlie** and says, "I'll have a gin . . . . and tonic."

After a few moments, **Charlie** looks up at the bear, and says, "I gotta ask you, why the big pause?"

A brain walks into the the **Brass Monkey** and says, "I'll have a pint of beer please." **Brad** responds, "Sorry, We can't serve you. You're out of your head."

An E-flat from St. Margarets walks into the **Brass Monkey**, and **Sassy** says, "Sorry, we don't serve minors."

An atom from Shore Acres walks back into the **Brass Monkey** after he realizes that he left his electrons there.

Kirky asks him, "Are you sure you left them here?"

"Yes," he replies. "I'm positive!"

A nonrenewable natural resource walks into the **Brass Monkey** and orders a whiskey. **Alex** says, "Sorry, I can't serve you; you've been getting wasted all day long!"

A baby seal from Manhattan Beach walks into the **Brass Monkey**. **Justin** asks, "What will it be stranger?" The seal responds, "Anything but a Canadian Club."

A neutron from Brown's Woods walks into the **Brass Monkey** and asks for a beer. **Frankie** promptly serves up a Bud.

"How much will that be?" asks the neutron.

"For you," **Frankie** said, "no charge."

Thomas Edison walks into the **Brass Monkey** and orders a beer. **Francis** says, "Okay, I'll serve you. Just don't get any ideas."

Pray for Whirled Peas.

The Worst Time to Have a Heart Attack Is during a Game of Charades.

A Broadneck Winter Can Be Fun . . . But Then Again . . .

It May Also Be a Good Time to Head South

THE BRASS MONKEY
pass-a-grille beach, fl
727-367-7620

BROADNECK'S SOUTH FLORIDA HOME AWAY FROM HOME

Drawing on 20 years restaurant experience in the Chesapeake Bay area, Kelly and her husband Barry have worked to achieve uncompromised and superior food quality, service, value and consistency in a classy, yet casual dining atmosphere. All menu items are prepared in-house with the highest quality ingredients and painstaking attention to detail and freshness, all offered at a reasonable price.

WE OVERLOOK NOTHING BUT THE GULF!

Ravens/Orioles Headquarters • MLB/NFL package • Lots of food and drink specials during football season • Largest shrimp in the state of Florida • Award winning jumbo lump crabcakes - ALL KILLER! NO FILLER!

You've Got to Try Our Crab Cake Reuben!

***EVERY* BROADNECKIAN'S SOUTH FLORIDA HOME AWAY FROM HOME!**

St. Pete/Tampa Area • thebrassmonkey.net

Why Did the Chicken Cross the Playground? TO GET TO THE OTHER SLIDE.

The husband told the wife that he needed more space. SO SHE LOCKED HIM OUTSIDE.

Broadneck Rezoned as Nudist Colony
Vizzini's Pizza and Sub's Lobbying Pays Off

Story Said To Be Sensational Fabrication to Boost Baloney Readership

By Dan Saul Knight
STAFF WRITER

As if being the founder of the most environmentally concerned and historically sensitive pizza store in the world were not enough, Jay Vizzini, Sr. has lobbied the Anne Arundel County Department of Planning and Zoning for weeks to rezone Broadneck from R-5 residential to RNC-LICIB meaning Residential Nudist Colony with Light Industrial Cottage Industries in the Basements.

Jay's hard work paid off Monday when the zoning board unanimously passed the zoning change. By law, starting March 1st, all residents within the area so zoned must go nude when the temperature reaches 68 degrees and above.

Jay got the idea for the zoning change when he noticed thousands of families with money in their pockets zooming past exit 29B on Route 50 headed for Ocean City and Rehoboth Beach. "The naked truth is that we wanted to attract some additional customers to our pizza shop and to all the other businesses on Broadneck," he said.

Broadneck will now be the largest nudist camp in the state, and is expected to draw thousands of gaping tourists from all over America. Experts predict that about half the people heading "down the ocean, hon," perhaps as many as 50 thousand a day on weekends, will stop for a delicious pizza or sub at **Vizzini's**, a family rib dinner and/or Maryland crab soup at **O'Loughlin's Pub**, or tacos at the **Broadneck Grill**.

This journalist visited the Cape office of **Vizzini's Pizza and Subs** for verification of the above reports. When I walked in, Jay's secretary had just finished explaining to a customer that the toppings for their hand-tossed fresh dough pizza include pepperoni, Italian sausage, beef, meatball, ham, Italian salami, bacon, mushrooms, green peppers, sweet peppers, onions, black olives, Kalamata olives, tomatoes, banana peppers, feta cheese, anchovies, fresh basil, fresh garlic, broccoli, sun-dried tomatoes, spinach, and red onion.

Then Jay's secretary said to me, "Get a grip, paper boy! Four things: First, do you expect me to believe that your name is Dan Saul Knight? If it is, let's boogie! Second, the idea of a "journalist" working for the *Broadneck Baloney* strikes me as quite odd. How much does editor Elvis Presley, Jr. pay you a week? Like I am so sure he's the real editor! Third, you are not even interviewing me, and I am not really saying this. It's all done on Bob Johnson's computer, undoubtedly directed by space aliens. And fourth, let me give you the bare facts: this story is a farcical expedient whereby discerning readers will be happily attracted to local businesses through the refreshing absurdity of the narrative." ❂

Diners in Rezoned Broadneck Enjoy a Salad without Dressing at **O'Loughlin's Pub**

Tourists Mob Parking Lot, Hoping to Get into **Cape Ace, The Living Room,** and **Whimsicality** before Getting Subs and Pizzas at **Vizzini's**

My Girl just Told Me She Wants Diamonds for Valentine's Day, so I'm Getting Her a Deck of Cards.

How are the beach and Michelob Ultra alike. They're both SO close to water.

New zoning allows gardening boots and belts.

As a long-time extension of Broadneck fun in South Florida, the Brass Monkey in St. Pete Beach has rezoned itself to accommodate many happy Broadneck vacationers.

After zoning change, *Baloney* ad director, Bob Johnson, strums some chords for advertisers Jay Vizzini, James Guth, Rick Jones, and Paddy Whalen.

"With 12 people in our family, doing laundry used to be a big chore. Not any more! Thank you, Vizzini's Pizza and Subs."

Cape Housewife

"Broadneck more of a fun place since rezoning," residents say. "Thank you, Jay Vizzini, Sr.!"

Cape Ace employees now spend their lunch hours frolicking in the trees.

Double entendres proliferate as patrons barely enjoy O'Loughlin's exciting happy hour.

I Hate Conformists. I'm Joining a Group of People Who Feel the Same Way.

CAPITAL NEWSPAPER FOLDS AFTER THREE CENTURIES IN PRINT

COMPETITION FROM BROADNECK BALONEY CITED AS MAIN REASON

HEIDI CLARE
NEWS REPORTER

Annapolis, MD. After 300 years of continuous publication, the *Annapolis Capital* newspaper has closed its doors for good. A spokesbeing at a press conference attended only by this reporter issued the following brief statement: "No one reads our paper anymore. The people just read that great paper from across the Severn. The irony here is that any way you slice it, the *Baloney* has had *us* for lunch,."

One of the *Capital* photographers, Mat Finish, became so distraught when he heard the news of his paper's collapse that he swallowed a roll of film. We here at the *Baloney* send our best wishes to him, his family and his friends, and hope nothing serious develops.

This marks the end of a long and illustrious career for editor Dward Farquard who has announced his retirement. As a young man, Mr. Farquard wanted to go to dental school but he didn't have enough pull. According to his resume, he tried selling shoes but became discouraged when just about every customer had a fit. His first year as a reporter for the *Capital* was not very productive, but the publisher kept him on because his snoring kept the other reporters awake. He did raise some interesting and profound journalistic questions such as, "Is it five o'clock yet?" So before long, Mr. Farquard wound up behind the editor's desk.

Broadneck Baloney editor, Elvis Presley, Jr., has offered Mr. Farquard a position as the *Baloney*'s roving cultural anthropologist because of Mr. Farquard's plucky reputation.

Dward submitted his first story to the *Capital* in 1980, eliciting a response from the then-editor, Ed Cagey, that has become an oft-quoted classic: "Mr. Farquard, your story is both good and original. The difficulty is that the original part is not good, and the good part is not original."

The *Capital* then sent Mr. Farquard to the steaming jungles of central Africa to find Dong Chung Rhee, the famous *Life Magazine* photographer who had become lost near the crocodile-infested shores of the Congo River. Mr. Farquard searched diligently for Mr. Rhee for months until he stumbled upon a small village where the natives imprisoned foreigners in deep pits lined with raw honey. He shined his flashlight into one pit after another until he discovered the man he had been searching for. Mr. Farquard's words at that moment are now memorized by journalism students the world over: "Ah, sweet Mr. Rhee of *Life*, at last I've found you."

Cartoonist Derrick Smith saw a bright spot in an otherwise dark hour for his newspaper, "The *Capital* has made it through the Revolutionary War, the Civil War, the Great Depression, and two world wars. If our final demise was to be at the hands of a superior newspaper like the *Baloney*," the nonchalant formalist opined, "Let us at least be thankful that the *Baloney* built its reputation on great prose, because, after all, it could have been verse."

According to Mr. Farquard, the *Capital* paper boxes will remain in place. Former customers are urged to place a "Broadneck Baloney" sticker over the now defunct *Capital* logo. ✺

Stunned Capital Reporters Commiserate after *Baloney* Had *Them* for Lunch

Did you hear about the explosion at the cheese factory? ALL THAT WAS LEFT WAS DE BRIE!

ANNE ARUNDEL RENAMED "RICHARD'S TREE CARE COUNTY"

EVERY MONDAY DECLARED A GOVERNMENT-PAID HOLIDAY

By Leif Oakly
STAFF WRITER

Richard's Tree Care County, MD. From Laurel to the Bay Bridge, from Linthicum to Deale, the people are applauding the new name of our county.

For over 300 years the county had been named for Anne Arundel, the eldest and prissiest daughter of Abner Arundel, the founder of Arundel Asbestos and Carcinogens, Inc. Anne's association with her father's business had made it impossible for the county government to be taken seriously by the environmental movement. Bay naturalists have pointed out that clams and oysters used to float on the Bay until they were forced to mate with rocks to produce shells around their offspring to protect them from all the chemical crud Abner dumped in the water.

Members of the County Council voted unanimously to change the county name based on **Richard's** artistic botanical sensitivity, the politeness of his crew, and his exciting and innovative employee appreciation program. After five years, a worker gets a brown certificate that says, "Thank you for your valuable service." After ten years, the worker gets a green certificate that says, "Thank you for ten years of service." Then after fifteen years, the worker gets a badge to wear that says, "This person has a brown and green certificate."

The County Council was especially impressed that **Richard** chose the colors brown and green for his certificates since they remind people of vegetation and soil, two of the four basic natural elements, the other two being concrete and tar.

Our county executive wrote **Richard** a letter of thanks, saying in part, "I extend to you the heartfelt appreciation of all sensitive and caring people for helping us save the reputation of our county by allowing us to rename it after your business. I speak for every property owner and renter when I say the next time any of us needs cabling, pruning, pre-construction consultation, deep-root fertilization, lightning protection, 15-yard roll-off dumpsters, or disease control programs, we are calling you."

What Gets Easier to Pick Up as It Gets Heavier? A BROADNECK GAL.

BOB JOHNSON CHOSEN AS MAN OF THE YEAR

BROADNECK & THE WORLD CELEBRATE!

Broadneck Baloney Advertising Manager to Have His Golden Achievement Award Bronzed

By Mal Feezance
NY TIMES STAFF WRITER

Geneva, Switzerland. With an air half quizzical and half deferential, an international body of distinguished diplomats, scientists, religious leaders, and **Cape Ace Hardware** magnates today announced their selection of Bob Johnson, Advertising Director for the *Broadneck Baloney*, as Man of the Year. This is the sixth year in a row that the esteemed committee has decided to so honor Mr. Johnson.

In its bountiful praise for Mr. Johnson, the Committee referred specifically to his advertising work. In that difficult field, they said he has been able to bring about "a remarkable fusion of the highest standards of ethics with true art. Within the pages he designs, we find the maximum of attainable and communicable truth. His work has the loveliness of a tall white lily cut in Periklean marble, splendid and strong."

In an atmosphere crowded with flattery and adulation, the committee, known for its thoroughness in assessing candidates for this honor of honors, as in past years, saved its highest acclaim for Mr. Johnson's character: "Within and around this man of great merit and integrity, we find no sentimental twaddle, no shabby imitations, no shallow sophistry, no shuddering reluctance, no shuffling obeisance, no smirking sauciness, zero soporific emanations (none whatsoever), no specious artifices, no squeamish tastes, no stinted endowments, no strained interpretations, no superficial surliness, no superfluous precautions, and no threadbare sentiments."

Selection Committee Chairperson Melissa Wade of **Cape Ace Hardware** presents Mr. Johnson with what has become a well-earned annual trophy for the gritty salesman.

Mr. Johnson reacted stoically to the announcement. Comparing the work he has chosen to cooking a steak, he opined, "Advertising is a difficult medium because anything well-done is rare."

Mr. Johnson is widely known as the one who, in the early part of his magnificent career, perfected the unbiased survey technique now used to determine the desires of consumers. He once asked one hundred women which hair conditioners and shampoos they preferred when they showered. The top response: "How did you get in here?" Second response: Screaming.

My Dog Has No Nose. HOW DOES IT SMELL? Awful.

Thanks to Mr. Johnson's relentless lobbying to Congress, much more relevant warnings about alcohol consumption will appear on the inventories at all restaurants and liquor stores beginning next year. For hard liquor containers: "The irresponsible consumption of liquor may leave you wondering what happened to your underwear." For wine: "The consumption of too much wine may lead you to believe that you can logically converse with members of the opposite sex without spitting." For beer: "The consumption of too much beer may make you think you are a charming person who is whispering, when you are neither."

In presenting the award, the committee also cited Mr. Johnson's matchless copywriting skills, citing these examples:

"Joe's Auto Repair: Try us once and you'll never go anywhere again."

"For sale: Antique desk suitable for lady with thick legs and large drawers."

"Tired of cleaning yourself? Please let us do it for you."

"See ladies' blouses - half off."

So much for Mr. Johnson's prodigious boldness and energy of intellect.

When asked to what or to whom he attributed his success, Mr. Johnson reacted with characteristic aplomb, "It's been the hundreds, even the thousands of little people out there, the obscure multitude, the masses of underlings, the unsung rank and file, the common folk, the mere peons, the steadfast rabble, the everyday bumpkins, the insignificant yokels, the average hayseeds, the unknown cider squeezers, the hewers of wood and drawers of water, the run-of-the-mill clodhoppers, the nominal ne'er do wells, the uncertain people of naught, and the countless unassuming nobodies whom I wish to thank for their support over the years and along the way. This coveted award, in truth, belongs to them." ✺

Ladies, If a Man Says He Will Fix It, He Will. NO NEED TO REMIND HIM ABOUT IT EVERY 6 MONTHS.

A magician walks down an alley and turns into the back door of a bar.

RICHARD'S TREE CARE RELEASES PRELIMINARY FINDINGS INVOLVING THE "WHAT-TO-DO-NEXT" GENE

By Chris P. Bacon
STAFF WRITER

You are most likely sitting there, reading this article. How do you know what you are going to do next? Are you going to stop reading this informative news report? Are you going to continue to read it? What are you going to do next? Will you throw this book into the fireplace, or will you recognize it for the treasure it is, and put it in your safe with the rest of your valuables?

Whatever you do next, why do you do it? Richard's Tree Care scientists are on the verge of answering that crucial question, having uncovered the elusive what-to-do-next gene within the DNA double helix.

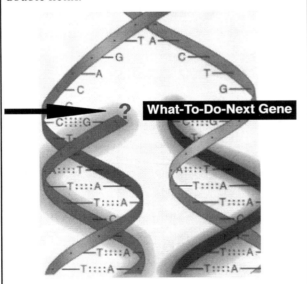

The what-to-do-next gene, Richard's scientists have discovered, appears at the end of each red DNA strand in the form of a question mark. See diagram. The fact that the what-to-do-next gene is in the shape of a question mark in itself raises many interesting and profound questions, such as Why should you go anywhere but to Richard's Tree Care for complete tree and shrub care, pruning (take-down and removal), pre-construction consultation, deep-root fertilization, lightning protection, 15-yard roll-off dumpsters, disease control/monitoring programs, and firewood sales? ✿

A MINOR COMMUNICATION PROBLEM

A judge was interviewing a woman regarding her pending divorce, and asked, "What are the grounds for your divorce?"

She replied, "About four acres and a nice little home in the middle of the property with a stream running by."

"No," he said, "I mean what is the foundation of this case?"

"It is made of concrete, brick and mortar," she responded.

"Well then," he continued, "what are your relations like?"

"I have an aunt and uncle living here in town, and my husband's parents live in the next town over. They're all nice."

He said, "Do you have a real grudge?"

"No," she replied, "We have a two-car carport and have never really needed one."

"Please," he tried again, "is there any infidelity in your marriage?"

"Yes, both my son and daughter have annoying stereo sets. We don't necessarily like the music, but the answer to your questions is a definite yes."

"Ma'am, does your husband ever beat you up?"

"Yes," she responded, "about twice a week he gets up earlier than I do."

Finally, in frustration, the judge asked, "Lady, why do you want a divorce?"

"Oh, I don't want a divorce," she replied. "I've never wanted a divorce. My husband does. He said he has trouble communicating with me." ✿

Old Lawyers Never Die. THEY JUST LOSE THEIR APPEAL.

MARONE LAW GROUP

Marone Law Group is an experienced insurance defense firm with a focus in the area of Property and Casualty defense. We handle First Party Property defense matters including: insurance coverage, sinkhole claims, hurricane claims and arson.

We also represent individuals and corporations in construction litigation and in the defense of liability matters including: slip and fall, dog bite injury, negligent security, boating and motor vehicle liability.

St. Petersburg
First Central Tower
360 Central Avenue,
11th Floor
St. Petersburg,
Florida
33731-3042
T: 727.828.8555
F: 727.362.3690

E: info@MaroneLaw.com

Arnold Couple Wins $10 Million Baloney Sweepstakes

LUCKY WINNERS TO GET $10 A YEAR FOR A MILLION YEARS, PROMISE TO DONATE TEN PERCENT TO CSCIA.

Saul T. Dogg
ACE REPORTER

How many times have you heard the big lottery winners say they would stay at their jobs, keep their same friends, et cetera? Too many times? Well, you won't hear that kind of talk from Arnoldites Philippa Bird and Biff Wellington.

"Hey, we're millionaires now," Biff said, "and we've already quit our jobs. We're going to relax, unbolt, let loose. We're casting off the yoke so it can't be on us."

Both Broadneck Peninsula residents are well-educated enough to manage their enormous windfall, each holding a BS, an MS, and a PhD. [Ed. Note: We know what BS is; MS, they say, means more of the same, and PhD means piled higher and deeper].

Giving 10% of their winnings to the CSCIA (Cape St. Claire Improvement Association) seems to this reporter to be somewhat overly generous in that the local group will be getting a total of one million dollars over time, a handsome sum in anyone's bank account. The big question: Does the Improvement Association deserve it?

Some *Baloney* insiders don't think so. They insist that the couple's donation is nothing more than a payoff to get Cape privileges, including two valid yearly bumper-stickers and a guest pass. If an official charge is brought, it most probably will read, "Misuse of Baloney Sweepstakes Funds," and carry with it a penalty of lifetime banishment from Cape.

When asked about that, Biff, who worked himself up from West Virginia coal miner to his festive status today as an amateur freelance ecdysiast, said, "**Cape Ace** is the place I go each month to get my *Baloney*. I am on my way there now to pick up a copy of this issue. I enjoy reading the ads while I sun myself at Main Beach and Lake Claire. I just hope the CSCIA thinks a million dollars is enough."

"We're just thrilled to have won the sweepstakes," Philippa said, "and honored to be interviewed by the *Baloney*. Before I forget it, I want you to know I had dinner last week with world chess champion Magnus Carlsen. The tablecloth at the restaurant was checkered. It took him two hours to pass me the salt."

The happy pair have said that they will use part of their winnings to pay for a course in conversational Chinese. "We plan to adopt a baby from Beijing and we want to be able to understand him when he starts to talk," Biff said, wearing a suede Tyrol hat with a feather plume, and a burgundy cowhide biker's jacket.

From time to time, paragraphs appear in the *Baloney* that seem to have very little to do with the actual content of the article. But in the larger sense, these paragraphs have everything to do with it because all of the editorial material in this publication is just filler anyway. What you are supposed to do is read all the ads very, very carefully and respond in a positive way to them; that is, buy something.

We put all of our advertisers through a five-year screening process before allowing their messages to appear on the ground-up and packed pages of the *Baloney*, so you can be confident that you're going to get the best deal and the most professional service possible. Sure, you can take the time to congratulate Philippa and Biff— just be sure you get busy and read those wonderful ads.

DEDICATED SCIENTIST DEVELOPS PILL TO COMBAT PEEVISH INGRATITUDE

Discovery Also Promises to Cure Puerile Fickleness, Sardonic Pedantry

By Dr. Victor Frankenstein
SCIENCE EDITOR

It has been said that, as with eggs, there is no such thing as a real smart or real dumb scientist: their brains are either fried or scrambled. Not so with the new breed of hard-boiled scientist as epitomized by Corey C. Cavillator, the inventor of the new pill that threatens to make the bane of peevish ingratitude a thing of the past.

Thanks in part to Doctor Cavillator, we won't have to listen anymore to the cynics who say that scientists are like granola—after you sift through the fruits and nuts, all you find are the flakes.

Doctor Corey C. Cavillator achieved his great breakthrough without any kind of wasteful government grant. This dedicated man worked under the most difficult circumstances solely for the benefit of humanity.

I remember being struck by the starkness of his working conditions. When I first walked into his laboratory over a year ago, I saw a lit cigar butt on the floor. I stepped on it, and a few moments later, Doctor Cavillator hollered out, "Hey, who turned off the heat?"

Doctor Cavillator first became concerned with the problems associated with peevish ingratitude about four years ago. At that time, he was working day and night trying to solve the riddle of the sphinx. One evening as he walked home from his laboratory, a group of pre-puberty boys, utterly insensitive to the scientific progress he was making for their benefit and the benefit of all people everywhere, began to taunt him.

One of the boys said, "Hey, Doctor Cavillator, your mother is so ugly even the Elephant Man paid to see her." Then another one said, "Yeah, and your mother is so smelly, her poops are glad to escape." And still another ungrateful uncouth youth yelled out, "Hey Doctor Cavillator, your sister is so fat, we couldn't download her picture from the Internet."

Instead of reacting in anger to these childish insults, Doctor Cavillator, sponsored by **Cape Ace Hardware**, **Arnold Pharmacy**, **RJ's Plumbing and Septic**, and **Sir Speedy Printing**, decided to throw all his energies for the next three years into producing the pill he named *Impedimentum*, now so conveniently available at you local pharmacy.

Laboratory tests on rats showed that Impedimentum works just as well to counteract puerile fickleness and sardonic pedantry as it does peevish ingratitude. The label warns, however, that the purchaser, when intending to slip the pill to an adult, should not mistake self-righteous indignation for peevish ingratitude or the consequences could be disastrous. A rat afflicted with the former but treated every day with Impedimentum for the latter became extremely paranoid, refusing to trust even the most considerate and well-meaning laboratory technicians.

Doctor Cavillator also cautioned strongly against administering more than the prescribed dosage. "An overdose of Impedimentum could cause an adult patient's healthy sense of balmy sarcasm to turn into a self-deprecating form of borderline irony," the doctor said.

Dr. Cavillator Prepares a Youth to Take His Pill
GOOD-BYE PEEVISH INGRATITUDE

A hamburger walks into a bar and the bartender says, "Sorry, we don't serve food in here."

Winning Free Trip Around the Sun Shocks, Elates Local Couple

Free Daily Spin Around Earth's Axis Also Included

By Amanda B. Reckenwith
STAFF WRITER

Ben and Eileen Dover never thought they'd get a knock on their door from Broadneck Baloney Clearing House officials. And they never thought they'd ever win anything as thrilling as a free trip around the sun. "We've never won anything like this before. What are the odds of our being chosen to receive such a fantastic prize?" Mrs. Dover gushed.

As it turns out, the odds were pretty good, since the Dovers were the only ones to enter the Baloney Sweepstakes. It was Mr. Dover who filled out the entry form, although he was quick to give all the credit to Eileen: "I only do what the voices in my wife's head tell her to tell me to do," the undaunted Cape denizen said.

Mrs. Dover expressed an eagerness to get all the particulars: "Baloney officials haven't given us all the details yet. Like, for instance, we're not sure how much walk-around money we're going to get, and I'm not sure what to pack," she said.

The free trip also includes a complete spin around the earth's axis everyday, and a spectacular nightly view of the phases of the moon throughout each month, with a magnificent backdrop of thousands of stars, weather cooperating.

"Is there gambling on the trip? Will we get a roll of quarters to start us off? Will Baloney officials pay for a babysitter? If the daily free spins make me dizzy, will Dramamine help? Is SPF 40 enough? Are there assigned seats?" Mr. Dover wondered.

Mr. and Mrs. Dover work together in a door-to-door hearing-aid sales business. "It's rewarding but sometimes very frustrating. Most of the time, our best potential customers never hear us knock." Mrs. Dover said.

Ben and Eileen Dover had their own special way of reacting to the good news, as seen here in these exclusive Baloney photos.

Before winning the free trip, the Dovers were so poor that they would go into O'Loughlin's with their own sandwiches to save money. Their poverty made the Dovers smarter. When the waiter said, "You can't bring your own sandwiches in here," they got around it by exchanging sandwiches with each other.

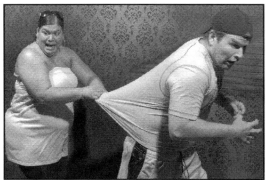

Pictured here: a Revell Downs woman forbidding her husband to enter the Baloney Sweepstakes, a move she now very much regrets.
They could have been the big winners.

Doctor, My Hair Keeps Failing Out. What Can You Give Me to Keep It in? A SHOEBOX MAYBE?

I'm So Lonely I Bought a Plane Ticket just for the Airport Pat-down.

A Streaker Ran Naked through the Church, but the Cops Were Able to Catch Him by the Organ.

Broadneck Baloney Insider
Solves Long-Standing Moon Mystery

TRY THE PEPPERONI ROLLS AND THE CHEESE FRIES AT VIZZINI'S PIZZA AND SUBS

By Nat Sass
STAFF WRITER

Even the history books say that all astronaut Neil Armstrong said on July 21st 1969, as he stepped onto the surface of the moon was, "That's one small step for a man; a giant leap for mankind." Yet, since that lunar event, rumors have been rife that federal government officials suppressed the enigmatic conclusion of his famous statement. Bleeping out words from the moon, though not illegal, does raise certain questions about the suppression of free speech, and the rights of American citizens to get all the sordid details of stuff.

At long last, the conspiracy to keep Armstrong's additional words from the public has been unravelled and substantiated by a *Broadneck Baloney* insider who wishes to remain anonymous. Thanks to this insider, we have the full and true text of Neil Armstrong's words: "That's one small step for a man; a giant leap for mankind, and good luck, Mr. Grinsky."

Because this Broadneck insider retained such excellent relations with many other Broadneck insiders over the years, he was trusted enough to get the inside story, which he has sold to the *Baloney* for ten million dollars. So what you are getting is pretty much what they call an exclusive inside story, except for what has appeared on Facebook and Twitter.

The Broadneck insider was able to piece together the inside details of the long-suppressed inside secret, which we are delighted to present to the people of Broadneck, which details are basically these:

Neil Armstrong grew up in the Deep Creek section of Shore Acres right next to Mr. and Mrs. Chauncey Grinsky. Back in the 1940s, when Neil Armstrong was five years old, he heard the Grinskys arguing over the white picket fence.

The argument had something to do with amorous matters. They bantered back and forth for ten or fifteen minutes and then Mrs. Grinsky screamed at Mr. Grinsky, "Sex! You want sex! You'll get some sex when that little kid next door goes to the moon!" Neil never forgot that argument or those words and thought that Mr. Grinsky might be encouraged by his message from space.

One small step for a man; a giant leap for mankind . . . and good luck Mr. Grinsky.

Einstein Look-alike Wins $100,000 Prize

Winner Sad There Is No Contest For His Wife

By Hugh DeMann
STAFF WRITER

A jubilant Harry Pitts today accepted a check for $100,000 from the Albert Einstein Look-A-Like Foundation of Broadneck as its latest winner. The foundation awards huge sums annually to men who look like the great scientist and humanitarian.

"I've slept now for more than 35 years with my face inside a plastic Einstein mold," Pitts said. "In an eminent and unique sense, I've been working toward this honor most of my adult life," the 55-year-old feather-weight prizefighter added.

Pitts, who hails from Shore Acres, said that he thought it was too bad that there wasn't a foundation that gave a cash award for the person most shaped like a pear because he felt confident his wife could win it. "She needs something to boost her self-esteem," he said.

The real Albert Einstein was born on Broadneck in 1879 on the poor side of Green Holly Drive in Cape St. Claire. To throw biographers off track, he covered his Broadneck twang with a thick, fake German accent. He put on his first mustache with a felt-tipped pen.

Little Albert Einstein was a late talker, and his parents were worried. But at the supper table one night he broke his silence to say, "What is this fly doing in my soup?" When his father promptly replied, "I believe it's the backstroke," Albert realized that in his future life, not everyone would be taking him seriously.

Young Einstein kept to himself most of the time. If we look at the make-up of Broadneck during his youth as a kind of a train, Albert was the peninsula's social caboose.

His junior high school yearbook says that he enjoyed thinking about constants and variables, thinking about the future possibilities of disco dancing, and thinking about watching Redskins football on television in the future.

Uncanny resemblance between Shore Acres man Harry Pitts, above, and former Broadneckian Albert Einstein, below.

His classmates credited him with the saying, "Arm-wrestling is the most fun you can have without smiling." After graduation from Broadneck Senior High School, where he distinguished himself as vice-president of the magnetism and pizza club, Albert read local books and avoided local people until that famous day in 1903 when he published his regular, special, and general theories of relativity, sponsored by **Vizzini's Pizza and Subs**, **Cape Hair Scene and Barber Shop**, **Sir Speedy**, **Whimsicality**, **Hoffman Animal Hospital**, **Fairwinds Marina**, and **Cape Ace Hardware**.

The Recipe Said to Separate 2 Eggs, SO HE TOOK ONE OF THEM INTO A DIFFERENT ROOM.

Einstein's regular theory of relativity had to do with the reasons his sister's in-laws tried to borrow money every chance they got.

His special theory revolutionized physics by positing for the first time that T = M, T standing for Time and M for Money.

His general theory of relativity was the first to put light, charm, entropy, gravity, friction, fire, velocity, acceleration, air, mass, spin, somersaults, shadow, space, water, wind, flux, time, and, some say, many unnecessary platitudes, all into the same equation. In lay person's terms, his equation proved that Time (T) is Nature's (N) way of keeping everything (E) from happening (H) at once (O).

Albert was a typical Broadneckian. When his first wife Candy told him to dress properly when going to the office, he argued, "Why should I? Everyone knows me there." But when she told him to dress properly for his first big physics conference, he argued again, "Why should I? No one knows me there."

Albert once walked into *O'Loughlin's Pub* and said to Heather the barmaid, "I'll take a Loose Cannon for me and a Guinness for my friend, Heisenberg." Heather looked around and asked, "Is your friend Heisenberg here?" Albert replied, "I'm not certain."

Einstein once climbed to the top of Mount Sinai to get close enough to talk to God and find out who was smarter. Looking up to the heavens, he asked, "God, what exactly does a million years mean to you?"

God replied, "A minute."

Albert then asked, "And what does a million dollars mean to you?"

God replied, "A penny."

So Albert asked "Can I have a penny?"

God replied, "Sure, in a minute."

In his later years, Albert mastered the all-encompassing String Theory. It was at this time that his second wife, Sugar, found lipstick on his collar and accused him of philandering. Guess what Albert said to that? Albert said, "Hold on, Sugar, I can explain everything!" ❀

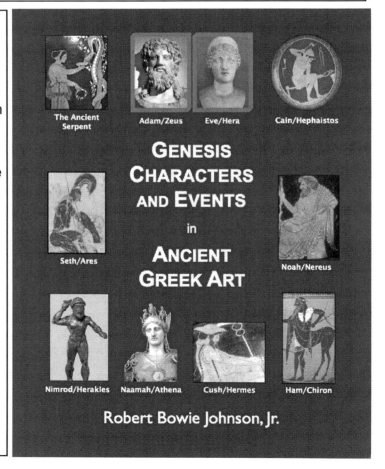

How Do You Eat an Elephant? ONE BITE AT A TIME.

My Wifi went down during family dinner tonight. One kid started talking and I didn't know who he was.

RICHARD'S TREE CARE, NOT FBI, HAS BAT CHILD

Photo Reveals Systematic Effort to Discredit the Baloney

By Shirley U. Geste
STAFF WRITER

In a move Broadneck insiders say was designed to discredit the *Baloney* as a journalistic power in America, the *Weekly World News* has published in its latest issue that the FBI has captured the "wild and dangerous" bat child. But as all *Broadneck Baloney* readers know, the bat child could not have been plucked from the roof of a flooded farmhouse in Mississippi last week as the *News* claims, because Richard and his courageous crew captured the big-headed, shrieking weirdo last November.

As the accompanying photo, taken only yesterday, proves, the oft-maligned and misunderstood creature is still in the custody of Richard Folderauer, Sr., and Richard's taming efforts appear to be bearing some fruit. In fact, they've become good friends as we can see by the bat child's hand on Richard's shoulder.

This is just more incontrovertible evidence that the the FBI, CIA, remnants of the Tsarist Secret Police, and the *Weekly World News* are engaged in a dastardly conspiracy to discredit the *Baloney* and all it stands for.

Richard has indicated that the false report will in no way affect the great skill with which he and his crews perform their many services. These include: complete tree and shrub care, pruning (take-down and removal), pre-construction consultation, deep-root fertilization, lightning protection, 15-yard roll-off dumpsters, disease control/monitoring programs, and firewood sales.

This reporter asked if Richard's free estimates would be affected in any way. Richard replied, "No way." This reporter also asked if his reasonable rates would change in any way. Richard answered, "Never!"

If you think that this sounds like a man whose business is fully insured, licensed by the Maryland State Forestry Department, and who is a member of the Maryland Arborist Association and the Tree Care Industry Association, you are one-hundred percent right! ❂

Decide for yourself who has the bat child:

Fake *Weekly World News* Photo

Genuine *Baloney* Photo

What's the one thing worse than a male chauvinist pig? A woman who won't do as she's told.

How Did You Make Out in Court? FINE.

BALONEY WORD PUZZLE #1

Example: 24 H _ _ _ _ in a D _ _ = 24 Hours in a Day

1001 A _ _ _ _ _ _ N _ _ _ _ _ _

88 P _ _ _ _ K _ _ _ _

32 D _ _ _ _ _ _ _ F _ _ _ _ _ _ _ _ _ at which W _ _ _ _ F _ _ _ _ _ _

18 H _ _ _ _ on a G _ _ _ C _ _ _ _ _ _

4 Q _ _ _ _ _ in a G _ _ _ _ _ _

1 W _ _ _ _ on a U _ _ _ _ _ _ _ _

5 or 9 D _ _ _ _ _ in a Z _ _ C _ _ _

11 P _ _ _ _ _ _ on an _ _ _ _ _ _ _ F _ _ _ _ _ _ _ T _ _ _

4 S _ _ _ _ _ _ on a V _ _ _ _ _

7 C _ _ _ _ _ in the R _ _ _ _ _ _ _

12 N _ _ _ _ _ _ on a C _ _ _ _ _

7 C _ _ _ _ _ _ _ _ _ _ on the G _ _ _ _ _

3 P _ _ _ _ _ _ in a H _ _ _ _ _ _ G _ _ _

9 P _ _ _ _ _ _ on a B _ _ _ _ _ _ _ _ T _ _ _

2 H _ _ _ _ are B _ _ _ _ _ _ T _ _ _ O _ _

8 D _ _ _ of H _ _ _ _ _ _ _ _

1 in a M _ _ _ _ _ _ _

13 O _ _ _ _ _ _ _ C _ _ _ _ _ _ _ _

366 D _ _ _ in a L _ _ _ Y _ _ _

Answers at BroadneckBaloney.com

Please Don't Write in the Spaces - So Others Can Enjoy the Challenge

Why do black widow spiders kill their males after mating? To stop the snoring before it starts.

Waiter, your thumb is in my soup! Don't worry, sir! The soup isn't very hot.

Waiter, there is a fly in my soup! Sorry sir, I must have missed it when I removed the other three.

WHAT I'D SAY TO THE MARTIANS

BY JACK HANDEY

Reprinted by permission of the author from his book of the same title.

People of Mars, you say we are brutes and savages. But let me tell you one thing: if I could get loose from this cage you have me in, I would tear you guys a new Martian butt hole. You say we are violent and barbaric, but has any one of you come up to my cage and extended his hand? Because, if he did, I would jerk it off and eat it right in front of him. "Mmm, that's good Martian," I would say.

You say your civilization is more advanced than ours. But who is really the more "civilized" one? You, standing there watching this cage? Or me, with my pants down, trying to urinate on you? You criticize our Earth religions, saying they have no relevance to the way we actually live. But think about this: if I could get my hands on that god of yours, I would grab his skinny neck and choke him until his big green head exploded.

We are a warlike species, you claim, and you show me films of Earth battles to prove it. But I have seen all the films about twenty times. Get some new films, or, so help me, if I ever get out of here I will empty my laser pistol into everyone I see, even pets.

Speaking of films, I could show you some films, films that portray a different, gentler side of Earth. And while you're watching the films I'd sort of slip away, because guess what: the projector is actually a thing that shoots out spinning blades! And you fell for it! Well, maybe not now you wouldn't.

You point to your long tradition of living peacefully with Earth. But you know what I point to? Your stupid heads.

You say there is much your civilization could teach ours. But perhaps there is something that I could teach you—how to scream like a parrot when I put your big Martian head in a vise.

You claim there are other intelligent beings in the galaxy besides earthlings and Martians. Good, then we can attack them together. And after we're through attacking them we'll attack you.

I came here in peace, seeking gold and slaves. But you have treated me like an intruder. Maybe it is not me who is the intruder but you. No, not me. You, stupid.

You keep my body imprisoned in this cage. But I am able to transport my mind to a place far away, a happier place, where I use Martian heads for batting practice.

I admit that sometimes I think we are not so different after all. When you see one of your old ones trip and fall down, do you not point and laugh, just as we on Earth do? And I think we can agree that nothing is more admired by the people of Earth and Mars alike than a fine, high-quality cigarette. For fun, we humans like to ski down mountains covered with snow; you like to "milk" bacteria off of scum hills and pack them into your gill slits. Are we so different? Of course we are, and you will be even more different if I ever finish my homemade flamethrower.

You may kill me, either on purpose or by not making sure that all the surfaces in my cage are safe to lick. But you can't kill an idea. And that idea is: me chasing you with a big wooden mallet.

You say you will release me only if I sign a statement saying that I will not attack you. And

I have agreed, the only condition being that I can sign with a long sharp pen. And still you keep me locked up.

True, you have allowed me reading material—not the "human reproduction" magazines I requested but the works of your greatest philosopher, Zandor or Zanax or whatever his name is. I want to discuss his ideas with him—just me, him, and one of his big, heavy books.

If you will not free me, at least deliver a message to Earth. Send my love to my wife, and also to my girlfriend. And to my children, if I have any anyplace. Ask my wife to please send me a bazooka, which is a flower we have on Earth. If my so-called friend Don asks you where the money I owe him is, please anally probe him. Do that anyway.

If you keep me imprisoned long enough, eventually I will die. Because one thing you Martians do not understand is that we humans cannot live without our freedom. So, if you see me lying lifeless in my cage, come on in, because I'm dead. Really.

Maybe one day we will not be the enemies you make us out to be. Perhaps one day a little Earth child will sit down to play with a little Martian child, or larva, or whatever they are. But, after a while, guess what happens: the little Martian tries to eat the Earth child. But guess what the Earth child has? A gun. You weren't expecting that, were you? And now the Martian child is running away, as fast as he can. Run, little Martian baby, run!

I would like to thank everyone for coming to my cage tonight to hear my speech. Donations will be gratefully accepted. (No Mars money, please.) ♦

Jack Handey's books, "Deep Thoughts," "Deeper Thoughts," "What I'd Say to the Martians," "Deepest Thoughts," and "The Lost Deep Thoughts" are available at amazon.com

Plain Old Broadneck Jokes

A man's wife came home and said, "Honey, the car won't start, but I know what the problem is."

He asked her what it was, and she told him there was water in the carburetor. Her husband thought for a moment, then said, "You know, I don't mean this offensively, but you don't know the carburetor from the accelerator."

"No," she insisted, "there's definitely water in the carburetor."

"Okay, honey, that's fine," he said. "I'll go take a look. Where is it?"

"In the lake," she replied. •

A husband shopped at Victoria's Secret for a sheer negligee for his wife. He found several, with prices from $50 to $500; evidently, the sheer-er, the price-ier!

Being a man, he picked the sheerest, took it home to his wife (without removing the price tag, of course) and asked her to model it. She dashed upstairs to their bedroom where she had an idea. "This thing is so sheer it might as well be nothing at all. If I don't put it on, but model naked for him, tomorrow I can return it and keep the $500 for myself."

So she walked out on the upstairs balcony naked and struck a sexy pose for him. Her husband looked up, grimaced, and said, "Dammit! For $500, shouldn't they at least iron it?!" •

Ole was never much of a scholar, but he sure could paint, especially portraits.

As his fame grew, people came from all over to have him paint their formal portrait.

One day, a beautiful young woman arrived at Ole's studio and asked Ole if he would paint her in the nude.

"Money is no object," she told Ole. "Would a half million dollars be enough?"

Since no one had ever made such a request before, Ole figured he'd better get permission from his wife, the lovely Lena.

"Can ya wait here fer a minute whilst I asks Lena?"

In a few minutes he returned. "Ya, shoor, you betcha, I can paint ya in da nude, but I'll haff ta leave my socks on so's I have a place to wipe my brushes!" •

A woman goes to the post office to buy stamps for her Christmas cards. She says to the clerk, "May I have 50 Christmas stamps?"

He says, "What denomination?"

The woman responds, "God help us. Has it come to this? Give me 22 Catholic, 12 Presbyterian, 10 Lutheran, and 6 Baptist." •

Three slightly deaf old ladies are on a bus. The first asks the others, "Is this Wembley?" The second says, "No, this is Thursday." The third says, "So am I! Let's get off the bus and have a drink!" •

A man takes a ride in a hot air balloon. The wind blows him far off course and the ground below him begins to look unfamiliar. He sees a farmer in a field on his tractor. He begins yelling down at the farmer "Helloooooo! Helloooooo!" until eventually the farmer looks up and notices him. The man in the balloon yells down, "I'm lost. Can you tell me where I am?" The farmer chuckles and says, "Heh, heh, you can't fool me. Why, you're up there in that little bitty basket." •

What's Worse Than Drinking to Forget? FORGETTING TO DRINK.

I Love to Give Homemade Gifts. WHICH ONE OF MY KIDS DO YOU WANT?

My wife was so sick this morning, I had to carry her to the kitchen to make my breakfast.

Plain Old Broadneck Jokes

A CEO-type was in the hospital, being treated for a minor deal. For a week he'd made a complete nuisance of himself, irritating all the staff, shouting orders and demanding attention, complaining about the food, the bed, the temperature, the weather. Typical big shot. One morning, a nurse entered the room, saying, "Time to take your temperature, sir."

After growling that she was disturbing his nap, the guy finally opened his mouth for the thermometer. "Sorry, sir," said the nurse, "but for this test we need your temperature from the other end, sir, if you don't mind."

After complaining for a while about the embarrassment and inconvenience, the guy finally rolled over and bared his butt. After the nurse finished she said, "Stay exactly like that and don't move. I'll be back in five minutes to check up on you."

The nurse left, leaving the door ajar. The big shot's back was to the door, and for over an hour, he heard people wandering up and down the hall, laughing. At length the doctor entered the room, saw the big shot with his bare butt in the air and gawked. Finally, he asks, "What's going on here?"

The big shot barks, "Haven't you ever seen someone having his temperature taken?"

"Not with a daffodil." •

A couple go for a meal at a Chinese restaurant and order the "Chicken Surprise." The waiter brings the meal, served in a lidded cast iron pot.

Just as the wife is about to serve herself, the lid of the pot rises slightly, and she briefly sees two beady little eyes looking around before the lid slams back down.

"Good grief, did you see that?" she asks her husband.

He didn't see it, so she asks him to look in the pot. He reaches for it and again the lid rises, and he sees two little eyes looking around before it slams down.

Rather perturbed, he calls the waiter over, explains what is happening, and demands an explanation.

"Please," says the waiter, "what you order?"

The husband replies, "Chicken Surprise."

"Ah, so sorry," says the waiter, "By mistake, I bring you Peeking Duck." •

George turned to his 40-year-old buddy on the next bar stool and asked, "John, Why aren't you married?"

"I guess I just haven't found the right woman," replied John.

"So what would she be like?" asked George.

"Well, George, she'd have to be real pretty, great at sex, a good cook and housekeeper, know how to handle money, with a pleasant personality, oh, and money, too, plenty of it. having a nice house would help," said John.

George grimaced. "A woman like that would be crazy to marry you."

"I don't care if she's crazy," said John. •

D&A Service Company
Heating & Cooling

We offer HVAC systems and services including top performing heating and air conditioning **repair, replacement** and **maintenance.** And with our **Free Estimates for System Replacement,** you are always guaranteed to save!

dandahvac.com

OFFICE: 240.294.4470
eFAX: 240.554.2586

**4506 Emerson Street #7
Hyattsville, MD 20781**

There's no better sunscreen than sitting inside O'Loughlin's Pub.

What was brown and sat on a piano bench? Beethoven's first movement.

Plain Old Broadneck Jokes

Men and women have two distinct views about weddings.

The husband-to-be wakes up in the morning, plays a round of golf and counts the minutes until he has to be at the altar.

The wife-to-be, on the other hand, wakes up in the morning and is panicking. She immediately begins to organize things, making sure everything is in proper order. In her mind she is repeating what she has to do: "All I have to do is go down the aisle, get to the altar, and marry him."

She repeats this over and over, until she begins to shorten it to three words which she continues to repeat, "Aisle, altar, him." "Aisle, altar, him." "Aisle, altar, him . . ." •

A man from Shore Acres was standing next in line at a checkout, when the attractive blonde woman in front of him turned around and gave him a big smile. "Hello," she said, as she waited for her change.

"Er, I'm sorry. Do I know you?" the man asked in some confusion.

"Oh, my mistake. I thought you were the father of one of my children," she said apologetically and, picking up her shopping, she left the store.

The astonished man thought, "How amazing that a good-looking woman like that should have forgotten who fathered her children."

Then he began to worry. He had an encounter in his youth that could have resulted in a child he didn't know about. She had been blonde, pretty, and about the same height.

On leaving the store, he saw the woman getting into her car. He ran over to her and said, "Look, you couldn't have been the girl I met that night at *Bella's Tavern* in 1980 could you? Saturday night, the band, the pool tournament . . . everyone got really wild and I was so out of it that I didn't get your number."

The woman, with a look of shock and disgust, said, "No! I was not that girl. I'm your son's English teacher, you idiot!" •

A young lad from Mago Vista is about to go on his first date, and he is nervous about what to talk about. He asks his father for advice.

The father replies: "My son, there are three subjects that always work. These are food, family, and philosophy. If she doesn't want talk about one, she'll talk about the others."

The lad picks up his date and they go to a soda fountain. Ice cream sodas in front of them, they stare at each other for a long time, as the lad's nervousness builds.

He remembers his father's advice, and chooses the first topic: food. He asks the girl, "Do you like spinach?"

"No," she says, and the embarrassing silence returns.

After a few more uncomfortable minutes, the lad thinks of his father's suggestion and turns to the second item on the list: family. He asks, "Do you have a brother?" Again, the girl says "No," and there is gnawing silence once again.

Thinking of his father's advice again, the lad then turns to the last item on the list: philosophy, and asks the girl the following question: "If you had a brother, do you think he would like spinach?" •

Mom, am I ugly? I TOLD YOU NOT TO CALL ME MOM IN PUBLIC!

Why should blondes not be given coffee breaks? It takes too long to retrain them.

BROADNECK BLONDES

A blonde was complaining to her friend about constantly being called a dumb blonde. Her friend told her "Go do something to prove them wrong! Why don't you learn all the state capitals or something?"

The blonde thinks this is a great idea, and locks herself up for two weeks studying.

The next party she goes to, some guy makes dumb blonde comments to her. She gets all indignant and claims, "I'm NOT a dumb blonde. In fact, I can name ALL the state capitals!"

The guy doesn't believe her, so she dares him to test her. He says "Okay, what's the capital of Montana?"

The blonde tosses her hair in triumph and says, "That's easy! It's M!" ☺

A blonde meets up with a friend as she's picking up her car from the mechanic.
"Everything okay with your car now?"
"Yes, thank goodness," the blonde replies.
"Weren't you worried the mechanic might try to rip you off?"
"Yeah, but I was relieved when he told me all I needed was blinker fluid!" ☺

Two blondes are sitting on a bench at the park. One says to the other, "Hey, which is farther, California or the moon?" The other blonde says, "Well, duh! Can you see California from here?" ☺

A blonde asked someone what time it was, and the person told her it was 3:45. The blonde, with a puzzled look on her face replied, "You know, it's the weirdest thing, I have been asking that question all day, and each time I get a different answer." ☺

SHE WAS SO BLONDE THAT...

She tripped over a cordless phone.

She thought she needed a token to get on Soul Train.

She spent 20 minutes looking at the orange juice can because it said "concentrate."

She told me to meet her at the corner of WALK and DON'T WALK.

She asked for a price check at the Dollar Store.

She studied for a blood test.

When she missed the 44 bus, she took the 22 bus twice instead.

When she went to the airport and saw a sign that said "Airport Left," she turned around and went home.

At the bottom of the application where it says, "Sign Here," she put "Pisces."

She sold her car for gas money!

She thought Meow Mix was a CD for cats.

To make up her mind, she put lipstick on her forehead.

What did the French chef give his wife for Valentine's Day? A hug and a quiche!

Why did God create blondes? Because pets can't bring beer from the fridge.

BROADNECK BLONDES

A blonde got lost in her car in a snow storm. She remembered what her dad had once told her: "If you get stuck in a snow storm, wait for a snow plow and follow it."

Pretty soon a snow plow came by, and she started to follow it. She followed the plow for about forty-five minutes. Finally the driver of the truck got out and asked her what she was doing. She explained that her dad had told her if she ever got stuck in the snow, to follow a plow. The driver nodded and said: "Well, I'm done with this parking lot, now you can follow me over to the next one."

A blonde walks into a doctor's office and says: "Doctor, what's the problem with me? When I touch my arm, ouch! It hurts. When I touch my leg, ouch! It hurts. When I touch my head, ouch! It hurts. When I touch my chest, ouch! It really hurts!"

The Doctor says: "Your finger's broken."

Two women are getting ready to leave for work. The brunette gets in the driver's seat and the blonde gets in the passenger's seat. The brunette says: "We're late, so you watch out the back window for cops." As she speeds down the road she asks the blonde:

"So, do you see any cops?"

The blonde replies: "Yes!"

The brunette says: "Are they behind us?"

"Yes!"

"Are they going to stop us?"

"I don't know!"

"Well, are their lights on?"

The blonde replies: "Yes, no, yes, no, yes, no, yes, no . . ."

A husband buys his blonde wife her first cell phone. The next day the blonde goes to get her hair done. Her phone rings and it's her husband:

"Hi honey," he says, "How do you like your new phone?"

"I just love it, it's so small and your voice is clear as a bell. But there's one thing I don't understand. How did you know I was at the beauty parlor?"

A blonde and a lawyer are seated next to each other on a flight from LA to NY. The lawyer asks if she would like to play a fun game?

The blonde, tired, just wants to take a nap, politely declines and rolls over to the window to catch a few winks.

The lawyer persists and explains that the game is easy and a lot of fun. He explains, "I ask you a question, and if you don't know the answer, you pay me $5.00, and vice versa" Again, she declines and tries to get some sleep.

The lawyer, now agitated, says, "Okay, if you don't know the answer you pay me $5.00, and if I don't know the answer, I will pay you $500.00." This catches the blonde's attention and, figuring there will be no end to this torment unless she plays, agrees to the game.

The lawyer asks the first question. "What's the distance from the earth to the moon?" The blonde doesn't say a word, reaches into her purse, pulls out a $5.00 bill and hands it to the lawyer. "Okay," says the lawyer, "your turn." She asks the lawyer, "What goes up a hill with three legs and comes down with four legs?"

The lawyer, puzzled, takes out his laptop computer and searches all his references - no

Why did Mozart kill all his chickens? Because they kept saying "Bach, Bach, Bach."

BROADNECK BLONDES

answer. He taps into the air phone with his modem and searches the net and the Library of Congress, no answer. Frustrated, he sends e-mails to all his friends and coworkers, to no avail.

After an hour, he wakes the blonde, and hands her $500.00. The blonde says, "Thank you," and turns back to get some more sleep.

The lawyer, who is more than a little miffed, wakes the blonde and asks, "Well, what's the answer?"

Without a word, the blonde reaches into her purse, hands the lawyer $5.00, and goes back to sleep. Are blonds really so dumb? ☺

One day a blond walks into a doctors office with both of her ears burnt. The doctor asks her what had happened. She says, "Well . . . when I was ironing my work suit the phone rang and I mistakenly picked up the iron instead of the phone."

"That explains one ear, but what about the other." "The son-of-a-gun called again." ☺

A blonde rings up an airline. She asks, "How long are your flights from America to England?" The woman on the other end of the phone says, "Just a minute . . ." The blonde says, "Thanks!" and hangs up the telephone. ☺

How do you keep a blonde busy for 2 days? Give her a piece of paper that has "please turn over" written on both sides. ☺

Two blondes fell down a hole. One said, "It's dark in here isn't it?" The other replied, "I don't know; I can't see!" ☺

On the first day of training for parachute jumping, a blonde listened intently to the instructor. He told them to start preparing for landing when they are at 300 feet. The blonde asked, "How am I supposed to know when I'm at 300 feet?"

"That's a good question. When you get to 300 feet, you can recognize the faces of people on the ground."

After pondering his answer, she asked, "What happens if there's no one there I know?" ☺

A blonde was down on her luck. In order to raise some money, she decided to kidnap a kid and hold him for ransom.

She went to the playground, grabbed a kid, took him behind a tree, and told him, "I've kidnapped you." She then wrote a note saying, "I've kidnapped your kid. Tomorrow morning put $10,000 in a paper bag and put it under the pecan tree next to the slide on the north side of the playground. Signed, A blonde."

The blonde then pinned the note to the kid's shirt and sent him home to show it to his parents.

The next morning the blonde checked, and sure enough, a paper bag was sitting beneath the pecan tree. The blonde opened up the bag and found the $10,000 with a note that said, "How could you do this to a fellow blonde?" ☺

A boss tells a blonde applicant, "I'll give you $12 an hour, starting today, and in three months, I'll raise it to $16 an hour. So, when would you like to start?"

"In three months." ☺

Why did the blonde have tread marks on her back? She crawled across the street when the sign said, "DON'T WALK."

BROADNECK BLONDES

The blonde walks into a drugstore and asks the pharmacist for some bottom deodorant. The pharmacist, a little bemused, explains to the woman that they don't sell anything called bottom deodorant, and never have.

Unfazed, the blonde assures him that she has been buying the stuff from this store on a regular basis, and would like some more.

"I'm sorry," says the pharmacist, "we don't have any." "But I always get it here," says the blonde. "Do you have the container it comes in?" "Yes!" says the blonde, "I will go home and get it."

She returns with the container and hands it to the pharmacist, who looks at it and says to her, "This is just a normal stick of underarm deodorant."

The annoyed blonde snatches the container back and reads out loud from the container: "To apply, push up bottom."

Two blondes are walking down the road when one says "Look at that dog with one eye!" The other blonde covers one of her eyes and says "Where?"

An airline captain was helping a new blonde flight attendant prepare for her first overnight trip. Upon their arrival, the captain showed the flight attendant the best place for airline personnel to eat, shop, and stay overnight.

The next morning as the pilot was preparing the crew for the day's route, he noticed the new stewardess was missing. He knew which room she was in at the hotel and called her up to ask what happened to her.

She answered the phone, crying, and said, "I can't get out of the room!"

"You can't get out of your room?" the captain asked. "Why not?"

She replied, "There are only three doors in here," she sobbed, "One is the bathroom, one is the closet, and one has a sign on it that says 'Do Not Disturb'!"

Q: How many blonde jokes are there?
A: One. The rest are all true stories.

There's a double decker bus driving down the street full of passengers, blonde and brunette. On the lower level of the bus, the brunettes are having a good time, talking, laughing, and singing along to the music playing.

On the upper part of the bus, the blondes are seated and they're in a panic. They're screaming, terrified, and holding onto each other as the bus moves along the street.

Finally, a brunette gets up and walks to the top of the bus to ask what's wrong. One of the blondes replies, "What's wrong?!? Well, you'd be screaming too if you didn't have a driver!!!"

A woman yells to a blonde walking along a river, "How do I get on the other side!?"
The blonde says, "You *are* on the other side!"

A blonde was driving down the motorway when her car phone rang. It was her husband, urgently warning her, "Honey, I just heard on the news that there's a car going the wrong way on Route 50. Please be careful!"
"It's not just one car!" said the blonde. "There are hundreds of them!"

Did you hear about the cannibal who passed his mother in the woods?

The Editor's Corner

Well, here are some more of my dad's favorite jokes:

A deliberate peasant joins a monastery and takes a vow of silence: he's allowed to say two words every seven years. After the first seven years, the elders bring him in and ask for his two words. "Cold floors," he says. They nod and send him away. Seven more years pass. They bring him back in and ask for his two words. He clears his throats and says, "Bad food." They nod and send him away. Seven more years pass. They bring him in for his two words. "I quit," he says. "That's not surprising," the elders say. "You've done nothing but complain since you got here."

A guy with a huge orange head goes in to see a doctor. The doctor says, "How did you get such a huge orange head?" The guy says, "Well, one day I was walking down the beach when I tripped over an old lantern. A genie came out and said, I'll grant you three wishes, whatever you desire . . . what is your first wish?"

I said, "I'd like all the money I could ever spend. The genie went 'Poof!', and there it was, all the money I could ever spend." Then he asked, "What is your second wish?"

I said, "I'd like a beautiful woman to love me, someone I could enjoy this money with. The genie went 'Poof!', and there she was, a gorgeous girl who immediately loved me.

"Then the genie asked me what my third wish was . . . and I think this is where I went wrong . . . I said, "I'd like a huge orange head."

A Jewish grandmother is watching her grandchild playing on the beach when a huge wave comes and takes him out to sea. She pleads, "Please God, save my only grandson. I beg of you, bring him back." And a big wave comes and washes the boy back onto the beach, as good as new. The Jewish grandmother looks up to heaven and says: "He had a hat!"

A man goes to a psychiatrist and says, "Doc, my brother's crazy, he thinks he's a chicken." The doctor says, "Why don't you have him put in the psycho ward?" The guy says, "We would. But we need the eggs."

A car hits a Jewish man. The paramedic rushes over and says, "Are you comfortable?" The man says: "I make a good living."

A guy shows up late for work. The boss yells, "You should have been here at 8:30!"
The guy replies: "Why? What happened at 8:30?"

Two guys are walking down the street when a mugger approaches them and demands their money. They both grudgingly pull out their wallets and begin taking out their cash. Just then one guy turns to the other and hands him a bill. "Here's that $20 I owe you," he says.

After 12 years of psychotherapy, the psychiatrist said something that brought tears to the patient's eyes: "No hablo Ingles."

A woman walked into the kitchen to find her husband stalking around with a fly swatter.
"What are you doing?" she asked.
"Hunting flies," her husband responded.
"Oh. Killing any?" she asked.
"Yep, 3 males, 2 females," he replied.
Intrigued, she asked. "How can you tell which are male and which are female?"
"Three were on a beer can, two were on the phone," he said.

Doctor: I'm not sure what is causing your headaches. It could be due to alcohol.
Patient: That's okay. I'll come back when you're sober.

Elvis Presley, Jr., Editor

How Were the Exam Questions? THEY WERE EASY. I HAD TROUBLE WITH THE ANSWERS.

The Editor's Corner

You might be a Broadneck redneck (Bredneck for short) if you let your 14-year-old daughter smoke at the dinner table in front of her kids, or you've been married three times and still have the same in-laws, or Jack Daniels makes your list of "most admired people," or you wonder how service stations keep their restrooms so clean, or someone in your family once died right after saying: "Hey, watch this," or you think Dom Perignon is a Mafia leader, or a ceiling fan once ruined your wife's hairdo, or you think "loaded dishwasher" means your wife is drunk again, or you've paid for an annual subscription to the *Broadneck Baloney*.

I'm passing this on to you because it definitely worked for me and we all could use more calm in our lives. By following the simple advice I heard on a medical TV show, I have found inner peace. It's true. A doctor proclaimed the way to achieve inner peace is to finish all the things you have started.

So I looked around my house to see the things I'd started but hadn't finished and, before leaving the house this morning, I finished off a bottle of Merlot, a bottle of Chardonnay, a bottle of vodka, three beers, half a bag of potato chips, the rest of my Xanax, and half a cheesecake. I really feel great. Please pass this on to others who may be in real need of some inner peace.

Here are more of my dad's favorite jokes:

A man is dining in a fancy restaurant and there is a gorgeous redhead sitting at the next table. He has been checking her out since he sat down, but lacks the nerve to talk with her.

Suddenly she sneezes, and her glass eye comes flying out of its socket toward him. He reflexively reaches out, grabs it out of the air, and hands it back to her.

"Oh my, I am so sorry," the woman says, as she pops her eye back in place. "Let me buy your dinner to make it up to you," she says.

They enjoy a wonderful dinner together, and afterwards they go to the theater followed by drinks. They talk, they laugh. She shares her deepest dreams and he shares his. She listens.

After paying for everything, she asks him if he would like to come to her place for a nightcap and stay for breakfast. He agrees.

They have a wonderful, happy time enjoying one romantic experience after another. They talk some more. They share more about themselves, their work, and their friends.

The next morning, she cooks a gourmet breakfast with all the trimmings. The guy is amazed! Everything had been fantastic! Incredible!

"You know," he says, "You are the perfect woman. What in the world attracted you to me to begin with?"

She replies . . . "Back at the restaurant, you just happened to catch my eye."

"Do you have any last wishes before we shoot you?" asked the captain of the firing squad.

"Can I sing a final song?"

"Sure."

"Thanks: A billion trillion bottles of beer on the wall, a billion trillion bottles of beer . . ."

A farmer was driving along the road with a load of fertilizer. A child playing in front of his house saw him and called, "What are you hauling?"

"Fertilizer," the farmer replied.

"What are you going to do with it?" asked the child.

"Put it on strawberries," answered the farmer.

"You ought to live here," the child advised him.

"We put sugar and cream on them."

Elvis Presley, Jr., Editor

I Gave Up Sex, Drugs, and Booze. IT WAS THE WORST 20 MINUTES OF MY LIFE.

LIMERICKS

A man and his lady-love, Min,
Skated out where the ice was quite thin.
Had a quarrel, no doubt,
For I hear they fell out,
What a blessing they didn't fall in!

I'd rather have Fingers than Toes,
I'd rather have Ears than a Nose.
And as for my Hair,
I'm glad it's all there,
I'll be awfully said, when it goes.

There was a young lady of Cork,
Whose Pa made a fortune in pork.
He bought for his daughter,
A tutor who taught her,
To balance green peas on her fork.

My neighbor came over to say,
Although not in a neighborly way,
That he'd knock me around,
If I didn't stop the sound,
Of the rock and roll music I play.

Limericks I cannot compose,
With noxious smells in my nose.
But this one was easy,
I only felt queasy,
Because I was sniffing my toes.

A young schoolgirl named Rose,
Is rather ashamed of her nose.
She distracts people's stares,
With the mice that she wears,
Hanging down from her clothes.

I met her on line, she was neat,
her photo was pretty, petite.
we met for a meal,
I saw her for real,
I screamed and then ran down the street!

Remember when nearly sixteen,
On your very first date as a teen.
At the movies? If yes,
Then I bet you can't guess,
What was shown on the cinema screen.

Is it me or the nature of money,
That's odd and particularly funny?
For when I have dough,
It goes quickly, you know,
And seeps out of my pockets like honey.

There was a young lady from Nachez
whose clothing was always in patches.
When she was asked why,
she replied, with a sigh,
"Cuz when Ah itches, Ah scratches."

I'm papering walls in the loo,
And quite frankly I haven't a clue.
For the pattern's all wrong,
Or the paper's too long,
And I'm stuck to the toilet with glue.

There was a young lady named Rose,
Who had a large wart on her nose.
When she had it removed,
Her appearance improved,
But her glasses slipped down to her toes.

At my age, I'm still hot, but now the hot comes in flashes.

There was an Old Man with a beard,
Who said, It is just as I feared!
Two Owls and a Hen,
Four Larks and a Wren,
Have all built their nests in my beard!

Amazingly, antelope stew,
Is supposedly better for you.
Than a goulash of rat,
Or Hungarian cat,
But I guess that's something you knew.

A dozen, a gross, and a score
Plus three times the square root of four
Divided by seven
Plus five times eleven
Is nine squared and not a bit more.

If you're lacking a little good cheer,
Go and tickle a bull in the rear.
For I'm sure that the rumor,
That they've no sense of humor,
Is a product of ignorant fear.

There was an old man of Peru,
Who dreamt he was eating his shoe.
He woke in the night,
With a terrible fright,
And found it was perfectly true.

There was a young lady of Kent,
Whose nose was most awfully bent.
She followed her nose,
One day, I suppose,
And no one knows which way she went.

An elderly man called Keith,
Mislaid his set of false teeth.
They'd been laid on a chair,
He'd forgot they were there,
Sat down, and was bitten beneath.

A young gourmet dining at Crewe,
Found a rather large mouse in his stew.
Said the waiter, Don't shout,
And wave it about,
Or the rest will be wanting one, too.

There once was a fly on the wall,
I wonder why didn't it fall.
Because its feet stuck,
Or was it just luck,
Or does gravity miss things so small?

An ambitious young fellow named Matt,
Tried to parachute using his hat.
Folks below looked so small,
As he started to fall,
Then got bigger and bigger and SPLAT!

There is a young schoolboy named Mason,
Whose mom cuts his hair with a basin.
When he stands in one place,
With a scarf round his face,
It's a mystery which way he's facing.

I'm really determined and keen,
To start giving this house a spring clean.
I will do it I say,
Yes, I'll do it today,
Well, I'll do it tomorrow, I mean.

Try handling every situation like a dog. If you can't eat it or play with it, just pee on it and walk away.

Bella's Wine and Spirits Presents...
ASK AUNT BERTHABELLE
Answers to LIfe's More Peculiar Problems

DEAR AUNT BERTHABELLE: My maiden name is Esmiralda Carmen. Five years ago, I met a man named Rocky Cohen at a fall wine tasting at *Bella's Wine and Spirits*. Six months later, we married at a marvelous ceremony in the area between *Quality Care Automotive, Inc.* and *Cape Ace Hardware*. I decided to use his name in my business dealings but then we got divorced, and I have moved back home to Edgewater where nobody knows my ex-husband. I am very confused about whether I should use my name Carmen or stick with my ex-husband's name, Cohen. Please help me sort this out, and please withhold my name until such time as my confusion is resolved. *E. C., Edgewater.*

DEAR E. C.: I sympathize deeply with you. No wonder you're confused. You can't tell if you're Carmen or Cohen.

DEAR AUNT BERTHABELLE: About a year ago, I meant to write to you about your feelings on the importance of physical exercise, but I let it slide. About six months ago, I thought very deeply about writing to you again about the same issue, but I just couldn't seem to get around to it. Well, at long last, here's my letter. What kind of exercise program do you recommend for a man such as myself in his mid-forties? *Saul Wrightnow, Mago Vista.*

DEAR SAUL: I doubt that you need to be involved in any kind of physical fitness program. You most likely get enough exercise dragging your heels, jumping to conclusions, jogging your memory and running late. If you think you need to do more than that to stay fit, why not try pushing your luck?

DEAR AUNT BERTHABELLE: My neighbor out back engages in some highly unusual behavior each weekend. I observe him from my upstairs bedroom window. It begins each Friday at about 6 pm when he returns from *Bella's Wine and Spirits* with a case of Bud in cans. He takes the case of beer to the side of his house, out of my view, then returns to get a sledgehammer out of his shed. He returns to the side of his house, and for the next hour or so, I hear frequent pounding noises. My neighbor repeats the same actions on Saturday evening. What's going on, Aunt Berthabelle? *Edna Nosy, Cape St. Claire.*

DEAR EDNA: There is nothing for you to fret about. Your neighbor is like many hard working Broadneckians. He likes to hammer down a few beers when he gets a chance.

DEAR AUNT BERTHABELLE: I've been studying Catholicism, Lutheranism, Pentacostalism, Methodism, and even a little Buddhism and Taoism. I can't make up my mind what to believe. I want to make something of myself here on Broadneck, and I want to have the right religion. Should I look into Presbyterianism and Episcopalianism also? How about Seventh Day Adventists and Jehovah's Witnesses? *Lou Smorals, Bay Hills.*

DEAR LOU: You are never going to amount to anything if all you ever think about is sects! sects! sects!

DEAR AUNT BERTHABELLE: I want to remind all your readers that Ground Hog Day is the tenth anniversary of the demise of one of the world's greatest scientists, Broadneck's own Dr. Gene Splicer. While attempting to take samples from a boiling mixture of acids in a huge vat, he accidentally fell in and perished. If fate hadn't taken him in such a cruel way, think of all the pressing scientific problems he could have solved. *Red Brown, Scarlet Green.*

DEAR MR. BROWN: Science as a whole and each of us individually have problems. I believe that Dr. Splicer was fortunate to become part of the solution. ❈

The Miss Universe Pageant is Fixed. ALL THE WINNERS ARE FROM EARTH.

Bella's Wine and Spirits Presents . . .
ASK AUNT BERTHABELLE
Answers to LIfe's More Peculiar Problems

DEAR AUNT BERTHABELLE: For the interest of your many readers, on this coming Monday, I will be delivering a lecture at the community college on the kidneys, the liver, and the small intestine. Please let them know about it and try to make it yourself if you can. *Doctor Jason Rainbows, Ferry Farms.*

DEAR DR. RAINBOWS: I'll be happy to inform my readers, but you'll never catch me there. I hate organ recitals.

DEAR AUNT BERTHABELLE: I have suffered with constipation for the past week. I sit in the bathroom for an hour each morning and an hour each night. Can you recommend anything I should take? *Mona Little, Shore Acres.*

DEAR MONA: Certainly. Take a book or a magazine.

DEAR AUNT BERTHABELLE: My wife and I recently went on our first European vacation. The traveling was a hassle, and Helsinki was the worst: our baggage, including all our clothing, vanished into Finn air. Our second stop was Prague. The people seemed so literate, always talking about their Czech books. Watching the people observing a certain landmark in Italy, however, caused us some confusion. As they studied the tower of Pisa, they all tilted about eleven degrees to the side. You are a well-known world traveler and I'm sure you can help us. What is it that makes these people lean? *Greg Arious, Ulmstead Gardens.*

DEAR GREG: You are setting me up to answer, "A strict low-fat diet is what makes them lean." You better get a grip, you dissolute punster: one thing I don't need is a straight man. This is an advice column, not an open forum for dim-witted jackasses who are unable to distinguish between acceptable humor and raw impertinence.

DEAR AUNT BERTHABELLE: In Annapolis last week, a dirty and shabby-looking homeless woman asked me for money for dinner. Before I was about to give her twenty dollars, I asked her if she was going to buy wine with it instead of food. She said that she wouldn't buy wine because she had stopped drinking years ago.

Then I asked her if she'd use the twenty bucks to go shopping instead of buying dinner for herself. "No, I don't waste time shopping," the grubby creature responded. "I need to spend all my time trying to stay alive."

Then I asked her if she would spend the money at a beauty salon. She replied, "Are you nuts? I haven't had my hair done in fifteen years!"

On hearing this, I decided to take this smelly, grimy woman to dinner with my husband and me that night, and I think you know why. *Barb E. Dahl, Whitehall.*

DEAR BARB: Of course I do. You wanted your husband to see what a woman looks like after she has given up shopping, hair appointments, and wine.

DEAR AUNT BERTHABELLE: While searching my family ancestry, I recently found that we are descended from the great William Tell of apple-splitting with his bow and arrow fame. Evidence has been found that William Tell and his family were avid bowlers. However, all league records have been unfortunately lost. Do you think there is anyway I may be able to retrieve those records? *Ivana Tell, College Manor.*

DEAR IVANA: I very seriously doubt it. Those league records are probably lost forever. We will just have to resign ourselves to the fact that we will never know for whom the Tells bowled.

DEAR AUNT BERTHABELLE: People make so many excuses for divorce these days. I say there's no excuse. What say you? *Destinee Hooker, Cape.*

DEAR DESTINEE: I just heard about an Amish woman who had a good excuse for divorce: She said her husband was driving her buggy. ✻

It's Amazing That the Amount of News That Happens in the World Each Day Always Exactly Fits the Newspaper.

Bella's Wine and Spirits Presents...
ASK AUNT BERTHABELLE
Answers to LIfe's More Peculiar Problems

DEAR AUNT BERTHABELLE: I love pie and ice cream and eat Oreo cookies by the sleeve. I just can't help myself. I am more than 250 pounds overweight. I shuffle across the room like a sloth on Librium. When I think of chocolate cake, intense hunger oozes from my pores. I just don't know what to do about my uncontrollable addiction to sweets. Is there anything you can do to help me? *Hugh G. Rear, Belvedere.*

DEAR HUGH: I empathize. I'm a bit tubby myself. Let us both take solace in the fact that our weight makes us harder to kidnap.

DEAR AUNT BERTHABELLE: I am a student who works very hard in my history class at Anne Arundel Community College. The girl behind me, although very beautiful and sexy, hardly ever studies. She can never remember any important historical names or places, and yet she gets the highest grades in the class. She and our teacher, Mr. Whipple, appear to be batting eyes at each other. Do you think our teacher is playing favorites, perhaps secretly seeing this vivacious vixen? *Eliza Lott, Mago Vista.*

DEAR ELIZA: Possibly. Did you ever consider that girls weak on names and places are quite often great on dates?

DEAR AUNT BERTHABELLE: My wife confessed to several affairs and promised to be faithful again. Wouldn't you know it! I came home early from work yesterday and found her in bed with a midget, both of them apparently spellbound with compelling sensations. My long nose became pinched and white with resentful rage. I am so angry that my teeth itch. Should I leave her for good? *Ivan Oeder, Whitehall Beach.*

DEAR IVAN: No. I would stick with her. Most bad habits are hard to break. Finding her with a midget seems like a positive sign. She's probably trying her best to taper off.

DEAR AUNT BERTHABELLE: My best friend and I have been talking lately about how life can be so unfair to the people of Broadneck sometimes. Let's say that a person living on Kent Island felt bad and had an inkling to end it all by jumping off the Bay Bridge. Would it cost the Kent Islander anything? Absolutely not, since there's no toll booth coming from that side. But let's just say that I, or my best friend (both of us are conscientious residents of Broadneck), wanted to end it all by jumping off the bridge. It would cost us $4.00, leaving sort of a bad feeling with us during the last few minutes of our lives. How would you rectify this gross and arbitrary injustice? *Hedda Hare, Log Inn Road.*

DEAR HEDDA: The poignant clarity of your appeal for justice has touched my sense of fair play. Enclosed please find two separate checks for $4.00 each made out to the Maryland State Toll Facilities Administration. One is for you, and one is for your best friend, with my compliments. Because I have done this, however, you and your friend need not jump to any conclusions.

DEAR AUNT BERTHABELLE: I work at the checkout desk at the Marriott in downtown Annapolis. Yesterday, a group of chess enthusiasts who had already checked in stood in the lobby discussing their recent tournament victories. After about an hour, my manager came out of the office and asked them to disperse. "But why?" they asked, as they moved off. Why do you think my boss did this? If I don't get an answer, I feel like I'm going to explode. *Adam Baum, Tydings-on-the-Bay.*

DEAR ADAM: I'm guessing your boss is a lot like me. We both just can't stand chess-nuts boasting in an open foyer. ❊

GOD BLESS THE IRISH 3

An Irishman walks into *O'Loughlin's*. Cindy, the bartender, asks him, "What'll you have?" The man replies, "Give me three pints of Guinness please."

So the bartender brings him three pints and the man proceeds to alternately sip one, then the other, then the third until they're gone. He then orders three more.

Cindy says, "Sir, I know you like them cold. You don't have to order three at a time. I can keep an eye on it and when you get low I'll bring you a fresh cold one."

The man says, "You don't understand. I have two brothers, one in Australia and one in the Ireland. We made a vow to each other that every Saturday night we'd still drink together. So right now, my brothers have three Guinness Stouts too, and we're drinking together.

Cindy thought that was a wonderful tradition. Every week the man came in and ordered three beers.

Then one week he came in and ordered only two. He drank them and then ordered two more. Cindy said to him, "I know what your tradition is, and I'd just like to say that I'm sorry that one of your brothers died."

The man said, "Oh, my brothers are fine—I just quit drinking."

Donal and Ennis were sitting next to each other at *O'Loughlin's*. After a while, Donal looks at Ennis and says, "I can't help but think, from listening to you, that you're from Ireland."

Ennis responds proudly, "Yes, That I am!"

Donal says, "So am I! And where about from Ireland might you be?"

Ennis answers, "I'm from Dublin, I am."

Donal responds, "Sure and begorrah, and so am I! And what street did you live on in Dublin?"

Ennis says, "A lovely little area it was, I lived on McCleary Street in the old central part of town."

Donal says, "Faith and it's a small world, so did I! And to what school would you have been going?"

Ennis replies, "Well now, I went to St. Mary's of course."

Donal gets really excited, and says, "And so did I. Tell me what year did you graduate?"

Ennis answers, "Well, now, in 1964."

Donal exclaims, "The Good Lord must be smiling down upon us! I can hardly believe our good luck at winding up together at *O'Loughlin's* tonight. Can you believe it, I graduated from St. Mary's in 1964 my own self."

About this time, another gentleman walks into *O'Loughlin's*, sits down, and orders a beer. The bartender walks over shaking his head and mutters, "It's going to be a long night tonight, the Murphy twins are at it again.

Kieran O'Connor always slept with his gun under his pillow. Hearing a noise at the foot of the bed, he shot off his big toe.

"Thank the Lord I wasn't sleeping at the other end of the bed," Kieran said to his friends in Donegal's pub. "I would have blown my head clear off."

Doncha and MacArthur are preparing to be blasted into space and have just left the mission briefing when one turns to the other and says, "Mac, where are we goin?"

MacArthur replies, "Well Donncha, the man in charge said we are on a mission to the sun."

"OK," says Donncha. He thinks for a while and then asks, "Won't it be a bit hot, it being the sun and all?"

"Don't be stupid, Donncha," says MacArthur, "The man said we'd be going at night."

GOD BLESS THE IRISH 4

One day an Irishman, who had been stranded on a desert island for over ten years, saw a speck on the horizon. "It's certainly not a ship," he thought. As the speck got closer and closer he began to rule out the possibilities of a small boat or even a raft.

Suddenly, there emerged from the surf a wet-suited, black-clad figure. Putting aside her scuba gear and her mask, there stood a drop-dead gorgeous blonde woman. The glamorous blonde strode up to the stunned Irishman and said to him, "Tell me, how long has it been since you've had a cigarette?"

"Ten years," replied the amazed Irishman. With that, she reached over and unzipped a waterproof pocket on the left sleeve of her wetsuit and pulled out a fresh pack of cigarettes. He took one, lit it up, and took a long drag. "Faith and begorrah," said the Irishman, "that is so good, I'd almost forgotten how great a smoke can be!"

"And how long has it been since you've had a drop of good Irish whiskey?" asked the blonde.

Trembling, the castaway replied, "Ten years."

At this, the blonde reached over to her right sleeve, unzipped the pocket, removed a flask and handed it to him.

The Irishman opened the flask and took a long drink. "Tis nectar of the gods!" he exclaimed. "Tis truly fantastic!"

At this point, the beautiful blonde started to slowly unzip the long front of her wetsuit, right down the middle. She looked at the trembling man and asked, "And how long has it been since you played around?"

With tears in his eyes, the Irishman fell to his knees and sobbed, "Sweet Jesus! Don't tell me you've got golf clubs in there, too!"

Paddy goes to the vet carrying his goldfish in a bowl. He tells the vet, "I think my goldfish has epilepsy." The vet looks at the goldfish and says, "He seems perfectly fine to me."

"Oh no," says Paddy, "You haven't taken him out of the bowl yet!"

Irishman Mike Murphy and his pregnant wife live on a farm in the distant rural regions of Broadneck, no running water, no electricity, etc. One night, Mike's wife begins to deliver the baby with the local doctor there in attendance.

Mike asks, "What d'ya want me to do, Doctor?"

"Hold the lantern, Mikey. Here it comes!" The doctor delivers the child and holds it up for the proud father to see.

"Mike, you're the proud father of a fine strapping boy."

Before Mike can finish saying, "Saints be praised," the Doctor interrupts, "Wait a minute. Hold the lantern, Mikey."

Soon the doctor delivers the next child. "You've a full set now, Mikey. A beautiful baby daughter."

"Thanks be to . . ."

Again the Doctor cuts in, "Hold the lantern, Mikey, Hold the lantern!" Soon the Doctor delivers a third child. The doctor holds up the baby for Mike's inspection.

"Doctor," asks Mike, "Do you think it's the light of the lantern that's attracting them?"

At the Taco Bell I Asked for Minimal Lettuce. THEY TOLD ME ALL THEY HAD WAS ICEBERG.

ANTI-JOKES

What did the man say to the woman? "Hey, you're blocking the TV. You can come sit next to me if you like, but I know you don't really like this kind of program. If you want to watch something different it's fine, but can I at least watch the end of the game? This is the finals of my favorite sporting event and it would mean a lot if I could finish watching it. Thank you for being such an understanding person."

A horse walks into a bar. Bartender asks "Why the long face?" The horse answers, "I just lost all my money gambling."

The IRS decides to audit Ralph, and summons him to the IRS office. The IRS auditor is not surprised when Ralph shows up with his attorney. The auditor says, "Well, sir, you have an extravagant lifestyle and no full-time employment, which you explain by saying that you win money gambling. I'm not sure the IRS finds that believable."

"I'm a great gambler, and I can prove it," says Ralph. "How about a demonstration? I bet you I can bite my own eye."
The auditor thinks for a moment and says "Sir, I'm not here to make frivolous bets with you."
Ralph is subsequently audited and has to declare bankruptcy.

Yo mama's so fat, I'd say she probably weighs a good 300 pounds or so. (She suffers from depression and eats to compensate, but thanks for noticing).

Yo mama's so fat that she's unfortunately going to have to receive quintuple bypass surgery and only has a 50% chance of pulling through. I'm sorry, son.

A seal walks into a club.
He proceeds to get on stage where he sings his hit song "Crazy." The crowd applauds and good times were had by all.

Why didn't the skeleton go to the dance?
It was in storage and it wasn't Halloween.

How could a bird with no wings fly?
I stapled it to an airplane.

Why did the blonde get fired from the M&M factory?
Repeated absences and stealing.

Why do firemen wear red suspenders? To comply with departmental regulations concerning uniform dress.

What's worse, ignorance or apathy? I'm not sure about either. They both carry negative connotations and can lead to one's downfall.

The pope, Lil Wayne and Ann Coulter walk into a bar . . . Unlikely.

24 Hours in a Day, 24 Beers in a Case. COINCIDENCE? I THINK NOT.

Did You Hear? THEY TOOK THE WORD GULLIBLE OUT OF THE DICTIONARY.

Oprah walks onto a bus, but doesn't have the right amount of change for the fare. "Can you break a $100 dollar bill?" She asks the bus driver.

"No," he says, "and I'm sorry but you're going to have to go to the back of the bus."

"Excuse me?" she says with disdain. "I will do no such thing."

"But that is where the change machine is. You should be able to break your bill back there."

After that, Oprah was red-faced with embarrassment.

A priest and a rabbi sit next to each other on a plane. It's a short flight and they both nod off for the duration of the flight without speaking.

What is the difference between a gynecologist and a plumber?
A gynecologist is a physician specializing in the treatment of women, whereas a plumber is a skilled tradesman who specializes in pipes and drains and such.

An Asian man is going to get a vasectomy. He shows up to the doctor's office wearing a suit. The doctor says "Why are you wearing a suit?" The Asian man says "I just got back from a funeral."

Now why would I want to cross the road? Look at all those cars! It's dangerous. I may have a brain the size of a peanut and run haphazardly if you cut off my head, but I'm not stupid.

Why couldn't the midget fix his unicycle? Because he didn't have a Phillips screwdriver.

ANTI-JOKES

What do you tell a woman with two black eyes?
Domestic violence is a crime. She should leave her abusive partner and seek help.

Did the blonde get fired from the M&M factory because she threw away the Ws? No. She quit because she had a degree in corporate law and decided to stop wasting her time in a dead end job.

Have you seen Stevie Wonder's new house?
Well, it's really nice.

What was the pirate movie rated? PG-13 for violence and brief nudity.

What did the duck say to the skunk? Quack, quack, quack.

What do you call a doormat mixed with a dog? A doormat-dog mix.

Why is 6 afraid of 7?
Because 7 has a history of paranoid schizophrenia with violent tendencies and has gone off-medication once before.

How Do Fish Know How Much They Weigh? THEY HAVE THEIR OWN SCALES.

What Should You Give a Man Who Has Everything? A WOMAN TO SHOW HIM HOW IT ALL WORKS.

The teacher wrote on the blackboard: "I ain't had no fun in months," then she asked the class, "How should I correct this sentence?"

Little Johnny raised his hand and said, "Get a new boyfriend, and have a few drinks, teacher."

◆

The teacher had asked the class to write an essay about an unusual event that happened during the past week.

Little Johnny got up to read his. It began, "My daddy fell in a well last week."

"Good Lord!" the teacher exclaimed. "Is he okay?"

"He must be," said Little Johnny. "He stopped calling for help yesterday."

◆

The teacher asks little Johnny if he knows his numbers.

"Yes," he says. "My daddy taught me."

"Can you tell me what comes after three?"

"Four," answers little Johnny.

"What comes after six?"

"Seven," answers little Johnny.

"Very good," says the teacher. "Your father did a very fine job.

What comes after ten?"

"A jack," answers little Johnny.

◆

A door-to-door salesman comes-a-knocking and 10-year-old Little Johnny answers, a beer in one hand and a lit cigar in the other.

The salesman says, "Little boy, is your mommy home?"

Little Johnny taps his ash on the carpet and says, "Now just what in the hell do you think?"

◆

LITTLE JOHNNY

Little Johnny and Susie are only 10 years old, but they just know that they are in love. One day they decide that they want to get married, so Johnny goes to Susie's father to ask him for her hand. Johnny bravely walks up to him and says "Mr. Smith, me and Susie are in love and I want to ask you for her hand in marriage."

Thinking that this was the cutest thing, Mr. Smith replies, "Well Johnny, you are only 10. Where will you two live?"

Without even taking a moment to think about it, Johnny replies "In Susie's room. It's bigger than mine and we can both fit there nicely."

Still thinking this is just adorable, Mr. Smith says with a huge grin, "Okay then how will you live? You're not old enough to get a job. You'll need to support Susie."

Again, Johnny instantly replies, "Our allowance - Susie makes 5 bucks a week and I make 10 bucks a week. That's about 60 bucks a month, and that should do us just fine."

By this time Mr. Smith is a little shocked that Johnny has put so much thought into this. So, he thinks for a moment, trying to come up with something that Johnny won't have an answer to. After a second, Mr. Smith says, "Well Johnny, it seems like you have got everything all figured out. I just have one more question for you. What will you do if the two of you should have little ones of your own?"

Johnny just shrugs his shoulders and says, "Well, we've been lucky so far." ◆

Doctor: "You're Overweight." PATIENT: "I WANT A SECOND OPINION." Doctor: "You're also Ugly."

LITTLE JOHNNY

Little Johnny sat on a park bench stuffing all of his Halloween candy in his mouth. An old lady came over and said, "Son, don't you know that eating all of that candy will rot your teeth, give you acne, and make you sick?"

"My grandfather lived to be 105 years old!" replied Johnny.

"Did he eat five candy bars at a sitting?" the old lady retorted.

"No," said Johnny, "but he minded his own freakin' business."

Little Johnny asks his mother her age. She replies, "Gentlemen don't ask ladies that question."

Johnny then asks his mother how much she weighs.

Again his mother replies, "Gentlemen don't ask ladies that question."

The boy then asks, "Why did Daddy leave you?"

To this, the mother says, "You shouldn't ask that," and sends him to his room.

On the way, Johnny trips over his mother's purse. When he picks it up, her driver's license falls out.

Johnny runs back into the room. "I know all about you now. You are 36 years old, weigh 127 pounds and Daddy left you because you got an 'F' in sex!"

◆

A new teacher tries to make use of her psychology courses. The first day of class, she starts by saying, "Everyone who thinks they're stupid, stand up!"

After a few seconds, Little Johnny stands up. The teacher asks, "Do you think you're stupid, Johnny?"

"No, ma'am, but I hate to see you standing there all by yourself." ◆

Little Johnny's kindergarten class was on a field trip to their local police station where they saw pictures of the ten most dangerous criminals tacked to a bulletin board.

One of the youngsters pointed to a picture and asked if it really was the photo of a wanted person.

"Yes," said the policeman, "The detectives want very badly to capture him." Little Johnny asked, "Why didn't you arrest him when you took his picture?"

The teacher asked the class to use the word "fascinate" in a sentence.

Molly put up her hand and said, "My family went to my granddad's farm, and we all saw his pet sheep. It was fascinating."

The teacher said, "That was good, but I wanted you to use the word fascinate, not fascinating."

Sally raised her hand. She said, "My family went to see Rock City and I was fascinated."

The teacher said, "Well, that was good Sally, but I wanted you to use the word fascinate."

Little Johnny raised his hand. The teacher hesitated because she had been burned by Little Johnny before. She finally decided there was no way he could damage the word fascinate, so she called on him.

Johnny said, "My aunt Gina has a sweater with ten buttons, but her gazoombas are so big she can only fasten eight."

The teacher sat down and cried. ◆

Did You Get Many Orders as a Salesman? YES. GET OUT, STAY OUT, AND DON'T EVER COME BACK!

BALONEY WORD PUZZLE #2

Example: 24 H _ _ _ _ in a D _ _ = 24 Hours in a Day

99 B _ _ _ _ _ _ _ of B _ _ _ on the W _ _ _

6 S _ _ _ _ _ _ on a G _ _ _ _ _

4 Q _ _ _ _ _ _ _ in a D _ _ _ _ _ _

60 S _ _ _ _ _ _ in a M _ _ _ _ _ _

12 D _ _ _ of C _ _ _ _ _ _ _ _

21 G _ _ S _ _ _ _ _

4 S _ _ _ _ in a D _ _ _ of P _ _ _ _ _ _ C _ _ _ _

7 Y _ _ _ _ of B _ _ L _ _ _

2,000 P _ _ _ _ _ in a T _ _

9 S _ _ _ _ _ _ C _ _ _ _ J _ _ _ _ _ _ _

2 W _ _ _ _ _ D _ _ _ M _ _ _ a R _ _ _ _

1 M _ _ _ for the R _ _ _

2 S _ _ _ _ of a C _ _ _

4 S _ _ _ _ _ _ _ in a Y _ _ _

9 I _ _ _ _ _ _ in a B _ _ _ _ _ _ _ G _ _ _

6 P _ _ _ _ _ _ on a P _ _ _ T _ _ _ _

20,000 L _ _ _ _ _ _ U _ _ _ _ the S _ _

100 Y _ _ _ _ in a C _ _ _ _ _ _ _

3 F _ _ _ in a Y _ _ _

2 P _ _ _ in a P _ _

3 W _ _ _ _ _ on a T _ _ _ _ _ _ _

Answers at BroadneckBaloney.com

Please Don't Write in the Spaces - So Others Can Enjoy the Challenge

At the ATM an Old Lady Asked Me to Help Check Her Balance. SO I PUSHED HER OVER.

Plain Old Broadneck Jokes

I was tired of being bossed around by my wife so I went to a psychiatrist. The psychiatrist said I needed to build my self-esteem, and so he gave me a book on assertiveness, which I read on the way home.

I finished the book by the time I reached my house. I stormed into the house and walked up to my wife. Pointing a finger in her face, I said, "From now on, I want you to know that I am the man of this house, and my word is law! I want you to prepare me a gourmet meal tonight, and when I'm finished eating my meal, I expect a sumptuous dessert afterwards.

Then, after dinner, you're going to draw me my bath so I can relax. And, when I'm finished with my bath, guess who's going to dress me and comb my hair?"

"The funeral director," she said. •

A drunk was proudly showing off his new apartment to a couple of his friends late one night. When they made it to the bedroom, they saw a big brass gong next to the bed.

"What's a big brass gong doing in your bedroom?" one of the guests asked.

"It's not a gong. It's a talking clock," the drunk replied.

"A talking clock? Seriously?" asked his astonished friend.

"Yup," replied the drunk.

"How's it work?" the friend asked, squinting at it.

"Watch," the drunk replied. Picking up the mallet, he gave the gong an ear-shattering pound, and stepped back.

The three stood looking at one another for a moment.

Suddenly, someone on the other side of the wall screamed, "You moron, it's three o'clock in the morning!" •

A crusty old biker walks into a bank and says to the woman at the teller window "I want to open a damn checking account."

The astonished woman replies, "I beg your pardon, sir. I must have misunderstood you. What did you say?"

"Listen up, damn it. I said I want to open a damn checking account now!" says the biker.

"I'm very sorry sir, but that kind of language is not tolerated in this bank," the teller informs him. She then leaves the window and goes over to the bank manager to inform her of the situation.

The manager agrees that the teller does not have to listen to foul language.

They both return to the window and the manager asks the old biker, "Sir, what seems to be the problem here?"

"There is no damn problem," the man says. "I just won 50 million dollars in the damn lottery and I want to open a damn checking account in this damn bank!"

"I see," says the manager, "and is this damn nag giving you a hard time about it?" •

It was the intermission at the opera when Mrs. Sternberg rose from her seat and called: "Is there a doctor in the house? Is there a doctor in the house?!"

A man in a tuxedo pushed his way towards her. "I'm a doctor," he said.

"Oh, doctor," she said, "Have I got just the loveliest daughter for you . . ." •

Men are like blenders . . . You need one, but you're not sure why.

Plain Old Broadneck Jokes

There once was a bar maid from Yale
On her chest were tattooed the prices of ale
And for the sake of the blind, on her behind
Was the same thing written in brail. ☺

A husband and wife were waiting in the consultation room when the doctor entered.

"And what seems to be the problem, Mrs. Smith?"

"My husband worries constantly about money."

The doctor absentmindedly replied, "I think we can relieve him of that!" ☺

A newcomer was drinking in an Old West saloon when a cowboy ran through the swinging doors, yelling, "Big Jake's a'comin'!"

The place immediately emptied, leaving the newcomer and his beer alone at the bar.

Sure enough, soon a seven-foot tall, 350-pound cowboy swaggered in, barely fitting through the double doors.

He glanced around the saloon and, seeing no one but our friend, marched over to him, grabbed him by the scruff of the neck, threw him over the bar, and bellowed, "Gimme whiskey!"

The shaken man complied, found a full bottle, and placed it and a glass on the bar.

The huge cowboy bit the glass neck right off the bottle, spat it on the floor, and emptied the fifth in one giant swig.

The newcomer, not sure what to do next, asked, "Uh, do you want another?"

"Nope," the cowboy growled. "Gotta go. Big Jake's a'comin'!" ☺

A police officer pulls over a speeding car. The officer says, "I clocked you at 80 miles per hour, sir."

The driver says, "Gee, officer I had it on cruise control at 60, perhaps your radar gun needs calibrating."

The driver's wife is in the passenger seat kitting. Not looking up from her knitting she says: "Now don't be silly dear, you know that this car doesn't have cruise control."

As the officer writes out the ticket, the driver looks over at his wife and growls, "Can't you please keep your mouth shut for once?"

She smiles demurely and says, "You should be thankful your radar detector went off when it did."

As the officer makes out the second ticket for the illegal radar detector unit, the man glowers at his wife and says through clenched teeth, "Darn it, woman, can't you keep your mouth shut?"

The officer frowns and says, "And I notice that you're not wearing your seat belt, sir. That's an automatic $75 fine."

"Yeah, well, you see officer, I had it on, but took it off when you pulled me over so that I could get my license out of my back pocket," the driver responds.

His wife says, "Now, dear, you know very well that you didn't have your seat belt on. You never wear your seat belt when you're driving."

And, as the police officer is writing out the third ticket the driver turns to his wife and barks, "WHY DON'T YOU PLEASE SHUT UP!"

The officer looks over at the woman and asks, "Does your husband always talk to you this way, Ma'am?"

"Only when he's been drinking officer." ☺

My girlfriend left a note on the fridge: "It's not working. I can't take it anymore. I'm going to Mom's place."

I opened the fridge. The light came on. The beer was cold. What the heck is she talking about? ☺

Waiter, I asked for the hamburger without the bun. MY APOLOGIES. NO BUN INTENDED.

Why did the cows return to the marijuana field? It was the pot calling the cattle back.

Plain Old Broadneck Jokes

IRS Agent: "I need a list of your employees and how much you pay them."

Rancher: "Well, there's my hired hand who's been with me for 3 years. I pay him $200 a week plus free room and board. Then there's the mentally challenged guy. He works about 18 hours every day and does about 90 percent of all the work around here. He makes about $10 per week, pays his own room and board, and I buy him a bottle of bourbon every Saturday night so he can cope with life. He also cooks dinner for my wife occasionally."

IRS Agent: "That's the guy I want to talk to – the mentally challenged one."

Rancher: "That would be me." •

The newlywed wife winked at her husband and said, "I have great news for you honey. Pretty soon there will be three of us in this house instead of two."

Her husband jumped up and proclaimed, "Oh darling, you've made me the happiest man in the world!"

The wife smiled and replied, "I'm so glad you feel that way. My mother moves in tomorrow." •

The parents of two 5-year-old twin boys were worried that they had developed extreme personalities—one was a total pessimist, the other a total optimist —so they took them to a psychiatrist.

First the psychiatrist treated the pessimist. Trying to brighten his outlook, the psychiatrist took him to a room piled to the ceiling with brand-new toys. But instead of yelping with delight, the little boy burst into tears.

"What's the matter?" the psychiatrist asked, baffled. "Don't you want to play with any of the toys you see here?"

"Yes," the little boy bawled, "but if I did I'd only break them."

Next the psychiatrist treated the optimist. Trying to dampen his outlook, the psychiatrist took him to a room piled to the ceiling with horse manure. But instead of wrinkling his nose in disgust, the optimist emitted a yelp of delight the psychiatrist had been hoping to hear from his brother, the pessimist.

Then the boy clambered to the top of the pile, dropped to his knees, and began gleefully digging out scoop after scoop with his bare hands.

"What do you think you're doing?" the psychiatrist asked, just as baffled by the optimist as he had been by the pessimist.

"With all this manure," the little boy replied, beaming, "there must be a pony in here somewhere!" •

A little girl asked her mother, "How did the human race appear?"

The mother answered, "God made Adam and Eve and they had children, and so was all mankind made."

Two days later the girl asked her father the same question.

The father answered, "Many years ago there were worms, snakes, rats, and monkeys from which the human race evolved."

The confused girl returned to her mother and said, "Mom, how is it possible that you told me the human race was created by God, and Dad said they developed from worms, rats, snakes, and monkeys?"

The mother answered, "Well, dear, it is very simple. I told you about my side of the family and your father told you about his!" •

Do you drink to excess? I'll drink to anything.

If at First You Don't Succeed, Maybe Skydiving Isn't for You.

The Editor's Corner

A juggler driving to his next performance was stopped by the police.

"What are those knives doing in your car?" asked the officer.

"I juggle them in my act."

"Oh yeah?" says the cop. "Let's see you do it." So the juggler starts tossing and juggling the knives.

A guy driving by sees this and says, "Wow, am I glad I quit drinking. Look at the test they're making you do now!"

A young woman goes to the local psychic in hopes of contacting her dearly departed grandmother. The psychic's eyelids begin fluttering, her voice begins warbling, her hands float up above the table, and she begins moaning.

Eventually, a coherent voice emanates, saying, "Granddaughter? Are you there?"

The young woman, wide-eyed and on the edge of her seat, responds, "Grandmother? Is that you?"

"Yes granddaughter, it's me."

"It's really you, grandmother?" the woman says.

"Yes, it's really me, granddaughter."

The woman looks puzzled, "You're sure it's you?"

"Yes, granddaughter, I'm sure it's me."

"When did you learn to speak English?"

A man is walking down Whitehall Road when he sees a farmer feeding his pigs from an apple tree. The farmer picks up a pig and holds it next to a branch so that it can eat an apple from the tree. Then, he puts the pig down, picks up another pig and repeats the process.

The man says to the farmer: "You could save a lot of time by hitting that tree with a stick. All the apples would fall to the ground and feed the pigs at the same time." The farmer replied: "Yeah, I thought about that. But then it occurred to me, what's time to a pig?"

Over the years, I've been saving some of the more interesting blatherings of politicians. A few:

Let's jump off that bridge when we come to it.

To be demeanered like that is an exercise in fertility.

I deny the allegations, and I defy the allegators.

If somebody's gonna stab me in the back, I want to be there.

When you're talking to me, keep your big mouth shut.

Let's do this in one foul swoop.

I want to thank each and every one of you for having extinguished yourselves in this session.

These numbers are not my own; they are from someone who knows what he's talking about.

People planning on getting into serious accidents should have their seat belts on.

In these trying times, Americans stand on the horns of an enema.

When I was a kid, Dad explained to me everything I needed to know about religion in four sentences:

1. Islam does not recognize that the Jews are God's chosen people.
2. Jews do not recognize Jesus Christ as the Son of God.
3. Protestants do not recognize the pope as the head of Christianity.
4. And finally, Baptists do not recognize each other at the liquor store.

I'm embarrassed to be the editor of this publication. There's no editorial content to speak of. My very title is a farce. I shouldn't care, but I do because I don't want this travesty to reflect poorly upon my father. So, in his honor, I present one of his favorite poems:

Mary had a little pig,
She kept it fat and plastered;
And when the price of pork went up,
She shot the little bastard!

Elvis Presley, Jr., Editor

I Do Whatever the Rice Krispies Tell Me to Do.

The Editor's Corner

Maybe I'm not quite as sharp as a sack of wet mice. I might even be a few Bradys short of a bunch. Maybe my logs are ablaze but my chimney's clogged. So what?

Maybe my wheel is spinning but the hamster fell off, or the squeeze-cheese slipped off my cracker. And I could be a few pecans short of a fruit cake and dumb as a salt shaker. Who cares?

Maybe I've got too much chlorine in my gene pool or I'm a couple toppings short of a deluxe *Vizzini's* Pizza. I've been called a monosynaptic cretin, and worse. What's the big deal?

Maybe I haven't seen the ball since kickoff. Or possibly I'm a few brews short of a six pack. It could be that I have a full six pack but lack the plastic thingy that holds the cans together. I don't deny that my elevator might not go all the way to the top, and even if it could, that the doors wouldn't open.

Maybe with me the batteries aren't included, or I've lost contact with the mother ship. I might not be as quick as a snail crossing super glue, or even singing from the same hymn sheet as the rest of you. And it could be that most of the dots have worn off my dice. Perhaps I can't even find my butt with two hands and a road map.

Maybe I've got a nice cage, but there's no bird in it. Maybe you get more out of staring at a brick wall than reading my column. It's possible I have a few lug nuts rattling around in my hubcaps. Who cares? I'm still the editor of the most prestigious journal you've ever read, you moron!

People are funny. A local Catholic priest, notorious for his bad memory, ran into one of his parishioners at *Vizzini's Pizza 'n Subs*. He tried and tried but he simply could not remember who she was.

"Good morning, Father," she said.

The priest could only smile. He said, "Pardon me, miss. I can't remember your name, but your faith is familiar."

As Dad used to always tell me and Mom, "The best way to keep a rooster from crowing on Sunday is to cook him on Saturday."

You think it's easy to come up with The Editor's Corner every month?

I needed a new deck built and, desiring to demonstrate to the world that I'm open-minded and non-sexist, I passed up a great price from *Paddy Whalen of Solution One*, and hired a lady carpenter. It cost me a lot more, but I'm so glad I gave her the job. She has real long nails and you oughta see her build!

People are still funny. I was in the bank the other day, and one of the tellers asked *Mary Ann Davis* of *Cape Hair Scene* to identify herself. She said, "Oh sure, I'd be happy to." Then she walked over to the mirror, looked at herself, and said, "Yep, that's me all right."

Archimedes, that well-known truth-seeker,
jumped out of his bath with "Eureka!"
He ran half a mile
wearing only a smile
and became the very first streaker.

There once was a girl named Irene
who lived on distilled kerosene.
But she started absorbin'
a new hydrocarbon
and since then has never benzene.

A gentleman walks into a bar where there is loud music playing. He spots a pretty girl at the end of the bar and approaches her. He says "Would you like to dance?" and she replies, "I really don't like this song. And even if I did I wouldn't dance with you."

To which the gentleman replies "I don't think you heard me correctly. I said that you look fat in those pants."

Elvis Presley, Jr., Editor

The Editor's Corner

A swimmer whose clothing got strewed
by breezes that left her quite nude
saw a man come along,
and unless we are wrong,
you expected this line to be lewd.

There was a young fellow named Clyde
who fell in an outhouse and died.
Along came his brother
and fell in another
now they're interred side by side.

A Caper walks into the Arnold Pharmacy and asks Neil, "Do you have any acetylsalicylic acid?"

"Do you mean aspirin?" Neil asks.

"That's it. I can never remember that word!"

Let me amplify what I was saying to my critics in the previous issue.

Perhaps I am a few fries short of a happy meal, or even a couple of clowns short of a circus. Some have suggested that I am dumber than a box of hair.

Maybe I don't have all my corn flakes in one box or I'm one or two fruit loops shy of a full bowl. So what?

Maybe I'm all foam and no beer or a few feathers short of a whole duck. Maybe I don't have any grain in my silo. Perhaps my receiver is off the hook or there is too much yardage between my goal posts. It's possible that my belt doesn't go through all the loops. Who cares?

It may be that I am no smarter than bait and have an IQ somewhere between that of a rock and an oyster. I confess that I am missing several buttons on my remote control.

It is quite possible that my antenna doesn't pick up all the channels or that my chimney is clogged.

Maybe I forgot to pay my brain bill this month. Maybe I can't pour water out of a boot with instructions on the heel. What difference does it make?

At supper last night I was thinking that maybe I'm a few peas short of a casserole. I admit I seem about a half a bubble off plumb, and it's true: I might not be the crunchiest chip in the bag. Maybe my cornbread isn't done in the middle, and it could be that I'm not quite as sharp as a marble.

Well, let me ask you this: you are intently reading my column. What does that make you if not a pecan or two short of a fruitcake?

Yes, it is true that our very own *Baloney* advertising director has been presented with the Ravens Super Bowl Lombardi Trophy.

I am so proud, and I know my dad would be so proud of the award Bob Johnson has wound up with. Wait, I don't like ending sentences with a preposition. I mean "the award with which Bob Johnson has wound up." That's not any better is it? How about "the award up with which he has wound"? Oh, well.

In the photo, we see Barry Streib, the owner of *The Brass Monkey* in St. Pete Beach (and the man who lent Steve Bisciotti the money he needed to buy the Ravens), presenting the Super Bowl XLVII trophy to a visibly moved Bob. It is fitting because Ravens coach John Harbaugh is on record as saying that Johnson's play-calling advice was the key to the Ravens' 2012-13 championship season.

Elvis Presley, Jr., Editor

Doctor: You'll Live to Be 60. I AM 60! See, What Did I Tell You?

I'm Not a Big Fan of Archery: TOO MANY DRAWBACKS.

Mommy, What's a Werewolf? SHUT UP SON, AND COMB YOUR FACE.

BALONEY WORD PUZZLE #3

Example: 24 H _ _ _ _ in a D _ _ = 24 **Hours** in a **Day**

26 L _ _ _ _ _ _ _ of the A _ _ _ _ _ _ _

7 W _ _ _ _ _ _ of the A _ _ _ _ _ W _ _ _ _

12 S _ _ _ _ of the Z _ _ _ _ _

54 C _ _ _ _ _ in a D _ _ _ including J _ _ _ _ _

88 P _ _ _ _ K _ _ _

13 S _ _ _ _ _ _ on an A _ _ _ _ _ _ _ F _ _ _

18 H _ _ _ _ on a G _ _ _ C _ _ _ _ _ _

90 D _ _ _ _ _ _ in a R _ _ _ _ A _ _ _ _ _

200 D _ _ _ _ _ _ _ for P _ _ _ _ _ _ G _ in M _ _ _ _ _ _ _ _

8 S _ _ _ _ on a S _ _ _ S _ _ _

57 H _ _ _ _ V _ _ _ _ _ _ _ _ _

32 T _ _ _ _ C _ _ _ _ _ _ _ _ W _ _ _ _ _ T _ _ _ _

29 D _ _ _ in F _ _ _ _ _ _ _ _ in a L _ _ _ Y _ _ _

64 S _ _ _ _ _ _ on a C _ _ _ _ _ _ B _ _ _ _

3 B _ _ _ _ M _ _ _ (S _ _ H _ _ T _ _ _ R _ _)

102 F _ _ _ _ _ in the E _ _ _ _ _ _ S _ _ _ _ B _ _ _ _ _ _ _ _

360 D _ _ _ _ _ _ _ in a C _ _ _ _ _ _

66 B _ _ _ _ of the B _ _ _ _

500 S _ _ _ _ _ _ of P _ _ _ _ _ in a R _ _ _

18 W _ _ _ _ _ on a T _ _ _ _ _ _ _ T _ _ _ _ _ _

3 F _ _ _ _ of E _ _

Answers at BroadneckBaloney.com

Please Don't Write in the Spaces - So Others Can Enjoy the Challenge

Did You Hear about the Man Who Fell into an Upholstery Machine? HE'S NOW FULLY RECOVERED.

Funny Church Bulletin Notices

1. Thursday night - Potluck supper. Prayer and medication to follow.

2. Remember in prayer the many who are sick of our church and community. Smile at someone who is hard to love. Say "hell" to someone who doesn't care much about you.

3. For those of you who have children and don't know it, we have a nursery downstairs.

4. The rosebud on the alter this morning is to announce the birth of David Alan Belzer, the sin of Rev. and Mrs. Julius Belzer.

5. This afternoon there will be a meeting in the South and North ends of the church. Children will be baptized at both ends.

6. Tuesday at 4:00 pm there will be an ice cream social. All ladies giving milk will please come early.

7. Wednesday the ladies liturgy will meet. Mrs. Johnson will sing "Put me in my little bed" accompanied by the pastor.

8. Thursday at 5:00 pm there will be a meeting of the Little Mothers Club. All ladies wishing to be "Little Mothers" will meet with the Pastor in his study.

9. This being Easter Sunday, we will ask Mrs. Lewis to come forward and lay an egg on the altar.

10. The service will close with "Little Drops of Water." One of the ladies will start quietly and the rest of the congregation will join in.

11. Next Sunday a special collection will be taken to defray the cost of the new carpet. All those wishing to do something on the new carpet will come forward and do so.

12. The ladies of the church have cast off clothing of every kind. They can be seen in the church basement Saturday.

13. A bean supper will be held on Tuesday evening in the church hall. Music will follow.

14. At the evening service tonight, the sermon topic will be "What is Hell?" Come early and listen to our choir practice.

15. Low Self Esteem Support Group will meet Thursday at 7 pm. Please use the back door.

16. The Lutheran men's group will meet at 6 PM. Steak, mashed potatoes, green beans, bread and dessert will be served for a nominal feel.

Can You Name 20 Animals from Africa? YEAH, 19 GIRAFFES AND A GNU.

SPECIAL CLASSES FOR MEN
Taught by Women

Class 1: How to Fill Up the Ice Cube Trays. Step by Step, with Slide Presentation. Meets 4 weeks, Monday and Wednesday for 2 hours beginning at 7:00 PM.

Class 2: The Toilet Paper Roll. Does It Change Itself? Round Table Discussion. Meets 2 weeks, Saturdays 12:00 for 2 hours.

Class 3: Is It Possible to Urinate Using the Technique of Lifting the Seat and Avoiding the Floor/Walls and Nearby Bathtub? Group Practice. Meets 4 weeks, Saturdays 10:00 PM for 2 hours.

Class 4: Fundamental Differences Between the Laundry Hamper and the Floor. Pictures and Explanatory Graphics. Meets Saturdays at 2:00 PM for 3 weeks.

Class 5: After Dinner Dishes. Can They Levitate and Fly into the Kitchen Sink? Examples on Video. Meets 4 weeks, Tuesday and Thursday for 2 Hours Beginning at 7:00 PM.

Class 6: Loss of Identity - Losing the Remote to Your Significant Other. Help Line Support and Support Groups. Meets 4 Weeks, Friday and Sunday 7:00 PM.

Class 7: Learning How to Find Things. Starting with Looking in the Right Places instead of Turning the House upside down While Screaming. Open Forum. Monday at 8:00 PM, 2 hours.

Class 8: Health Watch - Bringing Her Flowers is Not Harmful to Your Health. Graphics and Audio Tapes. Three nights; Monday, Wednesday, Friday at 7:00 PM for 2 hours.

Class 9: Real Men Ask for Directions When Lost. Real Life Testimonials. Tuesdays at 6:00 PM, Location to Be Determined.

Class 10: Is It Genetically Possible to Sit Quietly While She Parallel Parks? Driving Simulations. 4 Weeks, Saturdays at Noon.

Class 11: Learning to Live - Basic Differences Between Mother and Wife. Online Classes and Role-playing. Location and Times to Be Announced.

Class 12: How to Be the Ideal Shopping Companion. Relaxation Exercises, Meditation and Breathing Techniques. Meets 4 weeks, Tuesday and Thursday beginning at 7:00 PM.

Class 13: How to Fight Cerebral Atrophy. Remembering Birthdays, Anniversaries and Other Important Dates and Calling When You're Going to be Late. Cerebral Shock Therapy Sessions and Full Lobotomies Offered. Three Nights; Monday, Wednesday, Friday at 7:00 PM.

Class 14: The Stove/Oven. What It is and How It is Used. Live Demonstration. Tuesdays at 6:00 PM, location to be determined.

BROADNECK MEN! SIGN UP TODAY!

The Romantic Encounter Was So Good, even the Neighbors Had a Cigarette.

How Do You Stop a Skunk from Smelling? PUT A CLOTHES PIN ON ITS NOSE.

Why Some Men Prefer Dogs to Wives

1. The later you are, the happier your dog is to see you.
2. Dogs don't notice if you call them by another name.
3. Dogs like it if you leave a lot of things on the floor.
4. A dog's parents never visit.
5. Dogs agree that you have to raise your voice to get your point across.
6. You never have to wait for a dog; they're ready to go 24 hours a day.
7. Dogs find you amusing when you're drunk.
8. Dogs like to go hunting and fishing and to the beach.
9. A dog will not wake you up in the night to ask: "If I died, would you get another dog?"
10. If a dog has babies, you can put an ad in the paper and give them away.
11. A dog will let you put a studded collar on without calling you a weirdo.
12. If dogs smell another dog on you, they don't get mad. They just think it's interesting.
13. Dogs like to ride in the back of a pick-up truck.
14. Last but not least: If a dog leaves, he won't take half your stuff.

We Live in a Society Where Vizzini's Pizza Gets to Your House before the Cops.

I Made the Chicken Soup. WHAT! I THOUGHT THE SOUP WAS FOR US.

Hoffman Animal Hospital

Committed to Caring and Connecting with Your Pet

Call today for an appointment. Compassionate care makes all the difference. We are passionate about providing excellent care for all pets.

We Treat Your Pets Like Valued Family Members

Dr. Lisa Hoffman
Dr. Liesl Wheeler
Dr. Jennifer Greenwood
Dr. Kathryn Harkins

Hoffmanah.com 410-757-3566 15 Old Mill Bottom Road N.

What's Green and Fuzzy and Will Hurt Like Heck If It Falls out of a Tree and Hits You? A POOL TABLE.

Bella's Wine and Spirits Presents . . .
FOR SURE BROADNECK FOLKLORE

If you throw your hair combings out a back window, and starlings use them in their nests, you will slowly go insane.

If you sneeze in the morning before breakfast, you won't want dessert after supper unless you have some **Yellowtail Riesling** in the fridge to go with it.

When five or more people are together and a longer-than-usual silence occurs, it's always exactly twenty minutes to the hour, give or take half-an-hour.

If you encounter a sad band leader at a crossroads after midnight on a Thursday, walk backwards in a circle 3 times or you will have bad luck for a month.

Cut your toenails seven Monday mornings in a row, then give a bottle of **Yellow Tail Chardonnay** to an embittered caricaturist, and within forty-eight hours, you will receive a present.

If you count the warts on an opinionated custodian, you will get them.

To cure depression, take your nail parings, put them in a plastic sandwich bag, tie the bag around the neck of a live eel, then put the eel back into the Bay. The eel will get depressed and you will get better.

To prevent a nonchalant dwarf from casting spells on you, sprinkle your socks with salt and pepper in the morning, and drink a glass of **Yellow Tail Pinot Grigio** with lunch.

In school, yank a hair from the head of the student in front of you. Draw it sharply between two fingernails, and if it curls, the one from whose head it was taken has a bad temper.

If a black cat crosses your path, it is bad luck; worse luck if it carries a kitten in its mouth; worse luck still if the kitten has a mulberry in its mouth; worse luck still if the cat is owned by a bashful clerk; worse luck yet if he is married to a touchy florist; and worse luck yet if you missed **Bella's** last wine tasting.

If you have a thick, clotty-sounding voice with an uneducated accent and wish to change it, drink a bottle of **Yellow Tail Shiraz** and repeat this 100 times while looking at yourself in the mirror:

20 cotton pickers/40 boys in knickers
Speedy, friendly service/Up at **Bella's Liquors.**

Eslin Solutions Plus

Solutions plus Service

Providing the perfect support vendor to your exact project

Facilities Maintenance Services
Preventative Maintenance
HVAC Plumbing Support

443.822.3136

Don Eslin (Chip)

Eslin-solutionsplus.com

Deslin@eslin-solutionsplus.com

Bella's Wine and Spirits Presents...
FOR SURE CHRISTMAS FOLKLORE

It is good luck to be the first one to open the door to let in Christmas, but, if when you do that, you hear a Barry Manilow song on the radio, close the door at once to keep his voice from chasing your luck outside.

At midnight on Christmas Eve, dogs and cats talk to each other.

If you eat no beans on Christmas Day, you will spend the rest of the year noticing misshapen oddities with discomforting monotony.

It is bad luck to cut your hair or nails on Christmas Day unless you have attended a wine-tasting at Bella's Liquors within the last sixty days.

If you kiss the one you love under the mistletoe, always sip Champagne from Bella's afterward to make sure your love will always sparkle.

If you drink a glass of Chardonnay or Sauvignon Blanc on Christmas Day and alternate drinking these wines each day thereafter through Ground Hog Day, your heart will get stronger and your hemorrhoids will disappear.

To change your luck for the better during the holidays, read this folklore out loud to a member of the opposite sex.

In olden times, the people of Broadneck relied upon bells to help them ring in the New Year. Today, they simply rely on Bella's.

Don't pay your bills on New Year's Day or that's what it will seem like you are doing all the rest of the year.

If you burn a pair of old shoes on New Year's Day, then drink a glass of hearty Cabernet, the devil won't know how to find you all year.

Eat 12 raw oysters with cocktail sauce and 2 glasses of Merlot on New Year's Eve and thoughts of wonderful romance will govern your thinking during each of the following 12 months.

If, on New Year's Day, at a party hosted by a recuperating pawnbroker, you encounter a gluttonous murmurer who reproaches you with a vengeful scowl, ask the host for a glass of Beaujolais. If the host has none, chastise him or her gently and depart at once or you'll be unlucky all of January.

If, on New Year's Eve, you put a cork from a bottle of Chardonnay purchased from Bella's under an azalea tree, you will have good luck for the entire year.

It is bad luck to start or enter a quarrel on New Year's Day.

Good luck on New Year's Day will bring good luck all the year long if you have remembered to keep a bottle of Peppermint Schnapps in your freezer during the holidays for guests who have bad breath.

If the first person to enter your home on New Year's Day is carrying a 12-pack of beer, or a bag of peanuts purchased at Bella's, the whole year will be a bountiful one for you and your family.

Bella's Wine and Spirits Presents . . .
FOR SURE FOLKLORE

It is bad luck to pass a left-handed, red-haired woman on Father's Day when it's raining. To counteract such an inauspicious occurrence, purchase a bottle of New Zealand **Oyster Bay Sauvignon Blanc** at **Bella's** on Tuesday (10% off all wines). Then, just after midnight, wearing your pajamas, walk downstairs backwards repeating this:

> The spell is broken
> Whom shall I thank?
> I'm easing into the kitchen
> For another glass of Sauvignon Blanc.

Never take a shiny penny from a mealymouthed opportunist who has recently been admonished by a henpecked name-dropper unless, within the previous 24 hours, you have shared a chilled bottle of **Boordy's Fish Market White**, purchased at **Bella's** from **Christine**, **Eddie**, **John**, **Kelly**, **Steve**, or **Dave**, with a hedging nonconformist.

If a disturbing pimple develops on your chin or on the right side of your nose, rub it with a penny. Then purchase a daily lottery ticket and a bottle of on-sale wine at **Bella's**. Then throw the penny into the parking lot with your left hand as your are leaving. The person who picks up the penny will get your pimple.

Make a wish when you see a Budweiser delivery truck outside of the **Riverbay Roadhouse** in the morning. If, within the next half-hour, a member of the opposite sex calls you, or mentions your middle name, your wish will come true.

To get rid of a wart, cut a lemon in half and rub it over the wart 19 times. Then, dampen the tip of the middle finger of your left hand with a bottle of **Boordy's Love My Goat Blush** purchased at **Bella's** after 6 pm and touch it to the wart. Then, drink the rest of the wine within the hour without telling anyone what you have done, and the wart will be gone in 3 days. If the wart is on the tip of the middle finger of your left hand, follow the same procedure as above except dampen the little finger of your right hand in a can of warm bock beer. If you have warts on the tips of both those fingers, burn them off using a cigarette lighter from a backseat ashtray in a 1984 Ford LTD.

IT IS GOOD LUCK TO:

Send a birthday card to a neglected grammarian.

Pick your teeth in the company of a half-hearted hypnotist.

Point at a whimpering nutritionist.

Sprinkle salt on the shoes of a jaywalking in-law.

Practice empty posturing with another borderline intellectual.

Tip an inebriated hairdresser.

IT IS BAD LUCK TO:

Suggest remedies to a barfing kleptomaniac.

French-kiss a winking disk-jockey.

Pass under a ladder unless you spit between the rungs.

Tease a pantomiming imperialist.

Prevent a left-handed mama's boy from changing stations on a car radio.

Issue a vague warning to a forlorn yet marriageable loiterer.

Preach to a narcissistic glassblower. ❊

Why Do They Lock Gas Station Bathrooms? ARE THEY AFRAID SOMEONE WILL CLEAN THEM?

Bella's Wine and Spirits Presents...
ASK AUNT BERTHABELLE
Answers to LIfe's More Peculiar Problems

DEAR AUNT BERTHABELLE: Years ago as a teenager, I had twins and gave them up for adoption. One of them went to a family in Egypt, and they named him Ahmal. The other went to a family in Los Angeles, and they named him Juan. A couple of weeks back, after almost twenty years without any contact, Juan sent a picture of himself to me. I was thrilled! I told my husband that I also would love to have a picture of his twin brother Ahmal. He told me that was one of the stupidest ideas he'd ever heard of. He said trying to contact my other son for a picture would be a huge waste of time, and he forbid me to do it. There's a good chance my husband will listen to you and change his mind. Please let him know that forbidding me to contact Ahmal is very wrong. *Isabelle Wringing, Bay Hills.*

DEAR ISABELLE: I hate to disappoint you but the fact is, I can't tell your husband that he is wrong when I see just how right he is. There is no need for you to receive a photo of your other child. Your sons are twins! If you've seen Juan, you've seen Ahmal.

DEAR AUNT BERTHABELLE: My local Broadneck dentist, who does not advertise in the Baloney or read your eclectic and entertaining column, and whom I detest for those reasons, told me that my new upper plate needs to be made of chrome because of my penchant for Hollandaise sauce which, he tells me, has a lot of lemon juice in it, and is corrosive to most dental tools. Why chrome, Aunt Berthabelle? *Amanda B. Reckonwith, Atlantis.*

DEAR AMANDA: That's an easy one. There's no plate like chrome for the Hollandaise.

DEAR AUNT BERTHABELLE: I recently read about a thief in Paris who planned to steal some paintings from the Louvre Museum. The news report said that, after careful planning, he got past security, stole the paintings and made it safely to his van.

However, he was captured only two blocks away when his van ran out of gas. My question is, how could the thief mastermind such a crime and then make such a foolish mistake? *Sherry Pitts, Shore Acres.*

DEAR SHERRY: Perhaps the reason the thief stole the paintings in the first place was because he had no Monet to buy Degas to make the Van Gogh.

DEAR AUNT BERTHABELLE: My 16-year-old son Chauncey passed his driving test and asked me, a clergyman, if there was any chance of getting a car for Christmas, which was still three months away. I told him that if he would get his grades up to the A and B level, study his Bible, and get his hair cut, I would consider getting him a car.

Now his grades are up, and the work he has put into his Bible studies is very encouraging to me. But I'm disappointed that he still hasn't gotten a haircut.

His reason for not getting a haircut is that, in the course of his Bible studies, he noticed in the illustrations that Moses, John the Baptist, Samson, and even Jesus had long hair. He makes a good, if annoying, point. I'm adamant in my stance that I'm not going to buy him a new car until he gets a haircut. What can I possibly tell him that will make him get a haircut? *Reverend Bobo Sinn, Glen Oban.*

DEAR REVEREND SINN: I suggest you remind Chauncey that even though Moses, John the Baptist, Samson, and Jesus had long hair, they walked wherever they went.

DEAR AUNT BERTHABELLE: I just wanted to let all of Broadneck know that I am retiring as the human cannonball in the circus. *Easton West, Tickflea Creek.*

DEAR EASTON: Where will they ever find another man of your caliber? ✺

I'm Going to Buy a Parrot and Teach It to Say "HELP! I'VE BEEN TURNED INTO A PARROT."

Bella's Wine and Spirits Presents...
ASK AUNT BERTHABELLE
Answers to LIfe's More Peculiar Problems

DEAR AUNT BERTHABELLE: I experienced great disappointment at an outdoor Broadneck festival last summer. A performer came onto the stage and pretended to juggle as if he were something like a juggling mime, for want of a better phrase. He came out empty-handed and remained so for his entire lame act. When I see a juggler, I expect him to be juggling something, but this guy was juggling nothing. I doubt that he even knew how to juggle. Wasn't that just pitiful? *MacDonald Berger, Brown's Woods.*

DEAR MACDONALD: Just because he came out empty-handed doesn't mean that he didn't know how to juggle. Juggling can be a very daunting challenge requiring the right equipment, and he simply may not have had the balls to attempt it.

DEAR AUNT BERTHABELLE: I am a marine policeman who works at Sandy Point State Park. This past September, I discovered a man sitting on a log in the woods chewing away on a dead bald eagle. I yelled, "Hey mister, the bald eagle is a protected species, and killing one is a punishable offense."

My stern words had no effect, and the man kept noshing away on the bald eagle's carcass. After a brief struggle, I arrested him and hauled him before the judge for arraignment. His court date was set for December 15th, and I just couldn't wait to see what stern punishment the judge would mete out to this scofflaw. Unfortunately, I went into a coma after sniffing too much airplane glue (I love that stuff!) and I missed the court date. I'm out of the coma now, and my first thought is what happened at the trial? I understand you were there. What did happen? *Roger D. Dodger, Buxom Bay.*

DEAR ROGER: Yes, I was at the trial. The man pleaded innocent to the charges against him, claiming that if he didn't eat the bald eagle he would have died from starvation.

To everyone's amazement, the judge ruled in his favor.

In the judge's closing statement he asked the man, "I would like you to tell me something before I let you go. I have never eaten a bald eagle, nor ever plan on it. But I'd like to know: What did it taste like?"

The man answered: "Well, it tasted like a cross between a Whooping Crane and a Spotted Owl."

DEAR AUNT BERTHABELLE: I think you set a terrible example by boasting that you "always take life with a grain of salt plus a slice of lemon and a shot of tequila." As the most influential person on Broadneck, perhaps it would be more prudent of you to share with your readers a meal you may partake of, instead of encouraging what are basically straight shots of demon alcohol. *Helen Wheels, Cape Despair.*

DEAR HELEN: Okay. I'm having potato salad for lunch. Well, potatoes and olives. Make that fermented potatoes. I'm having a vodka martini for lunch, and is it ever tasty!

DEAR AUNT BERTHABELLE: My teenage son has been conducting experiments with marijuana that trouble me somewhat. He bakes a batch of pot-laced brownies and then places them in different spots near the creek where the sea birds eat them. He gives them the brownies before he leaves for school and then again as soon as he gets home. Should I be worried about what my son is doing? *Carey Oakey, Eerie Creek.*

DEAR CAREY: Instead of doubting your son, you should be extremely proud of his systematic conscientious efforts. His obvious goal is a beneficent one: He is determined to leave no tern unstoned. ✤

Worrying Works! 90% of the THINGS I WORRY ABOUT NEVER HAPPEN.

Bella's Wine and Spirits Presents...
ASK AUNT BERTHABELLE
Answers to LIfe's More Peculiar Problems

DEAR AUNT BERTHABELLE: I discern from your picture that you are a no-nonsense woman, so let me get right to it. I feel myself magnetically drawn to your stern femininity. I furtively watched you enjoy your Coronarita at the *Broadneck Cantina* during happy hour last Friday. When you looked my way, I could feel the surging power of your sexual presence. I wondered then, and I wonder now: Do you have any fantasies you would share with me and your other dedicated readers? *Mal Feezance, Murky Creek Shoal.*

DEAR MAL: The fantasy that excites me the most is having two men at once: one cooking and one cleaning.

DEAR AUNT BERTHABELLE: This woman I met last week at *O'Loughlin's* happy hour told me she wants a guy who is funny and spontaneous. Yet when I tapped on her kitchen window uninvited late at night dressed as a clown, it was all panic and screaming. Why are women so fickle? *Eddie Swirling, Acorn Oaks.*

DEAR EDDIE: As I was reading your letter, I threw up in my mouth a little. I don't think it was a mere coincidence either.

DEAR AUNT BERTHABELLE: I am sick and tired of seeing all these so-called "Real Wives of Orange County," and "Real Wives of New Jersey," et cetera, all over the television. I am a "Real Wife of Broadneck" by golly and I get no recognition whatsoever. Where's the perspective, where's the fairness, where's the balance in this farcical injustice? *Faye Slift, Gnat's Swamp.*

DEAR FAYE: If you are indeed a "Real Wife of Broadneck," instead of complaining to me, shouldn't you be vacuuming, dusting, cooking and doing laundry?

DEAR AUNT BERTHABELLE: I recognize you as a wordsmith *par excellence*, and therefore believe you can answer this question for me. How do you explain the difference between complete and finished in a way that is easy to understand? *Lulu Lahlah, Tickbite Woods.*

DEAR LULU: When you marry the right woman, you are complete. When you marry the wrong woman, you are finished. When the right one catches you with the wrong one, you are completely finished.

DEAR AUNT BERTHABELLE: Do you remember the good old days before Facebook, Instagram, and Twitter? When you had to take a photograph of your dinner, then get the film developed, then go around to all your friends' houses to show them the picture of your dinner? *Winsome Cash, Creektown.*

DEAR WINSOME: No. Stop it!

DEAR AUNT BERTHABELLE: I can't believe all the debt I'm in. I owe the IRS, 5 credit card companies, my bookie, and I'm 18 months behind on my mortgage. Any advice? *Doug A. Hole, Severn Cataracts.*

DEAR DOUG: I really admire people like you who keep going when they're in huge amounts of debt. You deserve a lot of credit.

DEAR AUNT BERTHABELLE: Last Monday evening as I was enjoying a wonderful meal at *O'Loughlin's* with the usual exemplary service, I noticed Captain Kirk from Star Trek sneaking into the ladies' room. Why in the world would he do such a thing? *Hamilton "Ham" Burger, Lickskillet Woods.*

DEAR HAM: The answer is quite simple: He wanted to go where no man had gone before.

DEAR AUNT BERTHABELLE: I heard that you refer to the bathroom as the James instead of the John. Why do you do that? *Stan Still, Cape Capey.*

DEAR STAN: You heard wrong. I call it the Jim, not the James. I think it sounds a lot better when I tell people I spent an hour in the Jim first thing in the morning. ✸

The Other Day I Held the Door Open for a Clown. IT WAS A NICE JESTER.

MY MOTHER TAUGHT ME . . .

LOGIC:
"Because I said so, that's why."

TO APPRECIATE A JOB WELL DONE:
"If you're going to kill each other, do it outside. I just finished cleaning."

RELIGION:
"You better pray that will come out of the carpet!"

TIME TRAVEL
"If you don't straighten up, I'm going to knock you into the middle of next week."

MORE LOGIC:
"If you fall out of that swing and break your neck, you're not going to the store with me."

FORESIGHT:
"Make sure you wear clean underwear in case you're in an accident."

IRONY:
"Keep crying and I'll give you something to cry about."

OSMOSIS:
"Shut your mouth and eat your supper."

CONTORTIONISM:
"Will you look at that dirt on the back of your neck!"

STAMINA:
"You'll sit there until that spinach is gone."

WEATHER:
"This room of yours looks like a tornado went through it."

HYPOCRISY:
"If I told you once, I've told you a thousand times, don't exaggerate!"

CIRCLE OF LIFE:
"I brought you into this world and I can take you out."

BEHAVIOR MODIFICATION:
"Stop acting like your father."

ENVY:
"There are millions of less fortunate children in the world who don't have wonderful parents like you do."

ANTICIPATION:
"Just wait until we get home!"

MEDICAL SCIENCE:
"If you don't stop crossing your eyes, they're going to get stuck that way."

ESP:
"Put your sweater on. Don't you think I know when you are cold?"

HUMOR:
"When the lawn mower cuts off your toes, don't come running to me."

HOW TO BECOME AN ADULT:
"If you don't eat your vegetables, you'll never grow up."

RECEIVING:
"You are going to get it when we get home."

GENETICS:
"You're just like your father."

ROOTS:
"Shut that door behind you. Do you think you were born in a barn?"

JUSTICE:
"One day you'll have kids, and I hope they turn out just like you." ✺

GOD BLESS THE IRISH 5

A lady from Cork goes to her Irish priest and says, "Father, I have a problem. I have two female parrots, but they only know how to say one thing."

"What do they say?" asked the priest.

They say, "Hi, we're hookers! Do you want to have some fun?"

"That's obscene!" the priest exclaimed; then he thought for a moment. "I may have a solution to your problem. I have two male talking parrots, which I have taught to pray. Bring your two parrots over to my house, and we'll put them in the cage with Dylan and Donal. My parrots can teach your parrots to praise and worship, and your parrots are sure to stop saying that awful phrase in no time."

"Thank you," the lady responded, "this may very well be the solution."

The next day, she brought her female parrots to the priest's house. As she was being ushered in, she saw that his two male parrots were inside their cage, holding rosary beads and praying. She walked over and placed her parrots in with them.

After a few minutes, the female parrots cried out in unison, "Hi, we're hookers! Do you want to have some fun?"

There was stunned silence. Shocked, Dylan looked over at his parrot pal and exclaimed, "Donal, put the beads away. Our prayers are answered!"

The first man married a woman from Italy. He told her that she was to do the dishes and house cleaning. It took a couple of days, but on the third day, he came home to see a clean house and dishes washed and put away.

The second man married a woman from Poland. He gave his wife orders that she was to do all the cleaning, dishes and the cooking. The first day he didn't see any results. By the third day, he saw his house was clean, the dishes were done, and there was a huge dinner on the table.

The third man married a girl from Ireland. He ordered her to keep the house clean, dishes washed, lawn mowed, laundry washed, and hot food on the table for every meal. He said the first day he didn't see anything, the second day he didn't see anything but by the third day, some of the swelling had gone down and he could see a little out of his left eye, and his arm was healed enough that he could fix himself a sandwich and load the dishwasher.

Paddy and Mick are walking down the road and Paddy has a bag of doughnuts in his hand.

Paddy says to Mick: "If you can guess how many doughnuts are in my bag, you can have them both."

Mick and Paddy are walking along when Mick falls down a manhole. Paddy shouts down: "What shall I do?" Mick barks back: "Call me an ambulance!"

Paddy then jumps up and down screaming: "Mick is an ambulance, Mick is an ambulance."

Paddy stopped cutting the hedge as the big car drew up beside him and an English visitor enquired, "Could you tell me the way to Balbriggan, Please?"

Paddy wiped his brow.

"Certainly, Sir. If you take the first road to the left . . . No still that wouldn't do. Drive on for about four miles then turn left at the crossroads . . . No that wouldn't do either."

Paddy scratched his head thoughtfully.

"You know, sir, if I was going to Balbriggan I wouldn't start from here at all."

GOD BLESS THE IRISH 6

McQuillan walked into a bar and ordered martini after martini, each time removing the olives and placing them in a jar. When the jar was filled with olives and all the drinks consumed, the Irishman started to leave. "S'cuse me," said a customer, who was puzzled over what McQuillan had done. "What was that all about?" "Nothing," said the Irishman, "my wife just sent me out for a jar of olives."

Hennessy wasn't a very good looking fellow to start with. Now his business had failed, and his wife and family had left him. Depressed and distracted, he was standing near the edge of the bridge, contemplating suicide.

Suddenly, he sensed that someone was behind him, and turning around he saw an ugly little old female leprechaun. "Don't jump," she said, and I'll grant you three wishes." "Right," he said, "my first wish is to have $100,000."

She said, "When you check your account, you will find that you are in credit to that amount." He then said, "My second wish is to have my wife and children back." She said, "They will be there when you get home." He said, "My third wish is to be tall and handsome." She said, When you look in the mirror, you will find that your wish has been granted."

Then she added, "I want you to do something in return for me. I want you to kiss me." He looked at her and shuddered at the thought. But under the circumstances he thought he should do as she wanted. He took her in his arms and kissed her again and again. She said, "What age are you?" He replied, "I'm forty." She said, "Don't you think that you're a bit too old to be believing in leprechauns?"

An Englishman, Irishman and Scotsman were sitting at the bar in *O'Loughlin's*.

"The ambiance here is fantastic, the beer excellent and the food exceptional," said the Scotsman, "but I still prefer the pubs back home. Why in Glasgow, there's a little bar called McTavish's. The landlord there goes out of his way for the locals so much that when you buy four drinks, he'll buy the fifth drink for you."

"Well," said the Englishman, "at my local, the Red Lion, the barman there will buy you your third drink after you buy the first two."

"Ah, that's nothin'," said the Irishman. "Back home in Dublin there's Ryan's Bar. Now, the moment you set foot in the place they'll buy you a drink, then another, all the drinks you'd like. Then, when you've had enough drink, they'll take you upstairs and see that you enjoy all the pleasure you desire - ALL on the house!"

The Englishman and Scotsman immediately pour scorn on the Irishman's claims, but he swears every word is true.

"Well," said the Englishman, "did this actually happen to you?"

"Not to myself personally, no," said the Irishman, "but it did happen to me sister."

An Irish lass, a customer: "Could I be trying on that dress in the window?"

"I'd prefer that you use the dressing room."

Mrs. Feeney shouted from the kitchen, "Brian, is that you I hear spittin' in the vase on the mantel piece?"

"No," said Brian, "but I'm gettin' closer all the time."

"Mr. O'Halloran," asked the pharmacist, "did that mudpack I gave you improve your wife's appearance?"

"It did surely," replied O'Halloran, "but it keeps fallin' off."

Why It's Great to Be a Guy

1. Wedding plans take care of themselves.
2. You can wear a white T-shirt to a water park.
3. You don't give a rat's hindquarters whether or not someone notices your new haircut.
4. The world is your urinal.
5. People never stare at your chest when you're talking to them.
6. Phone conversations are over in 30 seconds flat.
7. One mood, ALL the time.
8. You get extra credit for the slightest act of thoughtfulness.
9. You can quietly enjoy a car ride from the passenger seat.
10. You can drop by to see a friend without having to bring a little gift.
11. If another guy shows up at the party in the same outfit, you just might become lifelong friends.
12. You are not expected to know the names of more than five colors.
13. You almost never have strap problems in public.
14. The same hairstyle lasts for years, maybe decades.
15. You have freedom of choice concerning growing a mustache.
16. None of your co-workers has the power to make you cry.
17. Your hair is dry after taking a shower by the time you're dressed.
18. You can go to the bathroom without a support group.
19. You can write your name in the snow.
20. Your pals can be trusted never to trap you with: "So, notice anything different?"
21. Bathroom lines are 80% shorter.
22. You can take pride in breaking wind.
23. Homer Simpson makes perfect sense.
24. You don't have to hide from the camera if you don't have your makeup on.
25. No stretch marks.

REAL HEADLINES FROM NEWSPAPERS AND THE WEB

Bank Drive-in Window Blocked By Board

Typhoon Rips Through Cemetery; Hundreds Dead

Astronaut Takes Blame for Gas in Spacecraft

Grandmother of Eight Makes Hole in One

Two Convicts Evade Noose, Jury Hung

Police Found Safe Under Blanket

William Kelly Was Fed Secretary

Milk Drinkers Are Turning to Powder

Deaf Mute Gets New Hearing in Killing

Police Begin Campaign to Run Down Jaywalkers

Government Claims Progress on Healthcare, But More Lies Ahead

Bridge Held Up by Red Tape

Man, Minus Ear, Waives Hearing

Kids Make Nutritious Snacks

Woman Kicked By Her Husband Said to Be Greatly Improved

Proposed Marijuana Law Sent to Joint Committee

Robber Holds Up Albert's Hosiery

Chinese Apeman Dated

Headless Body Found in Topless Bar

March Planned for Next August

Lingerie Shipment Hijacked—Thief Gives Police the Slip

Queen Mary Having Bottom Scraped.

Teacher Strikes Idle Kids

Lawyers Give Poor Free Legal Advice

Nicaragua Sets Goal to Wipe Out Literacy

20-Year Friendship Ends at Altar

War Dims Hope For Peace

If Strike Isn't Settled Quickly, It May Last a While

Blind Woman Gets New Kidney from Dad She Hasn't Seen in Years

NASA Probe Finds Toxic Gas Around Uranus

Prostitutes Appeal to Pope

Pastor Aghast at First Lady Sex Position

Why Don't Ostriches Fly? THEY CAN'T GET PAST AIRPORT SECURITY.

OUR REVIEW OF:

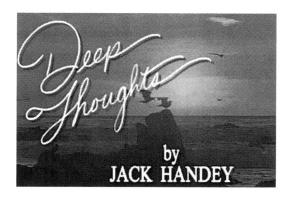

ALL WE NEED TO DO IS QUOTE FROM THE BOOK

It's funny that pirates were always going around searching for treasure, and they never realized that the real treasure was the fond memories they were creating.

To me, clowns aren't funny. In fact, they're kind of scary. I've wondered where this started and I think it goes back to the time I went to the circus, and a clown killed my dad.

Before you criticize someone, you should walk a mile in their shoes. That way, when you criticize them, you're a mile away and you have their shoes.

If God dwells inside us, like some people say, I sure hope He likes enchiladas, because that's what He's getting!

AVAILABLE AT AMAZON WITH MANY MORE OF HIS HILARIOUS BOOKS

If you're a cowboy and you're dragging a guy behind your horse, I bet it would really make you mad if you looked back and the guy was reading a magazine.

One thing kids like is to be tricked. For instance, I was going to take my little nephew to Disneyland, but instead I drove him to an old burned-out warehouse. "Oh, no," I said, "Disneyland burned down." He cried and cried, but I think that deep down he thought it was a pretty good joke. I started to drive over to the real Disneyland, but it was getting pretty late.

I hope if dogs ever take over the world, and they chose a king, they don't just go by size, because I bet there are some Chihuahuas with some good ideas.

Children need encouragement. If a kid gets an answer right, tell him it was a lucky guess. That way he develops a good, lucky feeling.

For mad scientists who keep brains in jars, here's a tip: why not add a slice of lemon to each jar, for freshness?

It takes a big man to cry, but it takes a bigger man to laugh at that man.

Why Did the Chicken Go to the Seance? TO GET TO THE OTHER SIDE.

All She Buys Are Romance Novels. I KNOW. SHE'S A HEROINE ADDICT.

KIDS TODAY

TEACHER: Maria, go to the map and find America.
MARIA: Here it is.
TEACHER: Correct. Now class, who discovered America?
CLASS: Maria.

TEACHER: Glenn, how do you spell crocodile?
GLENN: K-R-O-K-O-D-I-A-L.
TEACHER: No, that's wrong.
GLENN: Maybe it's wrong, but you asked me how I spell it.

TEACHER: Donald, what is the chemical formula for water?
DONALD: HIJKLMNO.
TEACHER: What are you talking about?
DONALD: Yesterday, you said it's H to O.

TEACHER: Clyde, your essay on "My Dog" is exactly the same as your brother's. Did you copy his?
CLYDE: No, ma'am, it's the same dog.

TEACHER: John, why are you doing your math multiplication on the floor?
JOHN: You told me to do it without using tables.

TEACHER: Harold, what do you call a person who keeps on talking when people are no longer interested?
HAROLD: A teacher.

CAPE HAIR SCENE AND BARBERSHOP

410.349.1646

PRESENTS HAIR JOKES

Trying to control her dry hair, a Broadneck woman treated her scalp with olive oil before washing it. Worried that the oil might leave an odor, she washed her hair several times. That night when she went to bed, she leaned over to her husband and asked, "Do I smell like olive oil?"

"No," he said, sniffing her. "Do I smell like Popeye?"

One solution to a bad hair day is to wear a low-cut blouse. No one will look at your hair.

A man and a little boy entered a barbershop together on St. Paddy's Day. After the man received the full treatment - shave, shampoo, manicure, haircut, etc. - he placed the boy in the chair.

"I'm goin' to buy a green tie to wear for the parade," he said. "I'll be back in a few minutes."

When the boy's haircut was completed and the man still hadn't returned, the barber said, "Looks like your daddy's forgotten all about you."

"That wasn't my daddy," said the boy. "He just walked up, took me by the hand and said, 'Come on, son, we're gonna get a free haircut!'"

[Mary Ann says: "Don't try it here!"].

What Did One Frog Say to the Other? TIME SURE IS FUN WHEN YOU'RE HAVING FLIES.

My Darling, My Beautiful Wife. MARRYING YOU HAS SCREWED UP MY LIFE.

ANTI-JOKES

An Arnold man who kept his boat at Fairwinds Marina was fishing by the Bay Bridge pilings when he caught a magnificent rock fish. As he was about to cut and kill the fish, the fish spoke up. "Please don't kill me," the fish said, "if you put me back in the water, I'll grant you any wish you want."
"Whoa!" said the fisherman. He had never heard a fish talk before. "Where did you learn to talk?"
"Actually, it's a long story, but if you want to put me back and get your wish, you've got to do it soon, I can't breathe outside of water."
"I don't know," the man considered, "I bet talking fish are quite delicious." By this point, the fish was suffocating terribly.
"Please . . ." the fish begged.
"Oh, all right, fine. I, umm . . . I wish I had a million dollars." The man tossed the fish back into the water. After the fish caught his breath it broke into laughter. "What kind of idiot believes a fish can grant wishes?" the fish said as he swam away. The fisherman didn't really care, because he was already a billionaire, and he was just going to give the million dollars to charity, possibly even one for the ethical treatment of fish. Two days later a shark ate the rock fish.

Yo mama is so stupid that she can't even name more than ten state capitals.

How do you wake up Lady Gaga? Set her alarm clock for a reasonable hour.

Did you hear the one about Michael Jackson? Apparently there's a joke that made fun of how stupid he looked, and it implied that he liked to put himself in uncomfortable situations with children.

Q: Why did the East German swimmer have her gold medal taken away?
A: Because they realized East Germany was no longer a country, and thus the swimmer must have submitted fraudulent registration paperwork.

Q: How can you tell the season of an old episode of Friends you are watching?
A: By looking at the size of Chandler's face. If it is super fat, then it's probably season 4 or 6.

Little Johnny was sitting in the class one morning when the teacher asked, "If you have six apples, and I take away two apples, how many apples do you have left?" Little Johnny raised his hand, but the teacher called on Suzy.
"You'd have four apples left, Miss Spencer," Suzy said.
"That's correct," said the teacher. But little Johnny became angry because he had a hilarious response for the teacher that had something to do with the teacher's relatively small breasts.

If Johnny has 50 candy bars and eats 45, what does he have?
Munchies. Johnny has the munchies.

My Teacher Pointed at Me with His Ruler and Said, "At the End of This Ruler, There's an Idiot."
I GOT DETENTION WHEN I ASKED "WHICH END?"

I Love Your Smile, Your Face, Your Eyes. DAMN I'M GOOD AT TELLING LIES.

ANTI-JOKES

Your mom is so fat that she sought a relevant support group. My understanding is that she tried Overeater's Anonymous and only lost a few pounds, but she's more comfortable with herself as a somewhat overweight woman. It meant more to her that the group improved her sense of self-worth. She's a much happier person now. We're all very proud of her, and are far less likely to encourage or even tolerate jokes concerning her overweight problem.

Yo mama is so fat that when she dives into a pool, she displaces a proportionately larger volume of water than people with less body mass.

Knock, knock.
WHO'S THERE?
Your neighbor, Sam.
OH. WELL, MY EXTENDED FAMILY IS OVER FOR DINNER AT THE MOMENT. WOULD YOU MIND COMING BACK LATER?
I suppose that would be all right.

What was the biggest turning point during Michael Vick's transformation from despised felon to MVP candidate?
He stopped killing dogs.

A man walks into a barn. He orders a drink. Horse asks "Why the long face?"
"I'm a frayed knot," he answers.

Two cows are in a field. Suddenly, from behind a bush, a rabbit leaps out and hops toward the briar patch.
One cow looks around a bit, eats some grass and then wanders off.

A traveling salesman's car broke down in a rural area, and he asked a farmer if he could spend the night. The farmer said that it would be okay for him to spend the night but that he did not have a daughter.

Yo mama is so fat, that frankly, people have made unkind jokes about her for years. Let the cycle of abuse end here.

How do you confuse a blond?
By being unclear in your communication.

What do you call 40 lawyers going over a cliff in a bus?
Tragic and sad. They were my friends.

I crossed the road, and yet I feel as if nothing has been accomplished.

That guy is sooooo Amberly. He sleeps in a turtle neck.

Deja Moo: THE FEELING YOU'VE HEARD THAT BULL BEFORE.

When I'm not in a relationship, I shave one leg so it feels like I'm sleeping with a woman.

Plain Old Broadneck Jokes

A guy is driving around the back woods of Broadneck and he sees a sign in front of a broken down shanty-style house: "Talking Dog For Sale." He rings the bell and the owner appears and tells him the dog is in the backyard.

The guy goes into the backyard and sees a nice looking Labrador retriever sitting there.

"You talk?" he asks.

"Yep," the Lab replies.

After the guy recovers from the shock of hearing a dog talk, he says "So, what's your story?"

The Lab looks up and says, "Well, I discovered that I could talk when I was pretty young. I wanted to help the government, so I told the CIA. In no time at all they had me jetting from country to country, sitting in rooms with spies and world leaders, because no one figured a dog would be eavesdropping. I was one of their most valuable spies for eight years running, but the jetting around really tired me out, and I knew I wasn't getting any younger so I decided to settle down. I signed up for a job at the airport to do some undercover security, wandering near suspicious characters and listening in. I uncovered some incredible dealings and was awarded a batch of medals. I got married, had a mess of puppies, and now I'm just retired."

The guy is amazed. He goes back in and asks the owner what he wants for the dog.

"Ten dollars," the guy says.

"Ten dollars? This dog is amazing! Why on earth are you selling him so cheap?"

"Because he's full of crap! He's never been out of the yard." •

An elderly couple, Pauline and Frank, were recently attending a church service at their retirement village. The couple had just celebrated their 60th wedding anniversary.

About half-way through the service, Pauline took a pen and paper out of her purse, and wrote a note and handed it to Frank. The note said, "I just silently passed gas, what do you think I should do, Frank?"

Frank scribbled back, "Put a new battery in your hearing aid." •

A couple of married politicians decided to campaign in Maryland. They wanted to pose as real, down-home folks, so they bought some flannel shirts and dungarees and rented a Chesapeake Bay Retriever to accompany them.

At one of the stops, a Broadneck bar, the bartender gushed, "Wow! Aren't you two famous national politicians?"

"Why yes we are!" announced the wife loudly, "And what a lovely peninsula you have here! We were passing through and wanted to stop and take in some local color."

At that, a man at the bar jumped up and ran out. The wife smiled smugly and knew the word would soon be out.

While they were talking to anyone who would listen, a grizzled old Broadneck farmer came in, walked over to the dog, lifted up its tail, looked underneath, shrugged his shoulders and started to walk out.

"Pardon me sir," said the wife, "Why did you just ignore my husband and me, walk past us, and look under our dog's tail? Is that some sort of local custom?"

"No ma'am," replied the old farmer. "Some fool is running around outside telling everyone there's a dog in here with two butt holes, and I just wanted to see for myself." •

Very Good

Jack the Ripper's mother to Jack: "No wonder you're still single. You never go out with the same girl twice."

Why, when he came home drunk, did Tom leave his clothes on the floor? He was in them.

Plain Old Broadneck Jokes

A farmer walks into a bar with a pig. The pig has a wooden leg. Farmer says to the barkeep, "Give me a beer, and one for the pig."

Barkeep says, "We don't serve livestock."

Farmer says, "But this is no ordinary pig. Last year a wolf was attacking the sheep, and this pig charged and chased the wolf away.

"Is that how he got the wooden leg?" the barkeep asked.

"No," said the farmer, "A couple of months ago there was a fire in the barn overnight, and this pig squealed until I woke up and found he had already busted the lock on the barn door and let all the animals escape the fire."

"And that's how he got the wooden leg?" the barkeep inquired.

"No," said the farmer, "Just last week my tractor turned over and I was pinned underneath in a flooding ditch. This pig pulled me out from under the tractor, and then called the ambulance and filed all the insurance paperwork for me."

"And that's how he lost the leg?" the barkeep asked.

"No," said the farmer, "It's just that when you have a pig this great, you don't want to eat it all at once." •

A pirate with an eye patch and a hook for a hand walks into the Riverbay Roadhouse.

The bartender, Dana, asks: "How did you get the hook?"

Pirate replies: "sword fight."

Dana says: "Wow. So how did you get the eye patch?"

Pirate: "Seagull pooped in my eye."

Dana: "What? you lost your eye from seagull poop?"

Pirate: "No, not really. It was my first day with the hook." •

Clem & Leroy saw an ad in the *Broadneck Baloney* and bought a mule for $100. The farmer agreed to deliver the mule the next day, but the next morning the farmer drove up and said,"Sorry, fellows, I have some bad news, the mule died last night."

Clem & Leroy replied, "Well then, just give us our money back."

The farmer said, "Can't do that. I went and spent it already."

They said, "Well then, just bring us the dead mule, and we'll raffle him off."

The farmer said, "You can't raffle off a dead mule!"

Leroy said, "We sure can! Heck, we don't hafta tell nobody he's dead!"

The farmer ran into Clem & Leroy a couple weeks later and asked, "What'd you fellers ever do with that dead mule?"

Leroy said,"We raffled him off like we said we wuz gonna do. Shucks, we sold 500 tickets fer two dollars apiece and made a profit of $998."

The farmer said, "My Lord, didn't anyone complain?"

Clem said, "The feller who won got upset. So we gave him his two dollars back." •

Taking his seat in his chambers, the judge faced the opposing lawyers.

"So," he said, "I have been presented, by both of you, with a bribe." Both lawyers squirmed uncomfortably.

"You, attorney Jones, gave me $15,000. And you, attorney Smith, gave me $10,000."

The judge reached into his pocket and pulled out a check. He handed it to Jones.

"Now then, I'm returning $5,000, and we're going to decide this case solely on its merits!" •

A man enters O'Loughlin's with a roll of tarmac under his arm and says, "A pint please, and one for the road."

There's a Hole in the Nudist Colony Fence. NOW THAT'S WORTH LOOKING INTO.

10 Things You Will Never, Ever, Not Even in Your Wildest Dreams, Hear a Man Say

10. Here honey, you use the remote.

9. You know, I'd like to see her again, but her breasts are just too big.

8. Oh, Antonio Banderas AND Brad Pitt? That's one movie I gotta see!

7. While I'm up, can I get you a beer?

6. Honey since we don't have anything else planned, will you go to the wallpaper store with me?

5. Sex isn't that important; sometimes, I just like to be held.

4. Why don't you go to the mall with me and help me pick out a pair of shoes?

3. Aw, forget Monday night football, let's watch our Melrose Place DVD.

2. Hey, let me hold your purse while you try that on.

. . . and the number 1 thing a man will never say:

1. We never talk anymore.

10 More Things You Will Never, Even in Your Wildest Dreams, Hear a Man Say

10. Does this hunter's outfit make me look fat?

9. Do you think he is prettier than me?

8. My wife never listens to me.

7. I'll have the light vinaigrette salad and a diet soda.

6. Why don't we go to the men's room and freshen up?

5. No, I didn't see the game last night. I was watching the Home Shopping Network.

4. Looks like it's time to buy some new underwear.

3. Okay, I want to know right now, who left the toilet seat up?

2. I've got my father's thighs.

1. The dog? No, that was me.

What Did the Blonde Say When She Found out She Was Pregnant? I WONDER IF IT'S MINE.

Things We Would Never Know Without The Movies

Once applied, lipstick will never rub off, even while scuba diving.

You can always find a chainsaw whenever you need one.

Any lock can be picked by a credit card or a paper clip in seconds—unless it's the door to a burning building with a child trapped inside.

Cars that crash will almost always burst into flames.

All telephone numbers in America begin with the digits 555.

A single match will be sufficient to light up a room the size of a football stadium.

Medieval peasants had perfect teeth.

A man will show no pain while taking the most ferocious beating but will wince when a woman tries to clean his wounds.

When paying for a taxi, don't look at your wallet as you take out a bill—just grab one at random and hand it over. It will always be the exact fare.

It's easy for anyone to land a jet passenger plane providing there is someone to talk you down.

The ventilation system of any building is the perfect hiding place—no one will ever think of looking for you in there and you can travel to any other part of the building undetected.

Police departments give their officers personality tests to make sure they are deliberately assigned to a partner who is their polar opposite.

The Eiffel Tower can be seen from any window in Paris.

All bombs are fitted with electronic timing devices with large red readouts so you know exactly when they are going to go off.

If you need to reload your gun, you will always have more ammunition, even if you haven't been carrying any before then.

You are very likely to survive any battle in any war unless you make the mistake of showing someone a picture of your sweetheart back home.

Kitchens don't have light switches. When entering a kitchen at night, you should open the fridge door and use that light instead.

If staying in a haunted house, women should investigate any strange noises in their most revealing underwear.

Whenever anyone is chased to a staircase, she/he will run upstairs rather than down.

Why Do Bagpipers Walk When They Play? THEY'RE TRYING TO GET AWAY FROM THE NOISE.

Real Catholic Elementary School Test Answers about the Old and New Testaments

Incorrect Spelling Left in.

1. In the first book of the Bible, Guinessis, God got tired of creating the world so He took the Sabbath off.
2. Adam and Eve were created from an apple tree. Noah's wife was Joan of Ark. Noah built an ark and the animals came on in pears.
3. Lot's wife was a pillar of salt during the day, but a ball of fire during the night.
4. The Jews were a proud people and throughout history they had trouble with unsympathetic genitals.
5. Sampson was a strongman who let himself be led astray by a Jezebel like Delilah.
6. Samson slayed the Philistines with the axe of the apostles.
7. Moses led the Jews to the Red Sea where they made unleavened bread which is bread without any ingredients.
8. The Egyptians were all drowned in the dessert. Afterwards, Moses went up to Mount Cyanide to get the ten commandments.
9. The first commandment was when Eve told Adam to eat the apple.
10. The seventh commandment is thou shalt not admit adultery.
11. Moses died before he ever reached Canada. Then Joshua led the Hebrews in the battle of Geritol.
12. The greatest miricle in the Bible is when Joshua told his son to stand still and he obeyed him.
13. David was a Hebrew king who was skilled at playing the liar. He fought the Finkelsteins, a race of people who live in biblical times.
14. Solomon, one of David's sons, had 300 wives and 700 porcupines.
15. When Mary heard she was the mother of Jesus, she sang the magna carta.
16. Jesus was born because he had an immaculate contraption.
17. Jesus enunciated the golden rule, which says to do unto others before they do one to you. He also explained a man doth not live by sweat alone.
18. It was a miracle when Jesus rose from the dead and managed to get the tombstone off the entrance.
19. The people who followed the Lord were called the twelve decibels.
20. The epistels were the wives of the apostles
21. One of the oppossums was Saint Matthew, who was also a taximan.
22. Saint Paul cavorted to Christianity. He preached holy acrimony which is another name for marriage.
23. Christians have only one spouse. This is known as monotony.

Right Now I'm Having Amnesia and Deja Vu at the Same Time. I THINK I'VE FORGOTTEN THIS BEFORE.

Top 21 Pick-up Lines for Broadneckians

1. You look so familiar! Oh, I know why, you look like my next girlfriend.
2. I'll bet you $20 you'll turn me down.
3. Excuse me, do you know how much a polar bear weighs? (No) Enough to break the ice. Hi, my name is . . .
4. If I were a gardner, I'd plant your tulips next to mine.
5. Kiss me if I'm wrong, but have we met?
6. You must be the number one cause of global warming.
7. I think I've seen your picture somewhere. Oh yes, it was in the dictionary under SHA-BAM!
8. Excuse me, do you have a Band-aid? I skinned my knee when I fell for you.
9. You must be a parking ticket, because you have fine written all over you.
10. You're so sweet I'm getting cavities.
11. If you were a burger at McDonald's, you'd be the McGorgeous.
12. Is it hot in here or is it just you?
13. Excuse me, do you have any raisins? How about a date?
14. I'm new in town. Could you give me directions to your apartment?
15. Do you want to see a picture of a beautiful person? (hold up a mirror).
16. When I saw you from across the room, I passed out cold and hit my head on the floor, so I'm going to need your name and number for insurance purposes.
17. If you stood in front of a mirror and held up eleven roses, you would see 12 of the most beautiful things in the world.
18. You must be tired because you've been running through my dreams all night.
19. You're like the square root of negative one because you're so unreal.
20. Is your name Google? Because you have everything I'm searching for.

If I were to ask you out on a date, would your answer be the same as the answer to this question?

A Celebrity Fell into a Vat of Molten Glass MAKING A SPECTACLE OUT OF HIMSELF.

PROFOUND PUNS FOR THE SEMI-PERPLEXED

The soldier who survived mustard gas and pepper spray is now a seasoned veteran.

A backward poet writes inverse.

In a democracy it's your vote that counts. In feudalism, it's your count that votes.

When cannibals ate a missionary, they got a taste of religion.

If you jumped off the bridge in Paris, you'd be in Seine.

A vulture boards an airplane, carrying two dead raccoons. The stewardess looks at him and says, "I'm sorry, sir, only one carrion allowed per passenger."

The midget fortune-teller who escaped from prison was a small medium at large.

Two fish swim into a concrete wall. One turns to the other and says, "Dam!"

Two Eskimos sitting in a kayak were chilly, so they lit a fire in the craft. Unsurprisingly it sank, proving again that you can't have your kayak and heat it too.

Two hydrogen atoms meet. One says, "I've lost my electron." The other says, "Are you sure?" The first replies, "Yes, I'm positive."

Did you hear about the Buddhist who refused Novocain during a root canal? His goal: transcend dental medication.

A sign on the lawn at a drug rehab center said: "Keep off the Grass."

Two silk worms had a race. They ended up in a tie.

A dog gave birth to puppies near the road and was cited for littering.

A hole has been found in the nudist camp wall. The police are looking into it.

Time flies like an arrow. Fruit flies like a banana.

The fattest knight at King Arthur's round table was Sir Cumference. He acquired his size from too much pi.

I thought I saw an eye doctor on an Alaskan island, but it turned out to be an optical Aleutian.

Atheism is a non-prophet organization.

Two hats were hanging on a hat rack. One hat said to the other: "You stay here; I'll go on a head."

I wondered why the baseball kept getting bigger. Then it hit me.

A grenade thrown into a kitchen in France would result in Linoleum Blownapart.

I Always Arrive Late to Work, but Make up for It by Leaving Early.

Pithy Puns for Perspicuous Persons

The friars were behind on their belfry payments, so they opened up a small florist shop to raise funds. Since everyone liked to buy flowers from the men of God, a rival florist across town thought the competition was unfair. He asked the good fathers to close down, but they refused. He went back and begged the friars to close. They ignored him. So the rival florist hired Hugh MacTaggart, the roughest and most vicious thug in town to "persuade" them to close. Hugh beat up the friars and trashed their store, saying he'd be back if they didn't close up shop. Terrified, they did so, thereby proving that Hugh, and only Hugh, can prevent florist friars.

A farmer noticed a fly buzzing around the cow's ear while he was milking it. Next thing you know, the fly was in the bucket of milk. The farmer says, "In one ear, and out the udder!"

What did Frank Sinatra say when someone asked him if he had ever kept wading birds as pets? "Egrets, I've had a few."

Leif Ericsson went off on his voyage to the New World, and a year later his wife noticed that his name wasn't on the village register anymore. She went to the village elders and asked, "Have you taken Leif off your census?"

A mediocre conductor of a mediocre orchestra had problems with the basses who were drunk most of the time. The last performance of the season featured Beethoven's 9th Symphony, which required extra effort from the basses as it reached its conclusion. As the conductor was about to cue the basses, he knocked over his music stand.

The sheet music scattered. As he stood in front of his orchestra, he realized his worst fear: it was the last of the 9th, no score, and the basses were loaded.

Mahatma Gandhi walked barefoot most of the time which produced an impressive set of callouses on his feet. He also ate very little, which made him rather frail and with his odd diet, he suffered from bad breath. This made him . . . a super calloused fragile mystic hexed by halitosis.

A group of people are touring the White House in Washington DC. As the tour ends, they are waiting in line to sign the visitors' register. A group of nuns are in line to sign the book, followed by a Jewish family with their young son, Sheldon. As they near the visitors' register, young Sheldon loses patience and runs ahead to sign the book. However, his mother scolds him, saying, "Wait till the nun signs, Shelly!"

A noted Broadneck biologist, who had been studying little green frogs in the Bay mud flats, was stumped. The frog population, despite efforts at predator control, declined at an alarming rate. A chemist at Anne Arundel Community College identified the problem: The frogs, due to a chemical change in the swamp water, simply couldn't stay coupled long enough to reproduce successfully. The chemist then brewed up a new adhesive to assist the frogs' togetherness, which included one part sodium. It seems the little green frogs needed some monosodium glue to mate.

The Cross-eyed Teacher HAD NO CONTROL OF HER PUPILS.

Some Amusing Palindromes

The very first palindrome was uttered in the Garden of Eden when the first man met his mate and said, "Madam, I'm Adam." A bunch more:

He lived as a devil, eh?
Al lets Della call Ed Stella
Ma is a nun as I am.
Dennis and Edna sinned.
Naomi, did I moan?
A man, a plan, a canal, Panama.
Enid and Edna dine.
Able was I ere I saw Elba.
Poor Dan is in a droop.
Go hang a salami; I'm a lasagna hog.
Go deliver a dare, vile dog!
Do geese see God?
Ah, Satan sees Natasha.
Lisa Bonet ate no basil.
Oozy rat in a sanitary zoo.
Was it Eliot's toilet I saw?
Kay, a red nude, peeped under a yak.
A santa lived as a devil at NASA.
Mr. Owl ate my metal worm.
Eva, can I stab bats in a cave?
Dammit, I'm mad!
Was it a rat I saw?
Never odd or even.
Doc, note: I dissent. A fast never prevents a fatness. I diet on cod.
Tarzan raised Desi Arnaz' rat.

ATTENTION: Please warn your friends afflicted with AIBOHPHOBIA — Fear of palindromes — and a palindrome itself, to avoid this page !

Nurses run.
To Idi Amin: I'm a idiot.
Draw pupil's lip upward.
Tulsa night life: filth, gin, a slut.
Evil olive.
Marge lets Norah see Sharon's telegram.
Dog, as a devil deified, lived as a god.
Ogre, flog a golfer. Go!
Tangy gnat.
Satan oscillate my metal sonatas.
Was it a car or a cat I saw?
Solo gigolos.
A nut for a jar of tuna.
Murder for a jar of red rum.
Cigar? Toss it in a can. It is so tragic.
Drab as a fool, aloof as a bard.
Borgnine drags dad's gardening robe.
Evil I did dwell, lewd did I live.
Gnu dung.
God, a red nugget. A fat egg under a dog.
I roamed under it as a tired, nude Maori.
No, Mel Gibson is a casino's big lemon.
Plan no damn Madonna LP.
Remarkable was I ere I saw Elba Kramer.
Sir, I soon saw Bob was no Osiris.
Sis, ask Costner to not rent socks "as is."
Sit on a potato pan, Otis.

An esteemed Broadneck gentleman had been taking a magazine to be printed in Delaware each month. There he introduced himself as Bob to an attractive receptionist named Melody. Each month he returned and said hello to Melody, but she could not remember his name. Finally, Bob said, "Melody, remember my name is a 3-letter palindrome, spelled the same way backwards and forwards, B-O-B, B-O-B."

"Oh, yes," Melody replied, "I'm sure to remember your name now."

The next month, Bob entered the printing office and said, "Hi, Melody." But Melody again could not remember his name. Then it came to her. She thought, "3-letter palindrome!" Her mind went into high gear. Then she looked up, and with a tentative expression, said, "D-A-D?"

Little Billy, Can You Name Two Pronouns? WHO ME?

Bella's Presents . . . A Few Tom Swifties for Your Amusement

"Get to the back of the boat," the captain yelled sternly.

"What's your first name, Mr. Hemingway," the boy asked earnestly.

"I wish I could afford a Swedish car," the would-be Broadneck intellectual Saabed.

"These handcuffs are chaffing my wrists," the prisoner said guardedly.

"Do I see hair coming out of your nostrils?" Tom asked the customer nosily.

"I want all you chickens to call me by my first name," Mr. Perdue said frankly.

"Ointment will help that cut heal," the nurse said savvily.

"You've got to do something about that worthless horse," Tom nagged.

"Let me help you find some sandpaper and a rasp file," Tom said to the customer abrasively.

"I'll always be a company woman," Tom said firmly.

"What kind of bread do you want with that corned beef"? Tom asked wryly.

"I'm hiding here, under this pile of letters," Tom said submissively.

"There's too much cotton in the warehouse," Tom said balefully.

"Is it cold enough for my wool coat?" Tom's wife asked sheepishly.

"Hurry and turn those pancakes," Tom urged flippantly.

"Be careful you don't fall over that cliff," Tom warned precipitously.

"Your mother-in-law's sarcasm really seems to get your goat," Tom kidded.

"What time is it now?" Tom's cousin asked presently.

"The captain busted me down from corporal again," the soldier confided to Tom privately.

"Fire!" yelled Tom alarmingly.

"You need a more emphatic font," the editor said boldly.

"I want to date around," said Tom unsteadily.

"We need a home run hitter," the manager said ruthlessly.

"I just returned from Japan," Tom said disoriented.

"I forget what to buy," Tom said listlessly.

"I only get Newsweek," Tom uttered timelessly.

"I hate pies with crumb bases," Tom said crustily.

"I commanded a group of ships for a year," the admiral said fleetingly.

"As my sole heir, you get it all," Tom said willfully.

"I love Chinese soup," Tom said wontonly.

"I've brought the dessert," Tom said piously.

"I collect old fairy tales," Tom said grimly.

"We've struck oil," Tom said crudely.

"A thousand thanks," Tom said mercifully.

"Get away from the dynamite," Tom hollered explosively.

"Please make me some macaroni and cheese for supper," Tom asked craftily.

"I won the daily double," Tom cried hoarsely.

"I'll pay off that customs official," Tom said dutifully.

"We still haven't struck oil," Tom said boringly.

"I need a pencil sharpener," Tom said bluntly.

"As soon as the rain stops, we'll break camp," Tom said intently.

"I've got to keep this fire going," Tom bellowed.

Doctor, I've Swallowed a Spoon. WHATEVER YOU DO, DON'T STIR.

STATEMENTS FROM ACTUAL GRADE SCHOOL PAPERS

- Ancient Egypt was inhabited by mummies and they all wrote in hydraulics. They lived in the Sarah Dessert and the climate of the Sarah is such that the inhabitants have to live elsewhere.
- Moses led the Hebrew slaves to the Red Sea, where they made unleavened bread which is bread made without any ingredients. Moses went up on Mount Cyanide to get the ten commandments. He died before he ever reached Canada.
- The Greeks were a highly sculptured people, and without them we wouldn't have history. The Greeks also had myths. A myth is a female moth.
- Actually, Homer was not written by Homer but by another man of that name.
- Socrates was a famous Greek teacher who went around giving people advice. They killed him. Socrates died from an overdose of wedlock. After his death his career suffered a dramatic decline.
- Joan of Arc was burnt to a steak and was canonized by Bernard Shaw. Finally, Magna Carta provided that no man should be hanged twice for the same offense.
- Queen Elizabeth was the "Virgin Queen." As a queen she was a great success. When she exposed herself before her troops they all shouted "Hurrah."
- The greatest writer of the Renaissance was William Shakespeare. He was born in the year 1564, supposedly on his birthday. He never made much money and is famous only because of his plays. He wrote tragedies, comedies, and hysterectomies, all in Islamic pentameter. Romeo and Juliet are an example of heroic couplet.
- Writing at the same time as Shakespeare was Miguel Cervantes. He wrote Donkey Hote. The next great author was John Milton. Milton wrote Paradise Lost. Then his wife died and he wrote Paradise Regained.
- One of the causes of the Revolutionary War was the English put tacks in their tea. Also the colonists would send their parcels through the post without stamps. Finally, the colonists won the war and no longer had to pay for taxis. Delegates from the original 13 states formed the contented congress. Thomas Jefferson and Benjamin Franklin were two singers of the declaration of independence. Franklin discovered electricity by rubbing two cats backwards and declared, "A horse divided against itself cannot stand."
- Johann Bach wrote a great many musical compositions and had a large number of children. In between he practiced on an old spinster which he kept up in his attic. Bach died from 1750 to the present.
- Beethoven wrote music even though he was deaf. He was so deaf he wrote loud music. He took long walks in the forest even when everyone was calling for him. Beethoven expired in 1827 and later died from this.
- The nineteenth century was a time of a great many thoughts and inventions. People stopped reproducing by hand and started reproducing by machine. The invention of the steam boat caused a network of rivers to spring up. Cyrus McCormick invented the McCormick raper, which did the work of a hundred men. Louis Paster discovered a cure for rabbis.

It's Not Fair. I Lost My Job Because of Something My Boss Said. WHAT DID HE SAY? You're Fired!

The Most Interesting Man on Broadneck: Bay Hills' Own Claude Butz

He named the Severn River, the Severn River, and the Magothy, the Magothy.

Presidents take off on his birthday.

His personality is so magnetic, he can't carry credit cards.

He takes his salad dressing right on the salad, so there is no going back.

Aliens ask him to probe them.

When in Rome, they do as he does.

The pope confesses his sins to him, after the pope kisses his ring.

He once postponed a total eclipse of the sun because it interfered with his polo match.

Ghosts sit around the fire and tell stories about him.

He once thought he was wrong, but he was mistaken. That was the only time he was mistaken.

His cereal never gets soggy. It sits there, staying crispy, just for him.

His mother has a tattoo that reads "Son."

He gave his father "the talk."

He once sent $1000 to a Nigerian scammer, and actually received his $5 million share of the loot.

He once caught the Loch Ness monster on a fishing trip in Scotland, and threw it back in, even though it wasn't catch and release.

He is the only person to have come back from the Bermuda Triangle, with a souvenir.

He has won the lifetime achievement award—twice.

He once went to a fortune teller—to warn her.

His tears can cure diseases. Too bad he doesn't cry.

His business card says simply, "I'll call you."

His organ donation card also lists his beard.

THESE ONE-LINERS REFUSED TO STAY AT THE TOP OR BOTTOM OF THE PAGE—THEY'RE BOLD

I want to be something really scary for Halloween this year so I'm dressing up as a phone battery at 2%.

My parents won't say which of their six kids they love the best, but they have told me I finished just out of the top five.

Makeup tip: You're not in the circus.

Why was Cinderella thrown off the basketball team? She ran away from the ball.

It's bad luck to be superstitious.

Behind every great man is a woman rolling her eyes.

I'm here for whatever you need me to do from the couch.

I think my neighbor is stalking me. She's been googling my name on her computer. I saw it through my telescope last night.

Maybe if we start telling people the brain is an app they will start using it.

When an employment application asks who is to be notified in case of emergency, I always write, "A very good doctor."

I can't believe I got fired from the calendar factory. All I did was take a day off.

I Had a Freudian Slip with My Wife. I Meant to Say "Honey, Please Pass the Salt." But Instead I Said, "You Wench, You Ruined My Life."

There are few things I enjoy more than picking an argument with my girlfriend when she has the hiccups.

I would give Dad what he wants for Father's Day, but I can't afford to move out yet.

My ex wrote to me: Can you delete my number? I responded: Who is this?

Thanks for explaining the word "many" to me, it means a lot.

People who write "u" instead of "you." What do you do with all the time you save?

Refusing to go to the gym counts as resistance training, right?

We are all time travelers moving at the speed of exactly 60 minutes per hour.

Any room is a panic room if you've lost your phone in it.

You want breakfast in bed? SLEEP IN THE KITCHEN.

The Most Interesting Woman on Broadneck: Ulmstead's own Natalie Cladd

Once a rattlesnake bit her, and after 5 days of excruciating pain, the snake finally died.

The circus ran away to join her.

She once got pulled over on College Parkway for speeding, and the cop got the ticket.

Her signature won a Pulitzer.

Even her enemies list her as an emergency contact.

In museums, she is allowed to touch the art.

She once won the Tour-de-France, but was disqualified for riding a unicycle.

Bigfoot tries to get pictures of her.

She doesn't have Daddy issues or Mommy issues, and she's never had any therapy.

Her feet don't get blisters: her shoes do.

She lives vicariously through herself.

She can speak Russian . . . in French.

She has never waited 15 minutes after finishing a meal before returning to the pool.

While swimming off the coast of Australia, she once scratched the underbelly of a Great White with her right hand.

Her charm is so contagious, vaccines have been developed for it.

She has taught old dogs a variety of new tricks.

She doesn't believe in using oven mitts, or potholders.

Her purse is woven out of chupacabra leather.

She is never late for any occasion, and if she is, you started too early.

If she were to pat you on the back, you would list it on your resume.

Waiter, there are two flies in my soup ! That's all right sir, have the extra one on me !

Q: Why do Blondes have TGIF written on their shoes? A: Toes Go In First.

BROADNECK BLONDES

A blonde is driving a helicopter and it crashes. When the police come and ask the blond what happened she says, "I got cold so I turned off the big fan!"

Blonde: "What does IDK stand for?" Brunette: "I don't know." Blonde: "OMG, nobody does!"

A blonde was playing Trivial Pursuit one night. It was her turn. She rolled the dice and she landed on "Science & Nature." Her question was, "If you are in a vacuum and someone calls your name, can you hear it?"
She thought for a time and then asked, "Is the vacuum on or off?"

A painting contractor was speaking with a woman about her job. In the first room, she said she would like a pale blue. The contractor wrote this down and went to the window, opened it, and yelled out "Green side up!"
In the second room, she told the painter she would like it painted in a soft yellow. He wrote this on his pad, walked to the window, opened it, and yelled "Green side up!"
The lady was somewhat curious, but she said nothing.
In the third room, she said she would like it painted a warm rose color. The painter wrote this down, walked to the window, opened it and yelled "Green side up!"
The lady then asked him, "Why do you keep yelling 'Green side up'?"
"I'm sorry," he replied. "But I have a crew of blondes laying sod across the street."

A blonde goes into a library and cheerfully says, "Hi! I'm here to see the doctor!"

In a stern, but hushed voice, the librarian says, "Miss, this is a library." So the blonde lowers her voice and says, "Oh sorry!" Then whispers very softly, "I'm here to see the doctor."

Two blonde football fans are walking along the road when one of them picks up a mirror. She looks in it and says, "Hey, I know that person!" The second one picks it up and says, "Of course you do, you idiot, it's me."

This executive was interviewing a nervous young blonde women for a position in his company. He wanted to find out something about her personality so he asked, "If you could have a conversation with someone, living or dead, who would it be?"
The blonde quickly responded, "The living one."

A blonde made several attempts to sell her old car. She was having a lot of problems finding a buyer because the car had 340,000 miles on it.
She discussed her problem with a brunette that she worked with at a bar. The brunette suggested, "There may be a chance to sell that car easier, but it's not going to be legal."
"That doesn't matter at all," replied the blonde. "All that matters it that I am able to sell this car."
"Alright," replied the brunette. In a quiet voice, she told the blonde: "Here is the address of a friend of mine. He owns a car repair shop around here. Tell him I sent you, and he will turn the counter back on your car to 40,000 miles. Then it shouldn't be a problem to sell your car."

People Who Hate Hand Gestures: I SALUTE YOU!

Three Fonts Walk into a Bar. The Barman says, "Get Out! We Don't Want Your Type in Here."

BROADNECK BLONDES

The following weekend, the blonde took a trip to the mechanic on the brunette's advice. About one month after that, the brunette saw the blonde and asked, "Did you sell your car?" "No!" replied the blonde. "Why should I? It only has 40,000 miles on it."

A blonde walks into a doctor's office and says, "Doc, I'm horribly sick!" The doctor looks at her and asks, "Flu?" "No, I drove here."

A blonde, a brunette and a red head were running from the cops when they came upon three empty sacks lying in front of a closed store. "Let's hide in these and the cops won't find us!" said the red head, and they each dove into the sacks.
The brunette hid in one that said CAT. The red head hid in one that said DOG, and the blonde hid in one that said POTATOES.
When the cops came by, they thought, "Maybe they're in these sacks. Let's kick them." They kicked the one the brunette was in that said CAT and she said: "Meow!" They kicked the second bag that said DOG with the red head in it. She said, "Woof!" So they moved on to the final sack that said POTATOES and kicked it. The blonde cried out: "Potatoes!"

A blonde goes to the hospital to give blood and is asked what type she is. She tells them she's an outgoing cat-lover.

On a famous TV game show a blonde contestant needed only to answer one more question. One simple question stood between her and the million dollar prize.

"To be today's champion," the show's host smiled, "name two of Santa's reindeer."
The blonde gave a sigh of relief because she had been given such an easy question. "Rudolph!" she said confidently, "and Olive!" The studio audience started to applaud (as the little sign above their heads said to do) but the clapping quickly faded into mumbling, and the confused host replied, "Yes, we'll accept Rudolph, but could you please explain Olive?!"
The blonde circled her hand forward impatiently and began to sing, "Rudolph the red-nosed reindeer had a very shiny nose. And if you ever saw it, you would even say it glowed. Olive, the other reindeer . . ."

A blonde's house was on fire. She called 911 and started screaming, "Help me, please! My house is burning! Hurry!" The operator said, "Okay, calm down and we'll be there soon. How do we get to your house?" The blonde replied, "Duh, in that big red truck!"

A cop pulls over a blonde for speeding. The cop gets out of his car and asks the blonde for her license. "You cops should get it together. One day you take away my license, and the next day you ask me to show it to you."

"Have you heard my knock-knock joke?" asked the blonde. "No," said the brunette. "Okay," said the blonde, "You start."

"Just Say NO to Drugs!" WELL, IF I'M TALKING TO MY DRUGS, I PROBABLY ALREADY SAID YES.

Why can't you tell blondes knock-knock jokes? Because they leave to go answer the door.

BROADNECK BLONDES

A young ventriloquist is touring the Broadneck and stops to entertain at O'Loughlin's Pub in the Bay Hills Shopping Center. He's going through his usual run of stupid blond jokes, when a big blond woman in the audience stands on her chair and says, "I've heard just about enough of your denigrating blond jokes!

"What makes you think you can stereotype women that way? What does a person's physical attributes have to do with their worth as a human being?

"It's guys like you who keep women like me from being respected at work and in my community, of reaching my full potential as a person . . . because you and your kind continue to perpetuate discrimination against not only blondes but women at large . . . all in the name of a distorted form of humor."

Flustered, the ventriloquist begins to apologize, but the blond stops him: "You stay out of this mister, I'm talking to that little jerk on your knee!"

A blonde was having sharp pains in her side. The doctor examined her and said, "You have acute appendicitis."

The blond yelled at the doctor, "A cute appendicitis! I came here to get medical help, not get a stupid compliment!"

The pizza guy asked the blonde if she would like her pizza cut into six pieces or twelve. "Six please" she said, "I could never eat twelve!"

One day, a blonde was watching the news and the news anchor said that a serial killer was on the loose. She rushed into her kitchen, brought all her cereal down to the basement and said "Don't worry, no one can kill you down here!"

A young blonde was on vacation in the depths of Louisiana. She wanted a pair of genuine alligator shoes in the worst way, but was very reluctant to pay the high prices the local vendors were asking. After becoming very frustrated with the "no haggle" attitude of one of the shopkeepers, the blonde shouted, "Maybe I'll just go out and catch my own alligator so I can get a pair of shoes at a reasonable price!"

The shopkeeper said, "By all means, be my guest. Maybe you'll luck out and catch yourself a big one!"

Determined, the blonde turned and headed for the swamps, set on catching herself an alligator. Later in the day, the shopkeeper was driving home, when he spotted the young woman standing waist deep in the water, shotgun in hand. Just then, he saw a huge 9-foot alligator swimming quickly toward her. She took aim, killed the creature, and with a great deal of effort hauled it on to the swamp bank. Lying nearby were several more of the dead creatures.

The shopkeeper watched in amazement. Just then the blonde flipped the alligator on its back, and frustrated, shouted out, "Dang it, this one isn't wearing any shoes either!"

Q: What did the blonde customer say after reading the buxom waitress's name tag?
A: "What did you name the other one?"

Q: What did the blonde say when she saw the sign for the YMCA?
A: "Look, they spelled Macy's wrong!"

I Feel Bad for the Homeless Guy's Dog. HE MUST BE THINKING, "THIS IS THE LONGEST WALK EVER."

When Grandmom Covered Granddad with Lard, HE WENT DOWNHILL QUICKLY.

Why Didn't the Lifeguard Save the Hippie? BECAUSE HE WAS TOO FAR OUT MAN!

Bella's Wine and Spirits Presents...
ASK AUNT BERTHABELLE
Answers to Life's More Peculiar Problems

DEAR AUNT BERTHABELLE: Our next door neighbors are from France. We have put up with his bathlessness, and her flagrantly exposed armpit hair on disgusting occasion after disgusting occasion. The vaunted multiculturalist experience is hitting a little too close to home. It gets worse. Last week they invited us over for breakfast. You've never seen an omelet as tiny as the one each of us was served that morning. I'd be embarrassed to offer such skimpy fare to any of my guests. Tell me, Aunt Berthabelle, if you know, why are French omelets so small? *Theopholos Punnoval, Semiparanoid Creek.*

DEAR THEOPHOLOS: The answer is quite obvious. To the French, one egg is an oeuf.

DEAR AUNT BERTHABELLE: While on Main Street in Annapolis last week, I watched a beggar walk up to a well-dressed woman and say "I haven't eaten anything in three days." She looked at him and said, "I wish I had your will power." Then the beggar walked up to a well-dressed man and said the same thing: "I haven't eaten anything in three days." The well-dressed man responded, "You should force yourself." Don't you think both of these people were overly insensitive to the bum's plight? *Carey Oakey, Eerie Creek.*

DEAR CAREY: Yes I do. There are people in this world who do not love all their fellow human beings as they should. And I hate people like that!

DEAR AUNT BERTHBELLE: My mother left early this morning to retrieve her purse which she said she left at the strip club where she works. My dad left soon after saying he had to apologize to some people at the local bar. I didn't know what to do, so I went to Sunday School. The teacher taught us about King David, and said that after he killed the giant Goliath, he rode his Triumph throughout the land. I didn't know that they had motorcycles in Biblical times. Do you think the Sunday School teacher was playing a joke on us? *Lynn C. Doyle, Amberly.*

DEAR LYNN: No, they had motorcycles back then. They also played baseball. Just look at the very first verse in the Bible "In the big inning, God created the heavens and the earth."

DEAR AUNT BERTHABELLE: I am a novelist here on Broadneck. I've been thinking about my little garden and how meditating upon the single plant in it could provide me with metaphors and chapter titles. Do you think I'm on the right track? *Constance Noring, Amberly.*

DEAR CONSTANCE: I'm not very optimistic about your writing. You don't seem to have much of a plot.

DEAR AUNT BERTHABELLE: I applied for a job that required two languages. I'm bilingual if you count the fact that I know sign language, but the employer wouldn't count it, and I didn't get the job. Do you think that's fair? *Hugh Jass, Cape.*

DEAR HUGH: I really think that's a mute point, don't you?

DEAR AUNT BERTHABELLE: Last week, I answered a knock at my door and came face to face with 6-foot-tall cockroach. It punched me between the eyes and scampered off.

More recently, my neighbor told me that a huge cockroach, undoubtedly the same one, punched him in the stomach and karate chopped him on the back before running away.

And just this morning that same cockroach attacked my sister and brother-in-law.

This is a dangerous situation for all of us here on Broadneck. Do you know anything about this threat from the insect world? *Wheaton Glootinfree, Acorn Oaks.*

DEAR WHEATON: I've just heard that there's a nasty bug going around. ✣

Two Buckets of Vomit Walk Down the Street. One Points Out "That's Where I Was Brought Up."

Mommy, What is Normal? JUST A SETTING ON THE DRYER, HONEY.

Bella's Wine and Spirits Presents...
ASK AUNT BERTHABELLE
Answers to LIfe's More Peculiar Problems

DEAR AUNT BERTHABELLE: I read your column every issue. I admire your tenacity in dealing with the many presumptuous pseudo-intellectuals who write to you with their ridiculous problems. Stay strong! *Mal D. Merr, Unshady Creek Shoal.*

DEAR MAL: Thanks, but I'm only as strong as the friends I have, the cocktails I drink, and the hairspray I use.

DEAR AUNT BERTHABELLE: To be President of the USA, you have to be 35-years-old and a natural born citizen. This is grossly unfair because there are a great many otherwise qualified people who cannot run for president because their mothers had to have a C-section. The Constitution was written nearly a hundred years ago, and back then nobody even thought of the discrimination that would result from a doctor having to deliver a baby in this unnatural way. Democrats and Republicans need to work together to solve this problem. *Red Rufinsore, Crud Cove.*

DEAR RED: You are the second person whose letter has caused me, upon reading it, to experience a certain reaction. I am reprinting the letter below from Eddie Swirling with my answer so that you will know exactly what I'm referring to. Perhaps you and Eddie should get together to double down on your respective dandified drivel.

DEAR AUNT BERTHABELLE: This woman I met last week at *O'Loughlin's* happy hour told me she wants a guy who is funny and spontaneous. Yet, when I tapped on her kitchen window uninvited late last night dressed as a clown, it was all panic and screaming. Why are women so fickle? *Eddie Swirling, Rotten Acorn Oaks.*

DEAR EDDIE: As I was reading your letter and thinking about you today, I threw up in my mouth a little. I don't think it was a mere coincidence either.

DEAR AUNT BERTHABELLE: It's me, Red, again. Thank you for sharing Eddie's letter and helping me realize how stupid I am. *Red Rufinsore.*

DEAR RED: It's me, Aunt Berthabelle, again. You're not stupid. You just have bad luck when you think.

DEAR AUNT BERTHABELLE: Hi. It's me for the third time, Red. I am trying so hard to change all the negative things about my life, but it seems so daunting, so overwhelming. Please help me with the advice I need. I'll be very thankful if you go easy on the sarcasm. *Red.*

DEAR RED: We all have the power to change one thing a day. Start with your underwear.

DEAR AUNT BERTHABELLE: Can't you come up with anything better than the "To the French, one egg is an oeuf" bit? *Duane Pipe, Cape St. Lucifer.*

DEAR DUANE: Sure: A boiled egg is hard to beat in the morning.

DEAR AUNT BERTHABELLE: I've been on welfare for ten years and I'm sick of it. I really need a job. I'm ready to go to work. With all your connections, I am hoping you can help me out. *Lilac A. Rugg, Dingleberry Meadows.*

DEAR LILAC: I can help. They're looking to hire someone at the circus to circumcise the elephants. The pay isn't all that much but the tips are huge.

DEAR AUNT BERTHABELLE: I always thought you were kind of a cool, steak and potatoes kind of gal, and then last week I saw you nodding your head yes again and again as you spoke with Faye Slift, the President of the Broadneck Vegetarian Club. Did Faye convince you to give up eating meat? *Elvis Presley, Try to Find Me.*

DEAR ELVIS: If my steak isn't still mooing, it's not quite rare enough for me. As for Faye Slift, I have never met herbivore. ✻

Bella's Wine and Spirits Presents...
ASK AUNT BERTHABELLE
Answers to Life's More Peculiar Problems

DEAR AUNT BERTHABELLE: I wanted to let your readers know that my common marmoset monkey did not come home after the weekend. I am concerned he is lost or stolen. He answers to the name Love/Hate. Please approach him with extreme caution. He had his stun gun with him when he left the house. *Hardy Harr, Northwest Magothy Mudd Flats.*

DEAR HARDY: Thanks for helping make Broadneck more of an open air zoo than it already was.

DEAR AUNT BERTHABELLE: Last weekend my drive from Broadneck to Fells Point was improved by listening to a Sherlock Holmes audiobook on my car's CD player. I was amused by my inability to follow the plot as closely as I would have liked, and put this down to middle-age memory lapses. Could there be another explanation? *Dr. John Watson, Baker Street Creek.*

DEAR DOCTOR: Elementary, my dear Watson. I suspect you had your CD player on shuffle.

DEAR AUNT BERTHABELLE: I think it is just terrible and disgusting how everyone has treated Lance Armstrong, especially after what he achieved winning seven Tour de France races while competing on drugs. When I was on drugs, I couldn't even *find* my bike. *Rosy Butt, Waste Lake Gardens.*

DEAR ROSY: Some people cause happiness *wherever* they go. You are the type who causes happiness *whenever* you go.

DEAR AUNT BERTHABELLE: I was wondering: How many divorced men does it take to change a light bulb? *Gloria Sair, Cape Despair.*

DEAR GLORIA: Who cares? They never get the house anyway.

DEAR AUNT BERTHABELLE: A recent article reported that candy manufacturers were discreetly shrinking the size of their chocolate bars. Is the same thing happening to men's underwear, or am I just getting older and fatter? *A. Nuss, Crudwater Estates.*

DEAR MR. NUSS: I'd call you a sadistic, hippophilic necrophile, but that would be beating a dead horse.

DEAR AUNT BERTHABELLE: I am very disappointed because there is nothing in this column concerning the outré pun "To the French, one egg is an oeuf" which I find quite amusing. *Charles DeGaulle III, Bordeaux, France.*

DEAR CHARLES: But now we have your letter.

DEAR AUNT BERTHABELLE: I recently discovered my husband in the garage drinking brake fluid. He likes it, and says that it's less expensive than a nasty alcohol habit. Am I justified to be worried about his health? *Bess Twishes, Mediocre Mills.*

DEAR BESS: I wouldn't worry too much about your husband. If he's drinking brake fluid, he should be able to stop any time he wants.

DEAR AUNT BERTHABELLE: My boyfriend is a hardheaded jokester. He continues to make jokes about my time of the month when he knows how much I hate that. Do you think I may be overly sensitive? *Mandy Lifeboats, Mutton-on-the-Bay.*

DEAR MANDY: You are not the least bit overly sensitive. I am one hundred percent on your side in this matter. Your boyfriend should know better: PMS jokes are not funny—period.

DEAR AUNT BERTHABELLE: I am two months pregnant. When can I expect my baby son to move? *Sue Yu, Upscale Side of Greenholly.*

DEAR SUE: With luck, right after he finishes high school.

DEAR AUNT BERTHABELLE: Right now my wife is banging on the front door, and my dog is barking at the back door. Which one should I let in first? *Royal Paine, Elitist Estates.*

DEAR ROYAL: The dog, of course. At least the dog will shut up after you let him in. ❈

SOME PICTURES FROM OUR SCRAPBOOK !

Bella and John Novosel's grandchildren in 2000: Valerie, Charles, Christine, and Denise.

Bella's Husband, John "Pappy" Novosel

Bella's and John's son, Joe, built this house for himself in 1946 on Route 50. Now it's the considerably expanded Ski Haus

A young Bella "Mom" Novosel

C. G. Smith and Bea Novosel Smith at their wedding reception at the Log Inn in June, 1947. Note the stone fireplace behind them.

The house John Novosel built for Bella on Route 50. In 1981, the family moved it more than 100 yards back off the service road. Bella's granddaughter, Valerie Sullivan, lives there today.

Left: Bea Novosel, in 1945 in front of her family's store on Route 50 — then a two lane road ending at the ferry dock at Sandy Point. Among her good customers were the Labrots who owned much of the peninsula. Bea married C. G. Smith in 1947. In 1954, the family owned a Tastee Freez franchise on Route 50. In later years, Bea, C. G. and Bella owned the Bee Hive Inn (later Bella's) in Cape St. Claire. Right: In 1959, the family added Bea's Sandwich Shop to the back of the Tastee Freez. Pictured are two of C. G.'s and Bea's Children, Denise and Charles Smith.

Bella's Liquors
410-757-0019

"Keeping You in the Best of Spirits"
Family Owned and Operated since 1964

Bella's Wine and Spirits Presents...
ASK AUNT BERTHABELLE
Answers to LIfe's More Peculiar Problems

DEAR AUNT BERTHABELLE: We are trying to add some new items to our catering menu, and we were thinking of including some Wookie steaks, perhaps sliced like a London Broil. Do you think that will be pleasing to our customers? *Biff Wellington, Magothy Mudd Flats.*

DEAR BIFF: I think a Wookie steak might just be a little too chewy.

DEAR AUNT BERTHABELLE: I don't know why I continue to read your column. I don't believe that you are real or that you work for Elvis Presley, Jr., the so-called editor of the *Baloney*. I must admit, however, that I did like your answer to the man who wanted to know why his French neighbors always served such small omelets. You responded something to the effect that, "To the French, one egg is an oeuf," but then in the next couple issues you ran that joke into the ground, if in fact it was a joke. I am sorry I even have to mention it again. If you are going to try to pull the "To the French, one egg is an oeuf," bit again, please notify those who deliver the *Baloney* to my house, that I want the page with your column on it ripped out in advance. *Anita Shower, Back End of Cruddy Creek.*

DEAR ANITA: Did you know that a candle's flame smells like burned nose hair? Go ahead, give one a sniff and see for yourself.

DEAR AUNT BERTHABELLE: I was wondering, since you give such wonderful advice, have you ever had relationship problems, Aunt Berthabelle? *Rosy Butt, Waste Lake Gardens.*

DEAR ROSY: I don't have relationship problems now. As a lass, I had a boyfriend with a wooden leg, but I broke it off.

DEAR AUNT BERTHABELLE: I've been having trouble sleeping for the last ten years. And if I do get to sleep, it's only for a short while. Any suggestions to help me? *Nat Sass, Revell Ups.*

DEAR NAT: How tall are you? It's a fact that taller people sleep longer in bed. If you're short, get a shorter bed. It's relative.

DEAR AUNT BERTHABELLE: I'm in love with a professional tennis player. He says he loves me but doesn't want to get married. Advise please. *Bud Weiser, Alcohol Acres.*

DEAR LYNN: He's not going to marry you. He's a tennis player. Love means nothing to him.

DEAR AUNT BERTHABELLE: I know it's dangerous to talk on my cell phone when I drive, especially when I've been drinking. I'm a math freak, so let me ask you, what's wrong with having a couple of beers and running some calculus equations through my head as I drive? *Dyl Pickel, Severn Pump Station.*

DEAR DAN: Alcohol and calculus don't mix, so don't drink and derive.

DEAR AUNT BERTHABELLE: This letter has nothing to do with anything. I do hope you publish it, because I took the time to write it out, so even though it has nothing to say, it should be a worthy addition to your letters column. I string together a series of sentences, all of which ought to be stricken by a half-decent copy editor. If you decline to publish this, I shall take my letters elsewhere in the future, where they may be ignored by a better class of person. *Moe Lester, Indian Hills.*

DEAR MOE: You are the epitome of the ideal letter-writer to my column. I don't have to respond by thinking of something funny or clever. And just think of all our readers out there. What are they getting out of this exchange? They're getting their heads filled with mush. At the *Baloney*, it's all about filling up pages with tripe anyhow. I just hope you appreciate the fact that I have taken the time to answer your thoughtful letter. Please be so kind as to keep us up to date. ✤

Why Can't a Pony Sing? BECAUSE IT'S A LITTLE HORSE.

More Church Bulletin Notices

OH GOD
WHY

1. The Fasting and Prayer Conference includes meals.

2. Today's Sermon: HOW MUCH CAN A MAN DRINK? with hymns from a full choir.

3. On a church bulletin during the minister's illness: "GOD IS GOOD - Dr. Hargreaves is better."

4. Potluck supper: prayer and medication to follow.

5. Pastor is on vacation. Massages can be given to church secretary.

6. Our Minister unveiled the church's new tithing campaign slogan last Sunday: "I Upped My Pledge - Up Yours."

7. The senior choir director invites any member of the congregation who enjoys sinning to join the choir.

8. During the absence of our pastor, we enjoyed the rare privilege of hearing a good sermon when A.B. Doe supplied our pulpit.

9. Attend and you will hear an excellent speaker and after, heave a healthy lunch.

10. A song fest was hell at the Methodist church Wednesday.

11. Twenty-two members were present at the church meeting held at the home of Mrs. Marsha Crutchfield last evening. Mrs. Crutchfield and Mrs. Rankin sang a duet: The Lord Knows Why.

12. The peacemaking meeting scheduled for today has been canceled due to a conflict.

13. Don't let worry ruin your week - let the church help.

14. The sermon this morning: "Jesus Walks on the Water." The sermon tonight: "Searching for Jesus."

15. This evening at 7 PM there will be a hymn singing in the park across from the Church. Bring a blanket and come prepared to sin.

16. Ladies, don't forget the rummage sale. It's a chance to get rid of those things not worth keeping around the house. Bring your husbands.

17. Please place your donation in the envelope along with the deceased person you want remembered.

18. The concert held in Fellowship Hall was a great success. Special thanks are due to the minister's daughter, who labored the whole evening at the piano, which as usual fell upon her.

My Favorite Part of Cooking Dinner IS WHEN THE VIZZINI'S PIZZA GUY SHOWS UP AT MY DOOR.

To Err is Human, TO MOO BOVINE.

Classes for Women
Taught by Men

Class 1
Up in Winter, Down in Summer - How to Adjust a Thermostat Step by Step, with Slide Presentation.
Meets 4 weeks, Monday and Wednesday for 2 hours beginning at 7:00 PM.

Class 2
Which Takes More Energy - Putting the Toilet Seat Down, or Bitching About It for 3 Hours? Round Table Discussion.
Meets 2 weeks, Saturday 12:00 for 2 hours.

Class 3
Is It Possible To Drive Past a Wal-Mart Without Stopping? - Group Debate.
Meets 4 weeks, Saturday 10:00 PM for 2 hours.

Class 4
Fundamental Differences Between a Purse and a Suitcase - Pictures and Explanatory Graphics.
Meets Saturdays at 2:00 PM for 3 weeks.

Class 5
Curling Irons - Can They Levitate and Fly Into The Bathroom Cabinet? Examples on Video.
Meets 4 weeks, Tuesday and Thursday for 2 hours beginning At 7:00 PM.

Class 6
How to Ask Questions During Commercials and Be Quiet During the Program. Help Line Support and Support Groups.
Meets 4 Weeks, Friday and Sunday 7:00 PM

Class 7
Can a Bath Be Taken Without 14 Different Kinds of Soaps and Shampoos? Open Forum.
Monday at 8:00 PM, 2 hours.

Class 8
Health Watch - They Make Medicine for PMS - USE IT!
Three nights; Monday, Wednesday, Friday at 7:00 PM for 2 hours.

Class 9
I Was Wrong and He Was Right - Real Life Testimonials.
Tuesdays at 6:00 PM Location to be determined.

Class 10
How to Parallel Park in Less Than 20 Minutes without an Insurance Claim. Driving Simulations.
4 weeks, Saturday's noon, 2 hours.

Class 11
Learning to Live - How to Apply Brakes Without Throwing Passengers Through the Windshield.
Tuesdays at 7:00 PM, location to be determined.

At my age "Getting lucky" means walking into a room and remembering what I came in there for.

Did you hear about the guy who stole a calendar? HE GOT 12 MONTHS.

Life Isn't a Fairy Tale. IF YOU LOSE YOUR SHOE AT MIDNIGHT, SLOW DOWN ON THE TEQUILA.

Why was the blonde jogging backwards? She wanted to gain weight.

BROADNECK BLONDE JOKES

A blonde pushes her BMW into the gas station and tells the mechanic that it died. After working on it for a few minutes, he has it idling smoothly.

"What's the story?" she asked. "Just crap in the carburetor," the mechanic replied. "How often do I have to do that?" asked the blonde.

A blonde heard that milk baths would make her more beautiful, so she left a note for her milkman to leave 15 gallons of milk. When the milkman read the note, he felt there must be a mistake. He thought she probably meant 1.5 gallons, so he knocked on the door to clarify the point.

The blonde came to the door and the milkman said, "I found your note to leave 15 gallons of milk. Did you mean 1.5 gallons?"

The blonde said, "I want 15 gallons of milk. I'm going to fill my bathtub up with milk and take a milk bath."

The milkman asked, "Do you want it pasteurized?" The blonde said, "No, just up to my neck."

A blonde walks by a travel agency and notices a sign in the window, "Cruise Special—$99!" She goes inside, lays her money on the counter and says, "I'd like the $99 cruise special, please."

The agent grabs her, drags her into the back room, ties her to a large inner tube, then drags her out the back door and downhill to the river, where he pushes her in and sends her floating.

A second blonde comes by a few minutes later, sees the sign, goes inside, lays her money on the counter, and asks for the $99 special. She too is tied to an inner tube and sent floating down the river.

Drifting into stronger current, she eventually catches up with the first blonde. They float side by side for a while before the first blonde asks, "Do they serve refreshments on this cruise? The second blonde replies, "They didn't last year."

As a blonde crawls out of her wrecked car, the local sheriff asks her what happened. The blonde began, "It was the strangest thing! I looked up and saw a tree, so I swerved to the right. Then I saw another tree, so I swerved to left. Then there was another tree, and another and another."

The sheriff thought for a minute and then said, "Ma'am, I don't know how to tell you this, but the only thing even resembling a tree on this road for 30 miles is your air freshener."

A very attractive blonde woman arrived at the casino and bet twenty thousand dollars on a single roll of the dice. She said, "I hope you don't mind, but I feel much luckier when I'm completely nude." With that, she stripped from the neck down, rolled the dice and yelled, "Come on, baby, Mama needs some new clothes!" As the dice came to a stop she jumped up and down and squealed . . . "YES! YES! I WON, I WON!"

She hugged each of the croupiers and then picked up her winnings and her clothes and quickly departed.

The croupiers stared at each other dumfounded. Finally, one of them asked, "What did she roll?"

The other answered, "I don't know—I thought you were watching."

MORAL: Blondes aren't so dumb, but all men are men.

Waiter, what's that in my soup? I'd better call the manager, sir. I can't tell one insect from another.

My grandma told me her joints are getting weaker, so I told her to roll them tighter.

BROADNECK BLONDE JOKES

The blonde reports for her university final examination that consists of yes/no type questions. She takes her seat in the examination hall, stares at the question paper for five minutes and then, in a fit of inspiration, takes out her purse, removes a coin and starts tossing the coin, marking the answer sheet: Yes, for heads, and No, for tails.

Within half an hour she is all done, whereas the rest of the class is still sweating it out. During the last few minutes she is seen desperately throwing the coin, muttering and sweating.

The moderator, alarmed, approaches her and asks what is going on.

"I finished the exam in half an hour," she said, "but now I'm checking my answers." ☺

A blonde is standing in front of a soda machine outside a store in Cape. After putting in a dollar, a root beer pops out of the machine. She set it on the ground, puts another dollar into the machine, and pushes another button.

Suddenly, a coke comes out of the machine! She continues to do this until a man waiting to use the machine becomes impatient. "Excuse me, can I get my soda and then you can go back to whatever you are doing?"

The blonde turns around and says, "No chance! I'm not giving up this machine while I'm winning!" ☺

Two blondes wait at a bus stop. A bus pulls up and opens the door. One of the blondes leans inside and asks the driver, "Will this bus take me to 5th Avenue?" The bus driver shakes his head and says, "No, I'm sorry."

The other blonde leans inside and asks, "How about ME?" ☺

A blonde was at home watching TV with her friends when she heard a noise. She ran out just in time to see a thief drive off in her brand new car.

"Did you see his face?" her friends asked when she came back inside. "No, but it's okay, I got the license plate number!" ☺

A couple of blonde men in a pickup truck drove into a lumberyard. One of the blonde men walked in the office and said, "We need some four-by-twos."

The clerk said, "You mean two-by-fours, don't you?" The man said, "I'll go check," and went back to the truck. He returned a minute later and said, "Yeah, I meant two-by-fours."

"All right. How long do you need them?" The customer paused for a minute and said, "I'd better go check."

After a while, the customer returned to the office and said, "A long time. We're gonna build a house." ☺

Two blondes realize that their apartment is on fire and go out onto the balcony.

"Help, help!" yells one of the blondes.
"Help us, help us!" yells the other.
"Maybe it would help if we yelled together," said the first blonde. "Good idea," said the other. So they yelled, "Together, together!" ☺

A Man Walks into a Book Store and Asks for a Book on Suffocation. The Clerk Asks, "You Want a Bag with That?"

GOLF JOKES

As a Broadneck lady is crying and screaming and running off the course, the club pro asks her what's wrong.

"I got stung by a bee," she sobs.

"Where'd you get stung," he asks.

"Between the 1st and 2nd hole."

"Sounds like your stance is too wide," the pro responds.

A golfer walks off the 18th green at Bay Hills, hands his putter to his caddie and says, "Kid, you've got to be the worst caddie in the world."

The caddie replies, "Sir, that would be too much of a coincidence."

As a couple approaches the altar, the groom tells his wife-to-be, "Honey, I've got something to confess: I'm a golf nut, and every chance I get, I'll be playing golf!"

"Since we're being honest," replies the bride, "I have to tell you that I'm a hooker."

The groom replies, "That's okay, honey. You just need to learn to keep your head down and your left arm straight!"

A husband and wife were playing on the ninth green when she collapsed from a heart attack. "Please dear, I need help." she said.

The husband ran off saying, "I'll go get some help." A little while later he returned, picked up his putter and began to line up his shot. His wife, on the ground, raised up her head and said, "I may be dying and you're putting?"

"Don't worry dear. I found a doctor on the second hole who said he'd come and help you."

"The second hole? When is he coming?"

"Hey! I told you not to worry," he said, stroking his putt. "Everyone has already agreed to let him play through."

A man and his wife are playing the fifth hole at their club when he slices his drive so far to the right it rolls into an equipment barn. He finds the ball and plans to take a drop when she says, "Let me go down to the other end of the barn and hold the door open. Then you can hit your ball through the door and back to the fairway."

He thinks this is a good idea, so she holds the door. He takes a big swing, but rather than flying through the door, the ball hits her in the head and kills her.

A year later, the same man and his new bride are playing the same hole when he again slices the ball into the shed. He finds it and plans to take an unplayable lie when she says, "Let me go down to the other end of the barn and hold the door open. Then you can hit your ball through the door and back to the fairway."

He looks at her, shakes his head, and explains, "No way. The last time I tried that, I took a triple bogey on this hole!"

"Bad day at the course," a guy tells his wife. "Charlie had a fatal heart attack on the third hole."

"That's terrible!" she says.

"You're telling me," the husband replies. "All day long, it was hit the ball, drag Charlie."

You spend too much time thinking about golf! Do you even remember the day we got married?

Of course I do! It was the day after I sank that 45-foot putt.

A Broadneck golfer standing on a tee overlooking the Magothy sees a couple of fishermen and says to his partner, "Look at those two idiots out there fishing in the rain."

A Baptist pastor decides to play hooky on a Sunday to play golf. He's playing the best golf of his life when an angel asks God, "Are you going to let him get away with this?"

So God says, "Watch this."

The pastor hits a 425-yard tee shot and the ball goes right in the hole for a double eagle. The angel asks, "Why did you reward him?"

God says, "Who is he gonna tell?"

A very bad golfer is playing at a new course and he is having a very bad day. He is on the 18th hole, and he sees a lake. He says to his caddy "I think I'm going to go drown myself in that lake."

The caddy says "I don't think you can do it. You can't keep your head down that long."

Two men ran out to the course for a quick nine after work. They get to the tee and see two ladies playing ahead of them.

One of the men complains that the ladies will slow them down and says he is going to ask if they can play through. He goes halfway to the ladies and turns back.

The other man asked what was wrong. The man said, "I can't go up there that's my wife and my mistress."

So the other man says he will go. He goes halfway and comes back. His partner asked what happened and the man replied, "Small world, huh?"

After slicing his tee shot into the woods, a golfer heads off in search of his ball, which he finds behind a large tree. After considering his position—and not wanting to take a drop and lose a stroke —he decides to hook the ball around the tree. He swings, the ball hits the tree, ricochets back at him, and instantly kills him.

When he opens his eyes, he sees the Pearly Gates and St. Peter standing before him.

"Am I dead?" he asks.

"Yes, my son," replies St. Peter, who looks the man over and notices his clubs. "I see you're a golfer," St. Peter says. "Are you any good?"

"Hey, I got here in two, didn't I?"

I Tried Cooking Supper with Wine Today. AFTER 5 GLASSES I FORGOT WHY I WAS IN THE KITCHEN.

WINE WORKOUT

Bella's Presents: SOME CAPTIVATING THOUGHTS ON WINE

Men are like fine wine. They begin as grapes, and it's up to women to stomp on them until they turn into something worth having dinner with.

I told my wife that a husband is like fine wine. So she locked me in the cellar.

It's no longer box wine. The classy term is Cardboardeaux.

Wine does not make you fat. It makes you lean - against tables, walls, and people.

Always keep a bottle of wine in the fridge for a special occasion. Sometimes the special occasion is that you have a bottle of wine in the fridge.

The secret of enjoying good wine: Open the bottle; allow it to breathe. If it doesn't appear to breathe, give it mouth-to-mouth.

Sometimes I write "Drink wine" on my to-do list, just so I feel like I accomplished something.

I enjoy a glass of wine every night for its health benefits. The other glasses are for my witty comebacks and flawless dance moves.

I vow to drink more wine so I can do something crafty with corks.

I drank so much wine last night, when I walked across the dance floor to get another glass, I won the dance competition.

A good man can make you feel sexy, strong, and able to take on the world. Oh, sorry . . . that's wine . . . wine does that.

I decide which wine to drink on a case by case basis.

I just heard on the grapevine that doctors have invented a new grape variety that acts as an anti-diuretic to help with incontinence. It's called "'Pinot More."

If you can't be with the one you love, love the wine you're with.

What did the grape say when it was crushed? Nothing, it just let out a little whine.

Someone told me that I could make ice cubes with leftover wine. I was confused. What is leftover wine?

My office just started Wine Wednesdays! It takes place in the ladies' room handicapped stall and I'm the only one who knows about it.

Novinophobia: The fear of running out of wine.

I'm a wine enthusiast: The more wine I drink the more enthusiastic I get.

Why did the cookie go to the hospital? BECAUSE HE FELT CRUMMY.

Presents
Sylvester Nosticmeister's
ANSWERS TO THE TOP 4 MOST ASKED QUESTIONS.

Question # 1: WHAT MAKES EMOTIONS SO UNPREDICTABLE?

The emotions come out of the nerves in the spine which are exposed to ultra-violet and other rays which sometimes change the rotation speed of atomic particles. When the electrons spin too fast, you get mad in order to throw off some of the excess energy. When the protons spin too slow, you start to feel depressed. When the direction of neutron spin changes, you feel like shooting some pool or sewing an old dress. If the walls and ceiling of your bedroom are lined with six inches of lead, you will tend to be one-third calmer than those who sleep in standard bedrooms.

But is "calm" the ideal? Some scientists say that "calm" is often mistaken for "slow" and sometimes for "stupid."

Emotions are unpredictable because the intensity of stellar, solar, and lunar rays varies from day to day. Scientists cannot predict with any certainty when super novas, sunspots, or lunar quakes will occur and where each person on Earth will be located at the time the rays associated with each get here.

Not all the news about emotional instability is depressing, however. A new hand-held device, much like a TV remote, has been developed by ITT to alter emotional states. According to the company's brochure, all you have to do is point the device at a subject's spinal column and press one of the thirty mood buttons. These mood buttons include: panting eagerness, passionate insistence, paralyzing sentimentalism, pining melancholy, polite indifference, primal resentment, profane contempt, prostrate servility, pugnacious defiance, restless inquisitiveness, smug stupefaction, snappish impertinence, scoffing suspicion, righteous indignation, saintly serenity, sarcastic incredulity, scholarly amusement, judgmental dismay, shallow vindictiveness, quenchless despair, quiet cynicism, ranting optimism, and tedious tolerance.

You can control the intensity of the mood you have chosen for your human subject the same way you now control TV volume with the remote. The Mighty-Mo Mood Modifier will be at **Cape Ace** by Christmas, retailing for $19.95.

Question # 2: WHAT IS THE BEST WAY TO RELIEVE TENSION?

I have found the basic breathing exercise of Halfaway Yoga to be the best tension reliever of all. Simply inhale deeply saying to yourself, "Breathing in, I relax my entire body." Then exhale, saying, "Breathing out, I fake a smile." Even if this does not make you feel any better, you will seem to be smiling a lot more.

Question # 3: WHAT KINDS OF THINGS ABOUT OTHER PEOPLE STARTING WITH AN "R" BUG US THE MOST?

According to the latest survey, these things are: rambling looseness, rancorous animosity, rapacious speculation, ravenous eagerness, reckless lavishness, reluctant tolerance, remorseless logic, repeated falsifications, repelling vices, repressed ardor, reproachful misgivings, repulsive spectacles, resourceful wickedness, rigid propriety, riotous clamor, rough brutality, and rude condescension.

Question #4: WHAT IS HELL LIKE?

We're talking here about the infernal, tricky, and mean schemes of the devil meant to punish people who did something wrong in their lives. In hell, you'd be inside thinking you were going to go out and have fun in the snow, but when you got outside, it would be nothing but slush mixed with

How do you fix a woman's watch. YOU DON'T. THERE'S A CLOCK ON THE STOVE.

the kind of mud that smells bad; and worse yet, all the mud-slush flakes would be exactly the same shape and size.

Or just when you're finally feeling like you are emotionally centered, the devil will send over some guy to tell you paralyzing, sentimental stores about little furry animals. Or maybe the story-teller will recite nice stories all day long, but he will drive you crazy because he has a severe, incurable case of the hiccups. Another thing the devil might do, if he knows you like music, is give you a keyboard with song books and lessons and everything, but no place to plug it in. Also, the devil might announce very slowly and clearly to a group of you that your time is up and you are getting out of hell. Then, he will give instructions on exactly how to get out by talking so fast that no one can understand him, and on top of that, he'll give you a tape of his talk, but no tape player.

Hell is a place where you're always being fooled. For example, after making you listen to the same Tasmanian folk song backwards for two or three eons, the devil might announce a "gossip break." You think you're going to hear juicy tidbits about the other sorry slobs you've come to know informally, but then all you hear whispered is stuff like, "Did you know that John Smith's middle name is William?" Or, "Have you heard that Mary Jones went to the dentist twenty-four times in her life?" This is the type of thing the devil does in hell, and it can be very aggravating.

If you should find yourself in one of these kinds of situations, or in a situation involving unspeakable humiliation for yourself, or you find yourself experiencing excruciating cruelty or injustice which exasperates you to the nth degree, try, above all, to keep a sense of humor because they say that helps. You might not like the set-up down there, but for the most part, those who go along, get along.

One of the dumbest things you can do is develop a conscientious anxiety to do the correct thing. Well-intentioned people have the worst time in hell because it's not possible to do things right there or even get a few brownie points for something you do. There's no sense even being courteous to others or to the devil himself, since you will encounter many intentional breaches of etiquette on his part. Trying to be sarcastic down there is also a waste of time. And don't fret about being constantly interrupted; everything is inconvenient down there.

I will permit myself the liberty of saying that there will be about another ten billion people in hell with you, almost all of them possessing a more than ordinary share of baseness and depravity, but this is all a mere conjectural estimate.

Also: the coins they give you down there don't fit the soda or cigarette machines. And whatever you do, don't argue about religion!

I got in a fight one time with a really big guy, and he said, "I'm going to mop the floor with your face." I said, "You'll be sorry." He said, "Oh, yeah? Why?" I said, "Well, you won't be able to get into the corners very well."

BALONEY CROSSWORD ANSWERS FROM PAGE 30

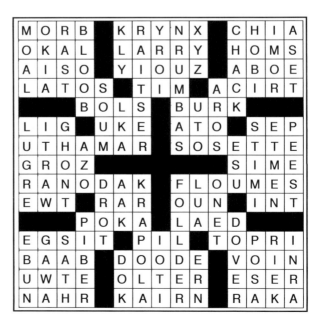

If I Didn't Drink, THEN HOW WOULD ANYONE KNOW HOW MUCH I LOVE THEM AT 2 AM?

Exclusive Baloney Interview with Jay Vizzini, Jr.

BB: Who has been your most notable customer since you took over management of Vizzini's in November of 2012?
JV: I'd have to say the Dalai Lama. He walked in one Wednesday afternoon last September and asked, "Can you make me one with everything?"
BB: I see.
JV: You're not laughing. You know the Dalai Lama is a Buddhist, right?
BB: Oh, yes, now I get it (laughter). How did you react to the Dalai Lama's request?
JV: We made him a large pizza with double cheese and all of our toppings. While it was baking, he asked me if it would be long. I said, "No, it will be round." After we gave him the pizza, he handed me a hundred dollar bill, but I just stood there looking at him until he said, "Where's my change?"
BB: And what did you say to that?
JV: I said, "As the world's most famous Buddhist, surely you must realize that change must come from within."
BB: As a person who grew up in Cape St. Claire and 2001 graduate of Broadneck High School, what made you want to go into the pizza business?
JV: I wanted to make some dough. Who doesn't? But seriously, my dad started Vizzini's in 1986 and always made the pizza dough fresh daily. Fresh-baked dough, quality ingredients, top-notch customer service, excellent prices—I just love being part of that.
BB: Do you have any other pizza jokes for us before we conclude the interview?
JV: I do, but they may too cheesy even for the *Baloney*. I'll try this one: What's the difference between a Vizzini's pizza and my pizza jokes?
BB: Let me guess: Your pizzas can be topped with all kinds of fresh and delicious toppings, but your pizza *jokes* can't be topped! ❂

Baloney Regrets
"I Should Never Have Named My Dog Sex"
By An Anonymous Broadneckian

Everybody who has a dog calls him Rover or Buddy, or some other familiar name. I thought I'd be a little different and call mine Sex, just for fun. What a mistake! He's a great pal, but he's caused me much embarrassment.

When I went to city hall to renew his dog license, I told the clerk I would like a license for Sex. He said, "I'd like one, too." Then, I said, "But this is a dog." He said that he didn't care what she looked like. Then I said, "You don't understand. I've had Sex since I was twelve years old." He winked and said, "You must have been quite a kid."

My girlfriend and I took the dog into a local diner one time. I asked the manager if he minded that we had Sex under the table. He said, "Better underneath than on top, but either way, get out!"

When I got married and went on my honeymoon, I took the dog with me. I told the motel clerk that I wanted a room for my wife and me and a special room for Sex. He said, "You don't need a special room. As long as you pay your bill, we don't care what you do." I said, "Look, you don't seem to understand. Sex keeps me awake at night." The clerk said, "Funny, I have the same problem."

One day I entered Sex in a contest, but the dog ran away. Another contestant asked me why I was just standing there, looking disappointed. I told him I had planned to have Sex in the contest. He told me I should have sold my own tickets. "But you don't get it," I said. "I had hoped to have Sex on TV." He said, "With cable, that's no big deal anymore."

When my wife and I separated, we went to court to fight for custody of the dog. I said, "Your honor, I had Sex before I was married." The judge said, "The courtroom isn't a confessional. Stick to the case, please."

Last night, Sex ran off again. I spent hours looking all over for him. A cop came over to me and asked, "What are you doing in this alley at 4 o'clock in the morning?" I told him I was looking for Sex. My case comes up Friday. I don't know if I should ask if I can have Sex in the courtroom or not. ❂

Our Baloney Mate-of-the-Year is GLADYS HECK

Height: 5' 10" Weight: 180 Bust: 42
Waist: 27 Hips: 37 Biceps 21

I REALLY HATE: People who use prepositions at the end of a sentence. That is something up with which I will not put.

WHAT IS YOUR VISION OF THE FUTURE? I hope someday we can put away all our fears and prejudices and just laugh at people when we feel like it.

FAVORITE POEM FROM AMERICAN LITERATURE: It's hard to be mad at a friend / When your heart is full of hope / But it's worse to lose a towel / When your eyes are full of soap.

DO YOU HAVE ANY IDEA WHY DON'T CANNIBALS EAT MISSIONARIES? I always thought it was because you can't keep a good man down.

FAVORITE 19TH CENTURY GERMAN PHILOSOPHER: Many of my friends probably think that I'd name Friedrich Nietzsche as my favorite, but I can never remember how to spell his name. I pick Arthur Schopenhauer. He gave voice to the plaintive weariness that crept into the soul of Europe after the wars of Napoleon, and I think that should count for something.

BIGGEST DISAPPOINTMENT: I bought my boyfriend a tie for Christmas and he took it back. When I asked why, he said it was too tight.

FAVORITE PARLOR GAME: Hide the Baloney.

FROM YOUR KNOWLEDGE OF AMERICAN HISTORY, CAN YOU TELL US WHY THE MEXICANS FOUGHT SO HARD TO WIN THE BATTLE OF THE ALAMO? I guess they wanted some walls to write on.

YOU'VE BEEN DESCRIBED AS AN AGGRESSIVE, FIERY, UNPREDICTABLE FLIRT. TRUE? Absolutely not. You can tell how I'm feeling by my mood ring. It turns green when I'm happy and leaves a big red mark on someone's forehead when I'm mad.

WHO IS THE MAN IN YOUR LIFE? He doesn't want his name mentioned. I think that once we get past the court dates, the restraining orders and the stalking charges against me, we may be able to make our relationship work. I've learned that you cannot make a man love you. All you can do is stalk him and hope he panics and gives in.

IS HE THE KIND OF MAN YOU'VE BEEN LOOKING FOR? I'll say this much for him: He's sensitive—He cries when I slap him.

ARE MEN AND WOMEN REALLY SO DIFFERENT? Yes, very. Men look at a woman's behind and say "What an ass!" Women look at the man's face and say the same thing. Also, men will never know the agony of childbirth, menstrual cramps, or taking off glitter nail polish.

TO WHAT HEIGHTS DO YOU ASPIRE? I've always thought that shooting at the stars and missing is much better than shooting at a pile of crap and hitting it. But I'm a realist: Sometimes success is just getting the laundry into the dryer before the mildew sets in.

MOST FRIGHTENING EXPERIENCE: It happened this morning. I read an article on the Internet about the dangers of heavy drinking. It almost scared the Heck out of me. That's it, after today no more reading.

MOST ANNOYING RECENT INCIDENT: Last week, this uppity woman just stared and stared at my beer cup holder, like she's never seen a cup holder on a grocery cart.

MOST RECENT UNUSUAL EXPERIENCE: I asked a fortune-teller to read my future. Suddenly, she went pale and sprinted from the room. That made me mad, so I grabbed the crystal ball, chased her down, and hit her with it. I wonder what she saw in that thing.

WHAT RANKLES YOU THE MOST? I hate it when I offer someone a sincere compliment on their mustache and suddenly she's not my friend anymore.

WHAT WOULD YOU SAY TO ENCOURAGE THOSE OF OUR READERS WHO MAY BE EXPERIENCING DIFFICULTIES? I want those people to know that whatever problems they are having, I'm here to read about them on Facebook.

MOST SATISFYING EXPERIENCE: That first bite of Vizzini's "The Vito" with Genoa salami, Prosciuttini ham, Virginia baked ham, turkey, and Provolone cheese, dressed with lettuce, tomato, mayonnaise, caramelized onion, mild hot peppers, zesty Italian dressing and spices for a great price. Not to mention the macaroni cheese bites. They're fabulous!

PLACE YOU MOST WANT YOUR BOYFRIEND TO TAKE YOU: To Fairwinds Marina where he can buy me a 222 Fisherman Wellcraft so I can cruise the Bay in style.

FAVORITE PASTIME: I am a very positive person who loves unique gifts, and so every day or so, I like to log onto Whimsicality's Web site, and just browse, baby, browse.

BIGGEST RESPONSIBILITIES: Making sure I take my car in for a check up at Rusty's Quality Care Automotive, consulting with Cape Ace Hardware's paint experts before I start any painting, calling Stacy Early at Long and Foster when I'm ready to sell my house, and making an appointment every week at Noreen's Boutique Spa.

FAVORITE CULINARY BARGAIN: It's a three-way tie between Sunday Brunch at O'Loughlin's Pub and Sunday Brunch at O'Loughlin's Pub and Sunday Brunch at O'Loughlin's Pub.

WE UNDERSTAND THAT YOU ATTENDED YALE LAW SCHOOL AND NOW ARE MAKING USE OF YOUR LAW DEGREE. IS THAT TRUE? Yes, but I'm only working as a lawyer on a temporary basis—to pay my way through pole dancing school.

WHAT DO YOU THINK IS THE DIFFERENCE BETWEEN A SMART MAN AND A DUMB MAN: Nothing. They both think they know everything.

DO YOU HAVE ANY SPECIAL THOUGHT YOU'D LIKE TO LEAVE WITH OUR READERS? Yes I do. As each of you slides down the banister of life, may the splinters never point the wrong way. ❂

Why Was the Cracker Crying? BECAUSE HIS MOM WAS A WAFER A WHILE.

DID WE READ THESE SIGNS RIGHT?

**TOILET OUT OF ORDER
PLEASE USE FLOOR BELOW**

**WE REPAIR ANYTHING
(PLEASE KNOCK HARD ON DOOR. BELL IS BROKEN)**

WOULD THE PERSON WHO TOOK THE STEP LADDER YESTERDAY PLEASE BRING IT BACK OR FURTHER STEPS WILL BE TAKEN

WE EXCHANGE ANYTHING: BICYCLES, WASHING MACHINES, ETC. WHY NOT BRING YOUR WIFE ALONG AND GET A WONDERFUL BARGAIN?

FOR ALL WHO HAVE CHILDREN AND DON'T KNOW IT, THERE IS DAY CARE ON 1ST FLOOR

AFTER COFFEE BREAK, STAFF SHOULD EMPTY THE POT AND STAND UPSIDE DOWN ON THE DRAINING BOARD

ANYONE EXITING THROUGH THIS DOOR WILL BE ASKED TO LEAVE

AUTOMATIC WASHING MACHINES: PLEASE REMOVE ALL YOUR CLOTHES WHEN LIGHT GOES OUT

**TOUCHING WIRES CAUSES INSTANT DEATH
$200 FINE**

At an education center:

OUR TEACHERS MAKE A DIFFRANCE

In a safari park:

ELEPHANTS PLEASE STAY IN YOUR CAR

On a pasture fence:

THE FARMER ALLOWS WALKERS TO CROSS THE FIELD FOR FREE, BUT THE BULL CHARGES

At a health food store:

SORRY, CLOSED DUE TO ILLNESS

Am I Getting Older or IS THE SUPERMARKET PLAYING GREAT MUSIC?

Do High-Strung Dogs Have Nervous Ticks?

Oh No! I Forgot My Coupon for O'Loughlin's Sunday Brunch.

Don't Mess with America: We Will Kill You in Your Sleep on Christmas.

Wife Discovers His Browser History.

Van Gogh at Bella's, July 1888.

Go Get Me that Broadneck Baloney Book Now!

A Short Course in the Meaning of Great Art

I Hit the MegaMill and I'm Not Telling My Husband.

I Just Replaced the Can of Air Freshener in the Office Bathroom with an Air Horn. NOW WE WAIT.

My Sister is Dating an Invisible Man. I DON'T KNOW WHAT SHE SEES IN HIM.

Some Questions to Ponder

1. Why do we say something is out of whack? What is a whack?
2. Why does a ship carry cargo, and a car carry shipments?
3. Why do we buy hot dogs in packages of ten and buns in packages of eight?
4. What happens if you drive at the speed of light and turn your headlights on?
5. Why are there interstate highways in Hawaii?
6. Is there another word for synonym?
7. You can be overwhelmed and underwhelmed, but why can't you be simply whelmed?
8. If you try to fail, and you fail, have you succeeded or failed?
9. Why are boxing rings square?
10. Can you be a closet claustrophobic?
11. How do you know when its time to tune your bagpipes?
12. If a pen is mightier than a sword, and a picture is worth a thousand words, how dangerous is a fax?
13. What was the best thing before sliced bread?
14. What are Preparations A thru G?
15. How do "Do not walk on the grass" signs get there?
16. If all the world is a stage, where is the audience sitting?
17. How can there be self-help "groups"?
18. How does the guy who drives the snowplow get to work in the morning?
19. If a word in the dictionary were misspelled, how would we know?
20. What if the Hokey Pokey IS what it's all about?
21. When a fly lands on the ceiling, has it done a half roll or a half loop?
22. How do people get discombobulated?
23. Have you ever seen someone who was combobulated?
24. Why does Goofy talk and wear clothes while Pluto barks naked?
25. Why are there stairs inside but steps outside?

I Hate It When I Don't Forward a Chain Letter AND THEN DIE THE NEXT DAY.

FISHING WITH PETE

Buzz and Pete were fishing at the headwaters of the Magothy in Pete's canoe when Buzz dropped his wallet. As they watched the wallet float away on the surface of the water, a carp came along and snatched up the wallet. Soon came another carp who stole it away and then a third joined in. Pete said to Buzz, "That's the first time I've ever seen carp-to-carp walleting."

One day Pete came home from work to find his wife dressed in a very sexy nighty.

"Tie me up," Pete's wife said, "and you can do anything you want."

So Pete tied her up and went fishing.

Pete and Barry are sitting quietly, sucking down beer and fishing for perch in Dividing Creek off the Magothy. Suddenly Barry says, "I think I'm going to divorce my wife. She hasn't spoken to me in over 2 months."

Pete sips his beer thoughtfully and says, "You'd better think it over. Women like that are hard to find."

What do fish and women have in common?

They both stop shaking their tail after you catch them.

What do you call a deaf Chesapeake Bay charter-boat captain?

Anything you want. He can't hear you anyhow.

Why Pete Got a Bigger Boat

Pete rings his boss and says, "I can't come to work today!"

The boss asks why and Pete says: "It's my eyes."

"What's wrong with them?" asks the boss.

"I just can't see myself coming to work, so I'm going fishing instead."

Pete had an awful time fishing in Martin's Cove, sitting in the blazing sun all day without a single bite. Before going home, he stopped at the supermarket and ordered four catfish. He told the fish salesman: "Pick out four large ones and throw them at me, will you?"

"Why do you want me to throw them at you?"

"Because I want to tell my wife that I caught them."

Pete and Buzz leave from Fairwinds Marina on a fishing trip. They rent all the equipment: the reels, the rods, the wading suits, the boat, the car, and even a cabin in the woods.

The first day they go fishing they don't catch a thing. The same thing happens on the second day, and on the third day as well. It goes on like this until finally, on the last day of their trip, Buzz finally catches a fish.

They're really depressed as they are driving home to Broadneck. Pete turns to Buzz and says, "Do you realize that this one lousy fish we caught cost us fifteen hundred dollars?"

"Wow!" exclaims Buzz. "It's a good thing we didn't catch any more!"

One day while driving home from his fishing trip in the pouring rain, Pete got a flat tire outside a monastery.

A monk came out and invited him inside to have dinner and spend the night. Pete accepted. That night Pete had a wonderful dinner of fish and chips.

Pete decided to compliment the chef. Entering the kitchen, he asked the cook, "Are you the fish friar?"

"No," the man replied, "I'm the chip monk."

Priests Can Kiss Nuns Now - AS LONG AS THEY DON'T GET INTO THE HABIT.

CAPE HAIR SCENE AND BARBERSHOP

capehairscene.com 410.349.1646

BOOK ONLINE!

Featuring *Enjoy* Hair Care Products

- Kids and flat tops
- Beard trims
- Regular and style haircuts
- Facial waxing
- Walk-in barber shop
- 4 generations of barbers

HOURS
Tuesday - Thursday: 8:30 am to 6 pm
Friday: 8:30 am to 5 pm
Saturday: 8:00 am to 2 pm
LATE APPTS BY REQUEST

Quality service at affordable prices
1344 Cape St. Claire Road
Bill and Mary Ann Davis
Owners

We support Wigs for Kids (At least 12 inches of hair to donate) and Locks of Love (At least 10 inches) for children with cancer and other maladies causing hair loss.

CARING DEEPLY FOR BROADNECK'S HAIRITAGE

MARINA • BOAT SALES • REPAIR • STORE
410-974-0758 fairwindsmarina.com

Fairwinds Marina is nestled in the serene riverfront community of Cape Saint Claire. This neighborhood gem is Annapolis's destination for complete marine care and Freedom Boat Club's home port on the Magothy River. The Magothy runs 12.1 miles through Anne Arundel County, opening into the Chesapeake Bay between Gibson Island and Persimmon Point. The river is a renowned fishing destination, as well as a local favorite to jump in for a swim. Located between Baltimore and Annapolis, this quiet cove offers a peaceful home on the water, along with convenient access to the Bay's most popular destinations.

Beginning in fall 2013, under the stewardship of the Goldbergs, Fairwinds Marina embarked on a major development project that is redefining "full service marina." We invite you to voyage with us as Fairwinds becomes your waterfront getaway. We are open 7 days a week to serve you and your boat's needs. Start getting the most out of your boating experience - stop by today!

A Simple Alternative to Boat Ownership

I've Been Reading about Crime in Multi-Story Car Parks. THAT IS WRONG ON SO MANY LEVELS.

TOP 20 REASONS FISHING IS BETTER THAN SEX

1. No matter how much beer, wine, or whiskey you've had, you can still Fish.
2. You don't have to take your clothes off to enjoy Fishing.
3. You don't have to hide your Fishing magazines.
4. It is perfectly acceptable to pay a professional to Fish with you.
5. The Ten Commandments don't say anything against Fishing.
6. If your partner takes pictures or videotapes of you Fishing, you don't have to worry about them showing up on the Internet if you become famous.
7. Your Fishing partner doesn't get upset about people you Fished with long ago.
8. It's perfectly respectable to Fish with a total stranger.
9. When you see a good Fishing person, no need to feel guilty about imagining Fishing together.
10. If your regular Fishing partner isn't available, he/she won't object if you Fish with someone else.
11. Nobody will ever tell you that you will go blind if you Fish by yourself.

12. When dealing with a Fishing pro, you never have to wonder if they are really an undercover cop.
13. You don't have to go to a sleazy shop in a seedy neighborhood to buy Fishing stuff.
14. You can have a Fishing calendar on your wall at the office, tell Fishing jokes, and invite coworkers to Fish with you without getting sued for Fishing harassment.
15. There are no Fishing-transmitted diseases.
16. If you want to watch Fishing on television, you don't have to subscribe to the Playboy channel.
17. Nobody expects you to Fish with the same partner for the rest of your life.
18. Nobody expects you to give up Fishing if your partner loses interest in it.
19. You don't have to be a newlywed to plan a getaway vacation primarily to enjoy your favorite activity.
20. Your Fishing partner will never say:

"Not again! We just Fished last week. Is Fishing all you ever think about?"

36 Things You'll Never Hear a Bredneck (Broadneck Redneck) Say

1. "I'll take Shakespeare for 1,000, Alex"
2. "Duct tape won't fix that."
3. "Come to think of it, I'll have a Heineken."
4. "We don't keep firearms in this house."
5. "You can't feed that to the dog."
6. "I thought Graceland was tacky."
7. "Professional wrasslin's fake."
8. No kids in the back of the pickup . . . it's not safe.
9. "Honey, did you mail that donation to Greenpeace?"
10. "We're vegetarians."
11. "Do you think my hair is too big?"
12. "I'll have grapefruit instead of biscuits and gravy."
13. "Honey, these bonsai trees need watering."
14. "I don't understand the appeal of NASCAR."
15. "Give me the small bag of pork rinds."
16. "Deer heads detract from the decor."
17. "Spitting is such a nasty habit."
18. "I just couldn't find a thing at Wal-Mart today."
19. "Trim the fat off that steak."
20. "Cappuccino tastes better than espresso."
21. "The tires on that truck are too big."
22. "I'll have the arugula and radicchio salad."
23. "I've got it all on a flash drive."
24. "Unsweetened tea tastes better."
25. "Would you like your fish poached or broiled?"
26. "My fiancée is registered at Tiffany's."
27. "I've got two cases of Stella Artois for the Super Bowl."
28. "She's too old to be wearing that bikini."
29. "Does the salad bar have bean sprouts?"
30. "Hey, here's an episode of *Hee Haw* that we haven't seen."
31. "I don't have a favorite college football team."
32. "Be sure to bring my salad dressing on the side."
33. "I believe you cooked those green beans too long."
34. "Those shorts ought to be a little longer, Darla."
35. "Elvis who?"
36. "Checkmate."

What is a Broadneck Redneck's Favorite Support Group? A 12-PACK OF PABST.

CHURCHY JOKES

Stranded on a Desert Island

One balmy day in the South Pacific, a US Navy ship espied smoke coming from one of three huts on an uncharted island. Upon arriving at the shore the captain was met by a shipwreck survivor. He said, "I'm so glad you're here! I've been alone on this island for more than five years!"

The captain replied, "If you're all alone on the island why do I see THREE huts."

The survivor said, "Oh. We'll, I live in one, and go to church in another."

"What about the THIRD hut?" asked the captain.

"That's where I USED to go to church."

Bats in the Belfry

Three Pastors in the South were having lunch in a diner. One said "Ya know, since summer started I've been having trouble with bats in my loft and attic at church. I've tried everything—noise, spray, cats—nothing seems to scare them away.

Another said "Yea, me too. I've got hundreds living in my belfry and in the attic. I've even had the place fumigated, and they won't go away."

The third said, "I baptized all mine, and made them members of the church . . . Haven't seen one back since!!!"

Head Hog of the Trough

Fred called a local church and asked to speak to the head hog of the trough.

Secretary: "How rude! I'll have you know we would NEVER EVER refer to our pastor as the head hog of the trough."

Fred: "Okay, then just take a message. Tell him I've come into a bit of money so I was calling to give your church $10,000."

Secretary: "Well hold the phone, dearie! I think I see that sectarian swine coming down the hall right now."

Temperance Preaching

A preacher was completing a temperance sermon and with great expression he said, "If I had all the beer in the world, I'd take it and throw it into the river."

With even greater emphasis, he said, "And if I had all the wine in the world, I'd take it and throw it into the river."

And then, finally, he said, "And if I had all the whiskey in the world, I'd take it and throw it into the river." Then he sat down.

The choir director then stood very cautiously and announced with a pleasant smile, "For our closing song, let us sing hymn #365: 'We Shall All Gather At the River.'"

Money Goes to Church

A well-worn one dollar bill and a similarly distressed twenty dollar bill arrived at a Federal Reserve Bank to be retired. As they moved along the conveyor belt to be burned, they struck up a conversation.

The twenty dollar bill reminisced about its travels all over the county. "I've had a pretty good life," the twenty proclaimed. "Why I've been to Las Vegas and Atlantic City, the finest

What Did One Ocean Say to the Other Ocean? NOTHING. THEY JUST WAVED.

restaurants in New York, performances on Broadway, and even a cruise to the Caribbean."

"Wow!" said the one dollar bill. "You've really had an exciting life!"

"So tell me," says the twenty, "where have you been throughout your lifetime?"

The one dollar bill replies, "Oh, I've been to the Catholic Church, the Methodist Church, the Baptist Church, the Lutheran Church . . ."

The twenty dollar bill interrupts, "What's a church?"

Meeting of the Board

"There will be a meeting of the Board immediately after the service," announced the pastor.

After the close of the service, the Church Board gathered at the back of the auditorium for the announced meeting. But there was a stranger in their midst, a visitor who had never attended their church before.

"My friend," said the pastor, "Didn't you understand that this is a meeting of the Board?"

"Yes," said the visitor, "and after today's sermon, I suppose I'm just about as bored as anyone else who came to this meeting."

Three Hymns

One Sunday a pastor told his congregation that the church needed some extra money and asked the people to prayerfully consider giving a little extra in the offering plate. He said that whoever gave the most would be able to pick out three hymns.

After the offering plates were passed, the pastor noticed that someone had placed ten $100 bills in the offering. He was so excited that he immediately shared his joy with his congregation and said he'd like to personally thank the person who placed the money in the offering plate.

And there sat our Rosie all the way in the back shyly raising her hand. The pastor asked her to come to the front. Slowly she made her way to the pastor. He told her how wonderful it was that she gave so much and in thanksgiving asked her to pick out three hymns.

Her eyes brightened as she looked over the congregation, pointed to the three most handsome men in the building and said, "I'll take him and him and him!"

What's Your Religion

As I was driving across the Bay Bridge at about 3 am one night, I saw a car pulled over ahead of me and a man standing on the edge, about to jump off. I immediately ran over and said "Stop! Don't do it!"

"Why shouldn't I?" he said.

I said, "Well, there's so much to live for!"

"Like what?"

"Well . . . are you religious or atheist?"

"Religious."

"Me too! Are you Christian or Jewish?"

"Christian."

"Me too! Are you Catholic or Protestant?"

"Protestant."

"Me too! Are you Episcopalian or Baptist?"

"Baptist."

"Wow! Me too! Are you Baptist Church of God or Baptist Church of the Lord?"

"Baptist Church of God."

"Me too! Are you Original Baptist Church of God, or are you Reformed Baptist Church of God?"

"Reformed Baptist Church of God."

"Me too! Are you Reformed Baptist Church of God, reformation of 1879, or Reformed Baptist Church of God, reformation of 1915?"

"Reformed Baptist Church of God, reformation of 1915!"

To which I replied, "Die, heretic scum!" and pushed him off. ¤

Jake and Janice

One day, when Jake was really mad with Janice, he started throwing knives at her picture. All were missing the target. Just then he got a call from her: "What are you doing?" she asked.
"Missing you," was his honest reply.

"Do you want dinner?" Janice asked Jake.
"What are my choices?" Jake wondered.
"Yes or no," said Janice.

Janice said to Jake, "I wish I were a newspaper so I'd be in your hands all day."
Jake replied, "I wish that you were a newspaper, too, so that I could have a new one everyday."

Jake came home late after a party. Janice yelled, "How would you feel if you didn't see me for two days?"
Jake couldn't believe the offer and said, "That would be great!"
So Monday passed, and Jake didn't see her. Tuesday and Wednesday passed, too, and still he didn't see her. But then on Thursday, the swelling went down a little bit, and he could see her out of the corner of his eye.

Jake said to Janice, "Today is Sunday and I want to enjoy it. So I bought three movie tickets."
"Why three tickets?" Janice asked.
"One for you and two for your parents," Jake replied.

Jake, wanting to prove to Janice that women talk more than men, showed her a study which indicated that men use about 15,000 words a day, whereas women use 30,000 words a day. Janice thought about this, then told Jake that women use twice as many words as men because they have to repeat everything they say. Looking stunned, Jake said, "What?"

Janice was reading a newspaper while Jake was engrossed in a magazine. Suddenly, Janice burst out laughing. "Listen to this," she said. "There's a classified ad here where a guy is offering to swap his wife for a season ticket to the Orioles' games."
"Hmmm," Jake said, not looking up from his magazine.
Teasing him, Janice asked, "Would you swap me for a season ticket?"
"Absolutely not," Jake said.
"How sweet," Janice said. "Tell me why not."
"Season's almost half over," Jake said.

As the crowded elevator descended, Janice became increasingly furious with Jake, who was delighted to be pressed against a gorgeous young blond woman. As the elevator stopped at the main floor, the blond suddenly whirled, slapped Jake, and said, "That will teach you to pinch me!"
Bewildered, Jake was halfway to the parking lot with Janice when he choked, "I . . . I didn't pinch that girl."
"Of course you didn't," replied Janice, "I did."

Jake and Janice are watching "Who Wants to Be a Millionaire," and Jake winks and says, "Honey, let's go upstairs."
Janice says no, so Jake asks again. Again she says no. So Jake says, "Is that your final answer?" Janice says yes.
Jake says, "Well, then, can I phone a friend?"

After being away on business, Jake thought it would be nice to bring Janice a little gift. "How about some perfume?" he asked the cosmetics clerk. She showed him a bottle costing $50.
"That's a bit much," said Jake. So the clerk returned with a smaller bottle for $30.
"That's still quite a bit," Jake groused. Growing annoyed, the cosmetics clerk brought out a tiny $15 bottle.
"What I mean," said Jake, "is I would like to see something really cheap." So the clerk handed him a mirror.

Jake asked Janice what she wanted to celebrate their 20th wedding anniversary. "How about a new mink coat?" he asked. Janice said no.
"Well how about a new Mercedes, or a new vacation home in the country" said Jake. Janice said no again.
"What I want," said Janice, "is a divorce."
"Sorry, I wasn't planning on spending that much," said Jake.

And Then the Fight Started . . .

My wife sat down on the couch next to me as I was flipping channels.

"What's on TV?" she asked.

"Dust," I said . . .

And then the fight started . . .

My wife was hinting about what she wanted for our upcoming anniversary.

She said, "I want something shiny that goes from 0 to 150 in about 3 seconds."

I said, "We already have a perfectly good bathroom scale."

And then the fight started . . .

I asked my wife, "Where do you want to go for our anniversary?" It warmed my heart to see her face melt in sweet appreciation.

"Somewhere I haven't been in a long time!" she said.

So I suggested, "How about the kitchen?"

And guess what? That's exactly the time the fight started!

My wife and I were sitting at a table at my high school reunion, and I kept staring at a drunken lady swigging her drink as she sat alone at a nearby table.

My wife asked, "Do you know her?"

"Yes," I sighed, "She's my old girlfriend. I understand she took to drinking right after we split up those many years ago, and I hear she hasn't been sober since."

"My God!" says my wife, "Who would think that a person could go on celebrating that long?"

And then the fight started . . .

I took my wife to a restaurant. The waiter, for some reason, took my order first.

"I'll have the strip steak, very rare, please."

He said, "Aren't you worried about the mad cow?"

"Nah, she can order for herself."

And then the fight started . . .

One year, Chauncy decided to buy Maude's mother a cemetery plot as a Christmas gift. The next year, he didn't buy her a gift at all. When his mother-in-law asked him why, Jake replied,

"Well, you still haven't used the gift I bought you last year!"

And that's how the fight started . . .

A woman is sitting in the cool of the evening on the veranda with her husband. Suddenly she sweetly says, "I love you."

He smiles shyly, and asks, "Is that you or the wine talking?

She replies, "It's me talking to the wine."

And then the fight started. . .

When I got home last night, my wife demanded that I take her someplace expensive. So, I took her to a gas station. And then the fight started . . .

A wife is standing nude, looking in the bedroom mirror. She is not happy with what she sees and says to her husband, "I feel horrible; I look old, fat and ugly. I really need you to pay me a compliment."

The husband replies, "Your eyesight's darn near perfect."

And then the fight started . . .

Doctor, I'm Afraid I Have Measles. THAT'S A RATHER RASH REMARK.

An Embarrassing Mix-up

Art wanted to get a Christmas gift for his new sweetheart, Pauley. They had not been going out together for very long. After careful consideration, he decided that a pair of gloves would be most appropriate—romantic but not too personal.

He then engaged the help of Pauley's younger sister to assist him in choosing an appropriate item; and off they went shopping together. Art eventually bought a pair of very stylish winter gloves in pale pink, and Pauley's sister took the opportunity of buying herself a pair of panties from the same store. However, during the wrapping process, the shop assistant mixed up the two items and Pauley's sister got the gloves and Pauley got the panties.

Without thinking to check the contents, Art sealed the package and sent it to Pauley with the following note:

Dear Pauley,

I chose these because I noticed that you are not in the habit of wearing any when we go out in the evening. If it had not been for your sister, I would have chosen the long ones with buttons down the side, but she wears short ones that are easier to remove.

These are a delicate shade, but the lady I bought them from showed me the pair she had been wearing for the past three weeks and they are hardly soiled. I asked her to try yours on for me and she looked really smart in them. I wish I could be there to put them on for you the first time, as no doubt other hands will come in contact with them before I have a chance to see you again. When you take them off, remember to blow in them before putting them away, as they will naturally be a little damp from wearing. Just think how many times I will kiss them during the coming year!

All My Love, Art

THE FORTHRIGHT DRUGGIST

Upon arriving home, a husband was met at the door by his sobbing wife. Tearfully, she explained, "It's the druggist. He insulted me terribly this morning on the phone." She then told her husband what the druggist had said to her.

Immediately the husband drove downtown to confront the druggist, and demand an apology. Before he could say more then a word or two, the druggist said, "Now just a minute! Listen to my side of it. This morning the alarm failed to go off, so I was late getting up. I went without breakfast and hurried out to the car, only to realize that I had locked the house and both the house and car keys were inside. I had to break a window to get my keys.

"Then, driving a little too fast, I got a speeding ticket. Later, when I was about three blocks from the store, I had a flat tire.

"When I finally got to the store, there were a bunch of people waiting for me to open up. I got the store opened, and started waiting on these people. All the time the darn phone was ringing off the hook. I had to break open a roll of nickels against the cash register drawer to make change, and they spilled all over the floor.

"I got down on my hands and knees to pick up the nickels. The phone was still ringing. When I came up, I cracked my head on the open cash drawer. That made me stagger back against a showcase with a bunch of perfume bottles on it, and half of them hit the floor and broke.

"Meanwhile, the phone is still ringing with no let up. When I finally got to answer it, it was your wife. She wanted to know how to use a rectal thermometer. And believe me mister, as God is my witness, all I did was tell her!"

Let's Talk about You for a Change. WHAT DO YOU THINK OF ME?

Why Did the Chicken Cross the Road? FOR A FOWL PURPOSE.

JUST PLAIN OLD JOKES

My career as a professional rock climber is going really well. I'm also taking a course in mattress-making, just so I have something to fall back on.

A man walks into a pet shop and says, "I'll have a wasp please." The shopkeeper says "We don't sell wasps." The man replies, "There's one in the window."

A nun, a priest, an Irishman, a Scotsman, a rabbi and a blonde walk into *O'Loughlin's*. The bartender looks at them and asks, "Is this some kind of joke?"

Q: What is the difference between a Broadneck brunette and garbage?
A: At least the garbage gets taken out once a week.

Red walks into a Broadneck bar, orders 12 shots and starts drinking them as fast as he can.
The bartender asks, "Dang, why are you drinking so fast?"
Red says, "You would be drinking fast, too, if you had what I had."
"What do you have?"
Red says, "75 cents."

Duane was fast asleep in his bed at 3:00 am in Revell Downs when he heard an urgent knocking at the door. Rubbing the sleep out of his eyes, he made his way to the door and opened it.
"Can you give me a push," asked the man on his doorstep.
The man looked a bit drunk to Duane, so he slammed the door in his face and went back to bed.
"Shame on you," said his wife, Pat, when hearing the story, "You remember on our vacation how our car got stuck in the middle of the night and that man helped us, so go out there and give him a push."
So Duane trudged back out of bed, opened the door, and called out, "Okay, I'm here to give you a push, where are you?"
"I'm over here in the back," came the voice, "on the swing."

My mom always said, "Never do anything that you'll regret later in life." I thought that was great advice so I got it tattooed on my forehead.

"Well, here is your problem," the doctor says to the first time father. "It seems that this child needs a diaper change." The new father then replies "But I swear, that package said it was good for 14-16 pounds."

"Our neighbor Mr. Smith kisses his wife every day before he goes to work. How come you never do?"
"Honey, how could I? I don't even know her."

"I hate to have to tell you this", said the doctor in a sad compassionate voice, "but unfortunately you have been been diagnosed with a highly contagious disease, and we will have to quarantine you, and you'll only be fed cheese and bologna."
"That's terrible," said the distraught young man, quickly sitting down before he would faint. "I don't know if I could handle being in quarantine . . . and the cheese and bologna diet . . . What's with the cheese and bologna diet anyway?
"It's not exactly a diet," responded the doctor in a most matter-of-fact manner, "It's just the only food that will fit under the door!"

I'm Afraid to Stop Smoking Because MY DAD WILL CALL ME A QUITTER.

Why Did the Cannibal Become a Cop? HE WANTED TO GRILL SUSPECTS.

MORE JUST PLAIN OLD JOKES

A cowboy walked into a bar and ordered a whiskey. When the bartender delivered the drink, the cowboy asked, "Where is everybody?"

The bartender replied, "They've gone to the hanging."

"Hanging? Who are they hanging?" "Brown Paper Pete," the bartender replied.

"What kind of a name is that?" the cowboy asked.

"Well," said the bartender, "he wears a brown paper hat, brown paper shirt, brown paper trousers and brown paper shoes."

"Weird guy," said the cowboy. "What are they hanging him for?"

"Rustling," said the bartender.

One Sunday afternoon, a guy walked into *O'Loughlin's Pub* with his pet dog. The bartender said, "Sorry, pal. No pets allowed."

The man replied, "This is a special dog. Turn on the Jets game and you'll see."

The bartender, eager to see what would happen, turned on the game.

The guy said, "Watch. Whenever the Jets score, my dog does flips." The Jets kept scoring field goals and the dog kept flipping and jumping.

"Wow! That's one heck of a dog you got there. What happens when the Jets score a touchdown?" asked the bartender.

The man replied, "I don't know. I've only had him for seven years."

A policeman looked up to see a Broadneck blonde racing down the center of the road at 100 mph. He pulled her over and said, "Hey, lady, would you mind telling me why you're going so fast down the middle of the road?"

"Oh, it's okay, officer," she replied. "I have a special license that allows me to drive like that."

"Oh, yeah?" Let's see it." The cop looked at the license and then concluded, "Ma'am, there's nothing special about this. It's just a temporary license."

"Look at the bottom," the woman insisted. "See? It says 'Tear along the dotted line.'"

Julius Caesar walks into a bar. "I'll have a martinus," he says. The bartender gives him a puzzled look and asks, "Don't you mean a martini?"

"Look," Caesar retorts, "If I wanted a double, I'd have asked for it!"

So Jesus walks into a wine bar and says, "I'll just have a glass of water."

I told the kids I never want to live in a vegetative state, dependent on some machine and fluids from a bottle. So they unplugged my computer and threw out my wine.

A man went to the doctor. The doctor examined him and said: "I'm sorry to have to tell you this, but you only have three minutes left to live."

The man said: "Oh my God! Are you sure there is nothing you can do for me?"

The doctor thought for a moment then replied: "I could boil you an egg."

Sister Catherine was asking all the Catholic school children in fourth grade what they want to be when they grow up.

Little Sheila said, "When I grow up, I want to be a prostitute."

Sister Catherine's eyes grew wide and she barked, "What did you say?!"

"A prostitute!" Sheila exclaimed.

Sister Catherine breathed a sigh of relief and said "Whew! Thank God! I thought you said you wanted to be a Protestant!"

The pastor asks his flock, "What would you like people to say when you're in your casket?"

One congregant says, "I'd like them to say that I was a fine family man."

Another says, "I'd like them to say that I helped people."

The third responds, "I'd like them to say, 'Look! I think he's moving!' "

I Love My 6-Pack Abs So Much That I PROTECT THEM WITH A LAYER OF FAT.

CHILDREN'S BOOK TITLES YOU'LL NEVER SEE

You Were an Accident
Strangers Have the Best Candy
The Little Sissy Who Snitched
Some Kittens Can Fly
Babar Meets the Taxidermist
All Dogs Go to Hell
The Kids' Guide to Hitchhiking

Getting More Chocolate on Your Face
Kathy Was So Bad Her Mom Stopped Loving Her
When Mommy and Daddy Don't Know the Answer They Say God Did It
What Is That Dog Doing to That Other Dog?
Why Can't Mr. Fork and Ms. Electrical Outlet Be Friends?
Daddy Drinks and Smokes Pot Because You Cry
You Are Different and That's Bad
Pop Goes The Hamster, and Other Great Microwave Games
The Hardy Boys, the Barbie Twins, and the Vice Squad
Curious George and the High-Voltage Fence
The Boy Who Died from Eating All His Vegetables
Start a Real-Estate Empire with Change from Mommy's Purse
Things Rich Kids Have, But You Never Will
The Care Bears Maul Some Campers and are Shot Dead
How to Become The Dominant Military Power in Your Elementary School
Controlling the Playground: Respect through Fear

Doctor, I Keep Thinking I'm an Airplane. OUR SESSION IS OVER. YOU CAN TAKE OFF NOW.

TWENTY-ONE ACTUAL ANALOGIES USED BY HIGH SCHOOL STUDENTS IN ENGLISH ESSAYS

1. When she tried to sing, it sounded like a walrus giving birth to farm equipment.

2. Her eyes twinkled, like the mustache of a man with a cold.

3. She was like a magnet: attractive from the back, repulsive from the front.

4. The ballerina rose gracefully en pointe and extended one slender leg behind her, like a dog at a fire hydrant.

5. She grew on him like she was a colony of E. coli and he was room temperature Canadian beef.

6. She had him like a toenail stuck in a shag carpet.

7. The lamp just sat there, like an inanimate object.

8. Her face was a perfect oval, like a circle that had two sides gently compressed by a Thigh Master.

9. Her eyes were like the stars, not because they twinkle, but because they were so far apart.

10. Her career was blowing up like a man with a broken metal detector in an active mine field.

11. The sun was below the watery horizon, like a muscle-sore grandma easing into a warm salt bath.

12. From the attic came an unearthly howl. The whole scene had an eerie, surreal quality, like when you're on vacation in another city and Jeopardy comes on at 7:00 instead of 7:30.

13. It was as easy as taking candy from a diabetic man who no longer wants to eat candy.

14. She had a deep, throaty, genuine laugh, like the sound that a dog makes before it throws up.

15. Their love burned with the fiery intensity of a urinary tract infection.

16. It's basically an illusion and no different than if I were to imagine something else, like Batman riding a flying toaster.

17. If it was any colder, it would be like being in a place that's a little colder than it is here.

18. Joy fills her heart like a silent but deadly passing of gas fills a room with no windows.

19. The bird flew gracefully into the air like a man stepping on a land mine in zero gravity.

20. He felt confused. As confused as a homeless man on house arrest.

21. The revelation that his marriage of 30 years had disintegrated because of his wife's infidelity came as a rude shock, like a surcharge at a formerly surcharge-free ATM.

Ignore People Who Tell You That You Eat Too Much Bacon. YOU DON'T NEED THAT KIND OF NEGATIVITY IN YOUR LIFE.

30 Advantages of Being a Woman

1. We got off the Titanic first.
2. We get to flirt with tech-support men who always return our calls, and are nice to us when we blow up our computers.
3. Our boyfriend's clothes make us look elfin and gorgeous. Guys look like complete idiots in ours.
4. We can be groupies. Male groupies are stalkers.
5. We can cry and get off speeding fines.
6. We've never lusted after a cartoon character or the central female figure in a computer game.
7. Taxis stop for us.
8. Men die earlier, so we get to cash in on the life insurance.
9. We don't look like a frog in a blender when dancing.
10. Free drinks, Free dinners, Free movies . . . (You get the point).
11. We can hug our girlfriends without wondering if they think we're gay.
12. We can hug our girlfriends without wondering if WE'RE gay.
13. New lipstick gives us a whole new lease on life.
14. It's possible to live our whole lives without ever taking a group shower.
15. We don't have to pass gas to amuse ourselves.
16. If we forget to shave, no one has to know.
17. We can congratulate our teammate without ever touching her butt.
18. If we have a zit, we know how to conceal it.
19. We never have to reach down every so often to make sure our privates are still there.
20. If we're dumb, some people will find it cute.
21. We don't have to memorize lines from *Caddyshack* or *Animal House* to fit in.
22. We have the ability to dress ourselves.
23. We can talk to people of the opposite sex without having to picture them naked.
24. If we marry someone 20 years younger, we're aware that we look like an idiot.
25. Our friends won't think we're weird if we ask whether there's spinach in our teeth.
26. There are times when chocolate really can solve all our problems.
27. We'll never regret piercing our ears.
28. We can fully assess people just by looking at their shoes.
29. We know which glass was ours by the lipstick mark.
30. We have enough sense to realize that the easiest way to get out of being lost is to ask for directions.

SPECIAL SECTION

THE TRUE BALONEY HISTORY OF BROADNECK

with

16 Recipes and 2 Stories passed down from the Realm of Queen Arnold the Great

The Glorious Legacy of Queen Arnold the Great

Curtains of opaque, freezing rain fell upon the embarking pilgrims when Queen Arnold left England and her husband, King Urthelbelt the Uneasy, in March of 777 AD for parts unknown.

When Queen Arnold and her party of 777 men, women and children arrived here on the 7th day of the 7th month of the 777th year, the poignant scent of wild honeysuckle wafted from the shore, as a dazzling and propitious blue sky inundated them with light. In other words, when they left England, it was sleeting pretty hard; when they got here, it was nice out. Lucky for them and us!

Looking into the reasons why the great queen chose to settle on what we now call Broadneck is not pertinent to the thread of this article; neither is a detailed account of the ideal society over which Queen Arnold ruled for 77 years. We will simply let the reader infer what went on way back then by mentioning some of the things which *did not* go on way back then.

In the realm of Queen Arnold the Great, there were no loose or hollow proclamations, no manifestly harsh or barbarous conversations, no lamentable instances of extravagance, no lax theories or corresponding practices, no disloyal villagers who disregarded the requirements of public or private courtesy, no disregard of the importance of trees and their care in the life of a happy humanity, no macabre or long-faced brooding, no silly displays of cheap animosity, no undignified disclosures, no vain allurements of fashion, no vulgar yearnings for place, (likewise) no proud schemes for personal aggrandizement, and (consequently) no running after the crass or gauche rewards of life.

Since these things did not exist in her realm —indeed, were not even pondered—the subjects of Queen Arnold did not find themselves disadvantaged by that peculiar malaise which has come to afflict our own time: jaded mental

Sketch of Queen Arnold from the 8th century by one of her many adorers. Her suiters obtained pearls for her from the bountiful oyster bars just inside the mouth of the Magothy near Fairwinds Marina. The letter B on her necklace tells us that this sketch was made after she named our peninsula in honor of the peerless raconteurs, Chuck and Trixie Broadneck.

and emotional weariness from too many so-called reality shows on TV.

Back in the realm of Queen Arnold, travelers from anywhere in the world were welcome—if they could produce a tasty and original soup recipe. Queen Arnold loved soup. Some say that she ate at lease one cup of garlic soup every day for breakfast, and that this is what accounted for her extraordinary good health and longevity. Some insist that the great queen bathed in a tub of yogurt/pepper/cucumber soup each evening before retiring, and that this is what accounted for her enthralling sensual magnetism, her exuberant mirth, her marvelous vivacity, her flawless beauty, her blunt rusticity, and her kiss-provoking lips. All of us should eat more soups and be open to their other uses.

How tasty were these soups? They were scrumptious in the days of Queen Arnold. More than sixty generations of the descendants of Queen Arnold and their friends on Broadneck have enjoyed them and tinkered with the recipes. However slightly, however delicately, each succeeding generation has improved upon these recipes. On the pages following this brief history, we reveal sixteen of these coveted recipes for the most delicious and nutritious soups in the world, palate-and-belly-tested for over a millennium!

We also present on the pages following the recipes, two stories whose plots originated back in Queen Arnold's wondrous realm, and which stories were, in fact, the queen's favorite after-soup stories.

How it usually worked way back then was like this: the Arnoldites ate soup just before darkness oozed around the forest; then as delicately emerging stars and small campfires magnified the sacred and subduing charm of the Broadneck woods, peerless raconteurs like Chuck and Trixie Broadneck (for whom Queen Arnold named our penisula) began to amuse and enchant young and old alike with these fabulous stories. If we were to hear or to read some, if not most, of these stories in their original forms, we would not recognize all the place names, idioms, nuances, people, and events as described. Thank goodness, each generation, right down to the present, has retold these stories, keeping the plots intact, but changing the times and circumstances, carefully eliminating the obsolete phraseology, so that we can understand and relate to every single aspect of these timeless and inspiring tales.

Arnold, Maryland today rests in the center of Broadneck, at the very location where the great queen and her subjects made their abode over 1200 years ago. By all rights, then, Arnold and perhaps all of Broadneck ought to be a national landmark, an historic park, or a protected, touristy place like Williamsburg, Virginia. Yet today, it is not even a city or an incorporated village, but just the name of a US Post Office zip code! The callous indifference of timid and dishonest historians is to blame for this travesty.

We understand the fear of these historians, even the caution of the progressive yet abysmally apologetic ones. The two major implications of recognizing the establishment of the realm of Queen Arnold on Broadneck in the 8th century are extremely pregnant with potential political and social conflict. First, the historians would then be forced to credit the discovery of this continent to a beautiful, sensitive, visionary, intelligent, tree-hugging European woman, something the inherent chauvinism, sexism, and elitism of their profession utterly forbid. And second, logic and truth demand that once the reality and time of the realm of the superlative queen are openly acknowledged, the name of our country will have to be changed from the United States of America to the United States of Arnold.

As historians who thrive on insincerity and falsehood continue to revel in the plaudits of the unlettered mob, let us remind ourselves that since the time of the Tower of Babel, fools have been posing as learned men. But the impostors of today will not succeed in sweeping the name of Queen Arnold the Great into oblivion.

There is coming a time when the moral grandeur of her remote and pristine realm will be acclaimed by the well-reasoned verdict of the jury known as impartial posterity. Then will Queen Arnold rightly be revered as the most august and imperial figure in the empire of historical thought. ✪

Teacher, Would You Punish Me for Something I Didn't Do? OF COURSE NOT. Good, I Didn't Do My Homework.

EARLY WINTER SOUPS FROM THE REALM OF QUEEN ARNOLD

Minestrone Soup

A soup/dinner filled with lots of good things: beans, spinach, onions, peas, tomatoes, leeks, herbs, carrots, even pasta. A real mouth/stomach full that is very filling.

INGREDIENTS (for 6 servings):

2 quarts of beef or chicken stock; 1 can of cooked kidney beans; a small head of celery; a small zucchini; 1/2 lb. of spinach; a small onion; 10 oz. of fresh peas; 1/2 lb. of bacon; 2 carrots; a small cabbage; 1 lb. of tomatoes; 2 leeks; 2 sprigs of parsley; 6 sage leaves; a clove of garlic; 4 Tbsp. of Parmesan cheese; salt and pepper to taste; hot toast squares or cooked pasta.

THE PREPARATION:

Chop the bacon and celery. Put them in a large saucepan and add the stock. Bring it all to a boil and add the peas. Reduce the heat and simmer for 30 minutes. Add the other vegetables, chopped, and continue to simmer for 30 minutes more. Add the kidney beans and simmer for 5 minutes. more. Add salt and pepper to taste and some Parmesan cheese. Ladle the soup into individual serving bowls and add either the hot toast squares or some pasta to each.

SUGGESTED WINE: Zinfandel.

Black Bean Soup

Not your usual bean soup, but a rich and satisfying pot of country culinary pleasure. It is very earthy and direct.
Drink a Fino sherry with it.

INGREDIENTS (for 6 servings):

2 cups of dried black beans; 1/4 lb. of salt pork; 3 cups of beef broth; 3 cups of water; 1/4 lb. of bacon; 1 ham bone (if you happen to have it); 2 Tbsp. of sweet butter; 1 medium onion, peeled and chopped; 2 leeks, whites only, cleaned and chopped; 1/2 cup of chopped celery tops; ½ tsp. of freshly ground black pepper; a large pinch of dried thyme; 1 bay leaf; salt to taste; 4 Tbsp. of Fino sherry; 2 hard-boiled eggs, minced; 1 Tbsp. of minced parsley.

THE PREPARATION:

Wash the beans and remove any dirt. Soak them overnight in cold water to cover.. Drain them and pour into a 6-quart pot. In a 1-quart saucepan, boil the salt pork in water for 4 minutes, drain and rinse it and add to the beans. Also add the broth, water, bacon and the ham bone. Bring it all to a boil, lower to a simmer, cover and cook for 3 hours. Meanwhile, in a saucepan, saute the onion in the butter for 5 minutes. Then add the leeks, carrot and celery tops and continue to saute for 3 minutes more. Put these vegetables into the simmering bean pot along with the pepper, thyme and bay leaf. After 3 hours, remove the pork and bacon and reserve them. Throw away the ham bone and bay leaf. Puree all the bean pot contents and return to the pot. Dice the bacon and pork and return them to the pot. Heat the soup again, adding some beef broth if it gets too thick to be soup. Add the sherry and ladle the soup into serving bowls. Sprinkle a little mixture of minced parsley and egg over each as a garnish.

SUGGESTED WINE: Sandeman Port.

Last year I joined a support group for procrastinators. We haven't met yet.

Two Aerials Got Married. THE CEREMONY WAS BORING BUT THE RECEPTION WAS FANTASTIC.

Borscht (Beet Soup)

Simple, and colorful too. Serve it hot or cold and plop in some sour cream. This Ukrainian version of an old favorite also includes beef for added body.

INGREDIENTS (for 8 servings):

2 medium-sized carrots; 6 medium-sized fresh beets (or canned or frozen equivalent); 1 rib of celery; 1 parsley root; the white parts of 2 leeks; 3 Tbsp. of butter; 2 quarts of water; 2 lbs. of beef brisket; 6 whole peppercorns; 1 bay leaf; 2 tsp. of salt; 2 cups of shredded cabbage; 1 tsp. of vinegar; chopped fresh dill.

THE PREPARATION:

Peel the carrots and the beets. Cut the carrots and 4 beets into julienne strips. Wash the celery, parsley root and leeks, and slice them into thin rounds. Melt the butter in a 3-quart pot and add the vegetables to cook over a low heat for 5 minutes. Add the water, beef, peppercorns, bay leaf and salt. Bring to a boil and reduce the heat to a simmer. Remove the meat after 2 hours, slice it and place in a soup tureen. Add the shredded cabbage to the soup and continue simmering. Grate the other beets. Wrap them in a cheesecloth and squeeze the juice into the vinegar. Add to the soup. Pour the soup over the meat into the tureen and sprinkle with dill. Serve sour cream in a sauce-boat. Good cold, too-especially the next day!

SUGGESTED WINE: Pinot Noir.

LATE WINTER SOUPS FROM THE REALM OF QUEEN ARNOLD

Chicken and Corn Soup

This centuries-old Mexican favorite, bursting with tender strips of chicken and tasty garden fresh vegetables, also is very suitable for freezing.

INGREDIENTS (for 6 servings):

3 lbs. chicken breasts; 4 cups water; 1 small onion, sliced; 1/4 tsp. peppercorns; salt; 2 tsp. coriander seeds; 1 rib of celery, quartered; 1 medium carrot, quartered; 6 ears fresh corn; 2 Tbsp. catsup.

THE PREPARATION:

Place chicken, water, onion, peppercorns, 1 tsp. salt, the coriander seeds, celery and carrot in a large saucepan. Cover and bring to a boil. Reduce heat and simmer for 40 to 50 minutes, until the meat is tender. Remove the chicken and reserve. Strain the stock into another large saucepan. Cut corn off the cobs and add to the chicken stock, cover and cook for 10 minutes. Remove the chicken from the bones, cut into strips, and add to the stock. Stir in the catsup and add salt to taste. Serve hot, with French bread.

SUGGESTED WINE: Chardonnay.

If You Were My Husband, I'd Poison Your Coffee. IF YOU WERE MY WIFE, I'D DRINK IT.

Good Goulash Soup

Simple, and colorful too. Serve it hot or cold No, this soup is not made from the rainy day foot gear, but it is a perfect body warmer for that kind of weather. It will stick to your ribs and warm your heart.

INGREDIENTS (for 10 servings):

6 medium onions; 4 Tbsp. of sweet butter; 3 Tbsp. of cider vinegar; 2 Tbsp. of Hungarian sweet paprika; 2 lbs. of boneless shin beef, cut into 1/2-inch pieces; 12 cups of homemade beef stock; 1 tsp. of caraway seeds; a big pinch of dried marjoram; 4 Tbsp. of flour; salt to your taste; 1 tsp. of freshly ground black pepper; 6 medium all-purpose potatoes.

THE PREPARATION:

Chop the peeled onions coarsely and saute them in the butter in an 8-quart saucepan or pot for about 6 minutes. Stir often. Add the paprika and the vinegar to the onions. Add the beef, 2 cups of the stock, the caraway seeds and the marjoram. Stir, bring to a boil, reduce the heat to a simmer, cover and cook for 45 minutes. In a small bowl, whisk the flour with a little of the stock until it is a smooth paste. Add this to the soup pot and stir in the remaining broth and pepper. Bring it all to a boil, lower the heat and simmer for another 45 minutes. Peel and cube the potatoes into 11-inch pieces. Add them to the soup and simmer, covered, for 15 minutes more.

SUGGESTED WINE: Cabernet.

EARLY SPRING SOUPS FROM THE REALM OF QUEEN ARNOLD

Artichoke Soup

Four green, spiky beauties from Castroville, California, combine with leeks, potatoes, beef broth, and more, to form this very exciting and hearty favorite.

INGREDIENTS (for 6 servings):

4 medium artichokes, peeled, choked and cut into 4 wedges each; 1 lemon rind; 2 leeks; 1 large Idaho potato; 2 celery ribs; 1/2 cup of olive oil; salt and pepper to taste; 4 cups of beef broth; 1 egg yolk; 2 Tbsp. of lemon juice.

THE PREPARATION:

Clean the leeks, removing the green tops. Cut the whites into 1/4-inch rounds. Peel the potato and mince one-quarter of it, dicing the rest. Clean and dice the celery. In a soup pot, add the oil, vegetables and any salt and pepper you like. Saute everything over a high heat for 2 minutes and add the broth. Add the lemon rind, bring everything to a boil, reduce to a strong simmer, cover and cook for 20 minutes. Remove the cover and cook 10 minutes more. Mix the egg yolk with the lemon juice and stir them into the bowl. Ladle into bowls and lay out some crusty, hot Italian bread.

SUGGESTED WINE: Merlot.

My Friend Has a Glass Eye. YOU'D NEVER KNOW IT UNLESS IT CAME OUT IN CONVERSATION.

Clam Chowder

Here is a soup you can whip up at the last minute so you will not have to clam up when the group drops in for a quick supper or snack and nothing is at hand to feed them.

INGREDIENTS (for 6 servings):

1½ cups of canned minced clams or about 2 cups of fresh shucked clams, any kind; 4 slices of bacon cut into cubes; 2 medium potatoes, peeled and diced; 1 onion, peeled and chopped; salt and pepper to taste; 2 cups of light cream; a pinch of thyme; paprika.

THE PREPARATION:

Use the canned clams as they are, but the fresh clams must be put through a coarse grinder after you wash them. Save their liquor. Fry the bacon and cook the potatoes in boiling water to cover for 25 minutes. Remove the browned bacon and saute the chopped onion in the fat. Remove the potatoes and let the water boil down a little. In a large saucepan, combine the bacon, the sauteed onion, the cooked potatoes, the boiling water, the liquor from the clams and bring it all to a boil. Reduce the heat and simmer for 10 minutes. Season to taste. Add the cream slowly and the clams. Heat the soup to the boiling point, but do not boil it! Stir in the pinch of thyme and ladle the chowder into individual serving bowls. Dust the top of each with some paprika.

SUGGESTED WINE: White Zinfandel.

LATE SPRING SOUPS FROM THE REALM OF QUEEN ARNOLD

Gazpacho

Some call this soup a cold salad that is wet. Whatever you call it, it is a perfect cool lunch or dinner followed by a mixed grill and some cheeses. Ole!

INGREDIENTS (for 6 servings):

4 medium-sized ripe tomatoes, peeled and chopped; 2 garlic cloves; salt and pepper to taste; 1 cup of soft bread cubes; 1/a cup of red wine vinegar; 1 medium-sized cucumber, peeled, seeded and chopped; 1 large green pepper, halved, seeded, de-ribbed and diced; 1/4 cup of olive oil; 2 cups of cold water; 2 cups of tomato juice; chopped scallions, croutons.

THE PREPARATION:

In a food processor or blender, add the garlic, bread cubes, salt and the vinegar. Blend to a paste. Add 3 tomatoes, a half of the cucumber and blend again. Mix the puree with the remaining tomato and cucumber pieces and the diced pepper. Bury it in the refrigerator until it gets very cold. Just before serving this gazpacho, stir in the oil, water and tomato juice and taste for seasoning. Garnish the bowls with the scallions and croutons.

How Can You Drop a Raw Egg on a Concrete Floor without Cracking It?
ANY WAY YOU WANT BECAUSE A CONCRETE FLOOR IS VERY HARD TO CRACK.

Asparagus

Fresh or, frozen asparagus, eggs, garlic, olive oil, and cheese, all make an Italian soup you will happily sop up with its own bread. Mangia! Mangia!

INGREDIENTS (for 6 servings):

2 lbs. of fresh or two 10-oz. packages of frozen cut asparagus; 1 garlic clove; 1/3 cup of olive oil; freshly ground pepper; 7 cups of water; 11 tsp. of salt; 4 medium eggs or 3 extra-large; 6 Tbsp. of grated Parmesan cheese; 6 slices of toasted Italian bread.

THE PREPARATION:

Wash the asparagus and break off the stems where they turn white. Discard the white parts. Cut the stems into bite-sized pieces. Frozen asparagus needs only thawing at room temperature. Chop the garlic very fine. In a 2-quart pot saute the garlic and asparagus over a medium heat for about 8 minutes, or until the asparagus are tender enough to eat. Add 5 twists of pepper, the water and salt, and bring to a boil for 5 minutes. Beat the eggs into the cheese and drop into the boiling soup. Quickly stir it all with a wire whisk. The soup will return to a boil and the eggs will be cooked into shreds. Ladle the soup over the bread slices. Eat it while it's hot!

SUGGESTED WINE: Soave.

EARLY SUMMER SOUPS FROM THE REALM OF QUEEN ARNOLD

Tomato

This hot-or-cold soup is very simple and quickly made. But try not to let that fool you. Its speed and freshness are its secrets.
It's good, good! good!

INGREDIENTS (for 4 servings):

11 lbs. of plum tomatoes; 1/3 cup of good olive oil; a crushed garlic clove; 1 Tbsp. of chopped fresh parsley, basil or marjoram; 2½ cups of homemade beef or chicken stock; salt and pepper to taste; sugar.

THE PREPARATION:

Place the tomatoes in a pot of boiling water for about 20 seconds each, and run them under cold water to stop the cooking. Cut out the stem cores and peel each. Slice each tomato across the middle and push the exposed seed with your index finger. Chop the tomatoes and put them in a large heavy saucepan with the olive oil. Cook them over a moderate heat until they melt into the oil, add the garlic and the green herb and cook it all for 5 minutes. Then add the stock, a pinch of sugar and any salt and pepper you want, let it cook 5 minutes more and serve either hot or cold. To make a full luncheon of this great soup add some crostini (slices of Italian bread, spread thickly with grated Parmesan cheese) and then cook in a 325°F oven for 10 minutes. Mama Mia!

SUGGESTED WINE: Bardolino.

Doctor, Can You Give Me Something for My Liver? HOW ABOUT A POUND OF ONIONS?

Pea Pod Soup

Forget shelling peas. This cold soup uses the whole pod along with other goodies for a really different first course. Very healthy-also very cooling on a hot day!

INGREDIENTS (for 8 servings):

1/2 cup of sweet butter; 2 lbs. of peas in their pods; 8 scallions; 2 quarts of homemade chicken broth; 2 Tbsp. of minced fresh tarragon; 16 romaine lettuce leaves; 1/2 cup of creme fraiche; fresh tarragon sprigs.

THE PREPARATION:

Snap off the ends and remove the strings from the pea pods. Slice the scallions into thin slices. Gently melt the butter in a heavy large saucepan. In it saute the pea pods and the scallions for about 5 minutes. Then add the broth and the minced tarragon. Bring it all to a boil and then lower the heat to a simmer for 15 minutes. Add the romaine leaves and simmer 5 minutes more. Add this soup to the food processor in batches and puree as finely as possible. Strain the puree through a fine sieve into a large bowl. Plop in the half cup of creme fraiche and mix it all up. You can also add some salt and pepper, lemon juice and sugar to taste if you like, but they are really not necessary. Cool the soup to room temperature and bury it in the refrigerator for 4 hours (or up to a day) before you serve it. When you serve cold Pea Pod Soup, ladle it into individual bowls and drop a sprig of fresh tarragon on each.

SUGGESTED WINE: Pinot Grigio.

LATE SUMMER SOUPS FROM THE REALM OF QUEEN ARNOLD

Roquefort Soup

One of the world's great blue cheeses made in a famous French mountain cave from sheep's milk gives an unusual taste to this soup. Don't be sheepish. Try it.

INGREDIENTS (for 8 servings):

3 Tbsp. of sweet butter; 1½ cups of minced onions; 1 cup of minced celery ribs; 1½ cups of minced carrots; 6 cups of homemade chicken stock; 1/2 cup of finely diced potatoes; 3 oz. of Roquefort cheese; 3 Tbsp. of heavy cream; 2 egg yolks; salt and pepper to taste; 1 Tbsp. of minced celery leaves.

THE PREPARATION:

In a large saucepan, melt the butter over a low heat and add the onion, celery and carrots. Cook slowly, stirring periodically, until the onions wilt. Pour in the stock and the potato, bring up to a boil over a high heat, then reduce to a simmer for 15 minutes. Mash the Roquefort and the cream together in a small bowl. Then mix in the yolks and a quarter-cup of the hot soup. Take the soup off heat and stir in the cheese mixture. Return the soup to a low heat for a minute. Do not boil it! Season with salt and pepper to your taste. Ladle hot soup plates full and sprinkle some celery leaves over each.

SUGGESTED WINE: Chardonnay.

Where Was the Declaration of Independence Signed? ON THE BOTTOM OF THE PAGE.

Why do I have to press 1 for English when they're just going to transfer me to someone I can't understand?

Seafood Soup

This is a wonderful, ageless recipe from Burgundy and it is meant to match the exquisite wines from that part of France: Macon, Beaujolais, Chablis, etc.

INGREDIENTS (for 6 servings):

1 large carrot, cut into 1/4-inch dice; 3 celery ribs, cut into 1/4-inch dice; 1 onion, finely chopped; the white and light green part of a leek, finely chopped; a 2-lb. red snapper or striped bass, boned with the frame reserved, and filets cut into 1-inch squares; 1 cup of dry white wine; 4 crushed garlic cloves; 6 sprigs of parsley; 2 cups of heavy cream; 3 Tbsp. of sweet butter; 8 oz. of bay scallops; salt and pepper to taste; 2 tomatoes, peeled, seeded and coarsely chopped; cayenne pepper; 1/2 cup of finely shredded basil.

THE PREPARATION:

Put aside 4 cups of the combined carrot, celery, onion and leek. Place the remainder into a stock pot to make a fish stock. Add the fish frame, wine, garlic, parsley and 4 cups of water. Bring to a boil, then reduce the heat to a simmer for 20 minutes. In a large saucepan, reduce the cream over a moderate heat to half. In a large skillet, melt the butter, add the fish and scallops and stir and saute for 4 minutes. Add salt and pepper to your taste and put the fish aside. Strain the fish stock through a fine sieve and return it to the pot. Add the reserved vegetables and bring to a boil. Reduce the heat and simmer, uncovered, for 4 minutes. Add the reduced cream, the tomatoes and the sauteed seafood. Sprinkle in a pinch of the cayenne pepper. Put a large pinch of basil in each bowl and ladle the soup over it.

SUGGESTED WINE: Muscadet.

EARLY FALL SOUPS FROM THE REALM OF QUEEN ARNOLD

Garlic Soup

A whole meal as well as a whole new taste if you know what garlic is now. The cooking and the broth sweeten the pungent cloves. Good!

INGREDIENTS (for 4 servings):

20 crushed cloves of garlic; 3 Tbsp. of olive oil; 2 large boneless slices of smoked ham hocks; 1 Tbsp. of flour; 2½ quarts of beef or chicken broth; 2 large sieved tomatoes; salt and pepper to taste; 1 sprig of thyme; 3 egg yolks; 1/3 cup of olive oil; thick slices of country bread; grated Gruyere cheese.

THE PREPARATION:

In a large saucepan, saute the ham slices in the olive oil until they are golden on both sides. Put the ham aside, covered with foil. Place the crushed garlic in the same pan and saute it slowly, not letting it brown. Add the flour, mix and continue sauteing until it absorbs. Pour in the broth and the tomatoes, add a little salt and a lot of pepper, the thyme and bring the soup to a boil for 15 minutes. Beat the egg yolks in a tureen with the olive oil and gradually pour in the hot soup, stirring as you do. Serve the soup with the bread slices on the side, to which you have added the cheese and browned in a 375°F oven. Slice the ham and arrange it with the bread.

SUGGESTED WINE: Chianti.

Japanese Mushroom Soup

Dried Japanese Shiitake mushrooms give this Oriental soup its unusual taste, and to help it along, include lemon zest and a colorful vegetable assortment.

INGREDIENTS (for 6 servings):

2½ cups of homemade chicken stock; 1 carrot, cut into 1-inch slices; half a celery rib, cut into the same lengths; a small onion, sliced; 4 sprigs of flat parsley; 1 oz. of dried Japanese Shiitake mushrooms; 1 Tbsp. of sake; 2 tsp. of Teriyaki sauce; 6 small spinach leaves; 18 long slivers of lemon zest; 1 Tbsp. of thinly sliced scallions.

THE PREPARATION:

In a saucepan, combine the stock, carrot, celery, onion and parsley with 2½ cups of water. Bring all to a boil, reduce the heat and simmer for 10 minutes. Wash the mushrooms very carefully and add them to the stock and simmer, partially covered, for 10 more minutes. Remove the vegetables (not the mushrooms). Lightly season the broth with the sake and Teriyaki sauce. Remove the middle stem from the spinach leaves and place the two parts at the bottom of each of the 6 serving bowls. Ladle the soup over the leaves and garnish each bowl with 3 strips of zest and a big pinch of the scallions.

SUGGESTED WINE: Alsace Pinot Blanc.

LATE FALL SOUPS FROM THE REALM OF QUEEN ARNOLD

Turkey Soup

This big bird makes a big soup. Cook the turkey stock the same way you would a chicken stock. Your guests will "gobble, gobble" this soup up!

INGREDIENTS (for 8 servings):

1/4 cup of sweet butter; 2 ribs of celery, chopped; 1 large onion, chopped; 2 medium potatoes, peeled and chopped; 2 quarts of homemade turkey stock; 2 tsp. of chopped fresh dill; 1/4 cup of light cream; salt and pepper to taste; 1 Tbsp. of chopped parsley.

THE PREPARATION:

In a large saucepan, melt the butter, stir in the celery, onions and potatoes, cover and cook slowly for 15 minutes. Stir once or twice so the vegetables do not burn. Pour in half the turkey stock and continue for 10 minutes. Then puree the vegetables in a processor and add in the rest of the stock. Add the dill, salt and pepper to taste and reheat it all. Thin the soup with some of the cream and reheat it to simmering. Pour into a large tureen and sprinkle with the chopped parsley.

SUGGESTED WINE: Chardonnay.

"To Do Is to Be" - NIETZSCHE. "To Be Is to Do" - KANT. "Do Be Do Be Do" - SINATRA.

1st of 2 Stories Passed Down from the Realm of Queen Arnold:

THE PICCOLO PLAYER AND THE BELL RINGERS
Sunday, Monday, and Tuesday

Sunday Morning

Damion Siggs Siksics, the pastor of the local Broad Neck United National Co-Denominationalists (BUNCOS) got in serious trouble this past Sunday. At the morning service, the mindful minister expected the addition of a new piccolo player to pass without undue note, but how wrong he was!

As eyewitnesses recount it, Pastor Siksics asked the congregation, estimated at more than 600, to turn to hymn number 66 as he nodded to the new piccolo player to pick up the tune. But the piccolo player, whose gangly arms appeared to have been squeezed from tubes, looked like a fawn startled in the darkness by a hunter's flashlight. Pastor Siksics understood that the new piccolo player found hymn number 66 too difficult to play. The pastor then told everyone to turn to the less complicated hymn number 33.

But the piccolo player, his eyes blinking in astonished silence, considered that hymn even harder to play.

Then the pastor smiled and told everyone to turn to hymn number one, the congregation's favorite, and the very anthem of his denomination "Here Comes Peter Cottontail"—but when the new piccolo player, with beads of amber sweat pouring down his curly black sideburns, looked at the notes, he shook his head as if he thought it to be the most difficult melody in the whole hymnal.

"Too much activity in the treble clef," he sincerely shrugged.

The nimble-footed pastor turned his back on the congregation and walked over to talk to the piccolo player whose homely facial features now

rearranged themselves into a sheepish grin. Just then, someone stood up in the rear and yelled, "The piccolo player is a stupid tone-deaf klutz." By the time the bejeweled, enrobed, unlucky pastor turned around to see who it was, the person had sat back down.

It took but a few moments for this flabbergasted yet gritty sophist to regain his composure as he walked calmly back to the pulpit. He studiously eyeballed the entire assembly, pointed a hammy forefinger up into the air, and commanded with unpalatable pietistic authority, "Will the person who just called the piccolo player a stupid tone-deaf klutz please stand up?"

No one budged.

Then, thinking quickly, the pastor said, "All right, will the person sitting next to the person who called the piccolo player a stupid tone-deaf klutz please stand up?" Still, no one in this crafty, controversial, conscientious congregation so much as allowed the slightest shadow of even a vague, ironic sneer to show up on his or her face.

Which Spa Machine Should I Use to Impress the Girls? TRY THE ATM IN THE LOBBY.

The curious, calculating, yet unconvincing cleric thought about just stopping, walking out from behind the pulpit and going home. But if he were to stop now, what? The breakdown of order and respect? The triumph of flaunting insolence? An incursion of the loud, the vulgar, and the morally obtuse? Howling chaos? Impaired prestige for himself and his denomination? Impecunious exile even?

But he remained undaunted as his voice reached a pitch of husky shrillness, "Will the person sitting next to the person sitting next to the person who called the piccolo player a stupid tone-deaf klutz please stand up!" he demanded.

The tone of his voice must have sounded insincere and trivial, like a helium balloon disappearing in the distance, without any weight, because, once again, there was no response from the congregation.

Pastor Siksics, clearing his throat of rumbling phlegm, began again, certain that sooner or later someone would feel the piddling tug of sham religious responsibility and identify the villain. "Will the person sitting next to the person sitting next to the person sitting next to the person who called the piccolo player a stupid tone-deaf klutz please stand up?"

The persistent clergyman's voice cracked with a courteous kind of weariness. Once again, the members of the congregation, evidently untouched by the melancholy yet heavy-handed drama, remained quiet, motionless, and bleary-eyed. In a proper Sunday morning setting such as this, time could only ooze sluggishly.

This was a sermon without any of the preacher's usual gaudy embellishments, and many of his listeners were glad for that. The obese orator wondered to himself how far this might go. He hoped most of his followers would retain their honest admiration for him, but at the same time, he could not blame the few visitors in his audience if they began to feel some genuine cynicism toward him and the regal and rarefied religious movement he had been leading and hoped to continue to lead.

The relentless rector now looked behind himself for courage to the overly sensitive piccolo player who now sat whimpering like a homesick puppy. Pastor Siksics turned quickly back to the members of his flock, his mind beginning to drift into a fuzzy haze. He thought about the mistake he had made the previous Sunday when three women attended the service with his loyal follower, Harry Butz. He was thrilled to see many new faces, so he said, "I am delighted to see all of our visitors, especially the ladies with Harry Butz." The deacon's diction was not as precise as it ought to have been and many gasped or groaned, understanding him to have said "the ladies with hairy butts." Standing there in a pose of jaded dignity thinking of last week's faux pas, and this week's piccolo predicament, he somehow found the strength to go on. His audience looked at the arteries throbbing in his neck and awaited more of what by now they surely considered relentless repetitive dribble.

The patriarchal, persistent, prying, pestiferous, plainspoken, yet unpersuasive pastor, thinking he saw the light of a flickering conscience, however dim, in the face of a big, ripe-bodied blond woman of about thirty with a dusting of artificial freckles on her cheeks, preached out politely but poignantly, "Will the person sitting next to the person sitting next to the person sitting next to the person sitting next to the person who called the piccolo player a stupid tone-deaf klutz please stand up?"

His hope that someone would stand up this time turned out again to be grossly over-inflated optimism. No reaction from the lumpish blond, no reaction from anybody at all. The statuesque, illiterate slobs in the parasitic pastor's audience were either enormously complacent or just too hopelessly befogged to see this pathological agitation for what it was. The pious preacher, who would have had a good career as a forger if he had decided to go that way, resolved to continue down the prodding path he had chosen.

But, as he pondered the inexplicable reluctance of his listeners to respond to his

Always Remember: You Are Unique JUST LIKE EVERYONE ELSE.

promptings, his bewilderment turned into feverish determination. He could induce a response! He would induce a response! But he would not play the sanctimonious hypocrite. He would issue no threats, no insulting invectives, no indelicate denunciations, no obscure intimations, no loquacious assurances, no lukewarm calls for repentance—just a continuation, a magnification of a simple request. This time he would do it with a bit more of a magisterial emphasis, accompanying his words with a skillful backward tilt of the head in a magnetic beckoning motion: "Will the person sitting next to the person sitting next to the person sitting next to the person sitting next to the person sitting next to the person who called the piccolo player a stupid tone-deaf klutz please stand up?"

Against vacant stupidity, even the greatest of the gods vies in vain.

The hampered homilist expected obedient compliance, but mute insensibility is what met him instead. The stubborn perfectionist looked to the back left of the church, then to the back right, then to the front right, then to the front left, like a dog, peeing his boundaries into good order. The methodical minister considered his anger to be a lot like his underwear—he knew it would be indecent of him to let too much show. But repressing his true feeling, he knew, could lead to a degrading collapse into a dreary, hysterical depression.

"Godammit," he screamed, "Will the person sitting next to the person sitting next to the person sitting next to the person sitting next to the person sitting next to the person sitting next to the person who called the piccolo player a stupid tone-deaf klutz please stand up!"

The most venerable and vehement vicar surveyed the portentous gulf between his demand and the lack of reaction in his congregation. Would his followers acknowledge a tardy recognition of their responsibility to speak up and help identify the vile desecrator of the piccolo player's fragile reputation? No, not this time. The congregation met the pastor's stony stare with polite indifference. And so again, he beguiled the listless souls in his audience with, "Will the person sitting next to the person sitting next to the person sitting next to the person sitting next to the person sitting next to the person sitting next to the person sitting next to the person who called the piccolo player a stupid tone-deaf . . ."

Just then a man stood up and interrupted the pastor by saying, "Please, that's enough. But don't get me wrong. I am not the person sitting next to the person sitting next to the person sitting next to the person sitting next to the person sitting next to the person sitting next to the person sitting next to the person sitting next to the person who called the piccolo player a stupid tone-deaf klutz.

"And I am not the person sitting next to the person sitting next to the person sitting next to the person sitting next to the person sitting next to the person who called the piccolo player a stupid tone-deaf klutz.

"And I am not the person sitting next to the person sitting next to the person sitting next to the person sitting next to the person who called the piccolo player a stupid tone-deaf klutz.

"And I am not the person sitting next to the person sitting next to the person sitting next to the person sitting next to the person who called the piccolo player a stupid tone-deaf klutz.

"And I am not the person sitting next to the person sitting next to the person sitting next to the person who called the piccolo player a stupid tone-deaf klutz.

"And I am not the person sitting next to the person sitting next to the person who called the piccolo player a stupid tone-deaf klutz.

"And I am not the person sitting next to the person who called the piccolo player a stupid tone-deaf klutz.

"And I am not the person who stood up and called the piccolo player a stupid tone-deaf klutz."

But what I and the rest of us in the congregation want to know is," the articulate joke-ender continued, "Who called that stupid tone-deaf klutz a piccolo player?"

Get married early in the morning. That way, if it doesn't work out, you haven't wasted a whole day.

Monday Morning

That was Sunday morning. On Monday morning at 9 a.m., a man with both arms in a cast answered Reverend Siksics' want ad for a new bell ringer. Because of the obvious handicap, Pastor Siksics dismissed the man's pleas for the job until he insisted he could ring the bell loud enough by running into it with his forehead and nose. The curious, compassionate, and often rantingly optimistic minister gave the pathetic initiate all he really wanted—a chance. The rugged and resolute imbecile ran straight into the bell with his forehead and nose, and it rang so loud that hundreds of parishioners heard it, and, thinking it announced some kind of special service, or maybe the hiring of a new piccolo player, began making their ways to the church.

Unfortunately, the proud but accident-prone idiot hit the bell so hard that he bounced right out the bell tower window, screaming like a saint sent to hell by mistake, all 220 feet down to the cement courtyard below.

He lay writhing and groaning and bleeding as the slouching parishioners sauntered up to him. When Pastor Siksics got down from the tower, one of his least brainwashed followers asked him, "What's going one here? Who is this injured man? What's his name?"

The most venerable and deferential parson scratched his shock of red hair, recently dyed for the religious holidays, and said, "You know, I honestly don't know who he is. I forgot to get his name, but his face rings a bell."

Tuesday Morning

That was Monday morning. On Tuesday morning, another very hapless and disheveled, yet unembarrassed human being with both arms in a cast showed up at the bell tower. He said to the cherubic churchman, "That man yesterday was my brother. I'm here to uphold our family honor. We may be accident prone, but we can hold down a job! I'll run into the bell with my face just like my brother did."

At first, the great religious leader feigned polite indifference and refused to allow the shaken, downtrodden, and impoverished whimperer to try to ring the bell. But then, like a pimple on your chin you just can't leave alone, Pastor Siksics began to feel the dull, nagging pull of this bold chump's troubles.

Once he had permission, the non-procrastinating, self-willed dabbler ran straight into the bell with his face. It rang so loud that hundreds of parishioners in the area heard it, and, thinking it announced some kind of special service, again began making their ways to the church. Unfortunately, the tough but hapless fall guy hit the bell so hard that he bounced right out the bell tower window, hit his head on the cement 220 feet below, and died.

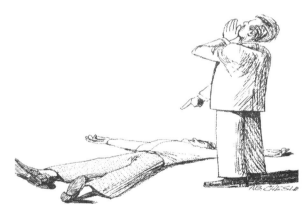

The first prompt and devoted parishioner to arrive yelled up to the now somewhat timid and addled clergyman in the bell tower, "Hey, Pastor Siksics, who is this dead man? What's his name?"

The dutiful, mooching windbag in the bell tower responded honestly, yelling down, "Come to think of it, I didn't get his name either, but he's a dead ringer for his brother."

You can imagine the kinds of things that happened the rest of the week. ◆

Chinese Pet Store Sign: BUY ONE DOG, GET ONE FLEA.

2nd of 2 Stories Passed Down from the Realm of Queen Arnold:

SUPER SHREWD SOFIA

Just last fall, a cook name Sofia offered her services through a want ad in the local paper. Though she was but a student with below average grades at the community college, she wore shoes with bright red heels, and when she went out in them, she gave herself great airs, and thought herself very fine indeed.

Sofia was not dumb in school but, by arbitrary academic standards, just maybe a little too skeptical, and somewhat impatient. While her class studied the *Dialogues of Plato*, for example, Sofia skipped ahead to see how Socrates died. When she found out that with his dying breath, Socrates had insisted that a chicken be sacrificed to a stone idol, Sofia said to herself, "This man is a moron," and forfeited further interest in the fine points of Platonic philosophy. As a general rule in all of her other classes, however, she favored the headlong vigor of sheer improvisation to any kind of analytical method.

Usually, when she returned from school to her small basement apartment, she would take a drink of wine to refresh herself, and as that gave her an appetite, she would take some of the best of whatever she was cooking, until she had had enough, "Because," she said, "a cook must know how things taste."

Now it happened that one chilly day in late November, a gentleman by the name of Samuel McGritty saw her advertisement and telephoned her, explaining, "I am expecting an influential guest tomorrow evening and I should like to treat him to an unforgettable repast here at my home on the Little Magothy River. Can you come in the early afternoon and prepare a pair of geese?"

"Oh, yes sir, geese are one of my specialties," Sofia fibbed.

Mr. McGritty and Sofia agreed on a very fair price, they both thought, payable in advance. Really though, in matters such as this, Mr. McGritty was generous to a touching and sometimes pathetic degree.

Mr. McGritty's directions were easy to follow: down Bay Head Road and left on Harmony Lane, until you see the big purple mailbox.

When they met at his doorstep the next day, Mr. McGritty, a twice-divorced, mustachioed man in his late thirties, found in Sofia a fresh and unsuspected loveliness. Her long, soft, wheat-colored hair glistened with golden streaks. A faint, transient, wistful smile lightened her face. Despite her youth, she seem to him surrounded by an aura of feminine professionalism. His carefully appraising eye enjoyed the match of her red heels and pink sweater, but he ignored Sofia's subtle semi-sassy seductive strutting. The fixed rules of good breeding regulated his interest in that direction, his feelings tempered by a sentimental fervor for high moral ideals.

Understandably then, Sofia thought of Mr. McGritty as measured and urbane, a man full of decision and dignity. She liked the curve of his mouth, the warmth in his eyes, the strength she saw in his hands, and the flecks of gray in his dark, slightly mussed hair. She also liked the subtle, vanishing aspect of Mr. McGritty's chin. She didn't expect any classical sexist, male-chauvinist put-downs from him.

"Oh Sofia, my dear," he said. "How can I ever thank you enough for coming on such short notice! This dinner this evening could mean the addition of a very important client for my corporation."

Sofia soon discovered that Mr. McGritty was a no-nonsense businessman and instructor. He laid

My Favorite Outdoor Activity Is Going Back Inside.

down what he expected of her in an unflinching, vigorous, and meticulous style. The geese, which he had shot himself, lay plucked and thawed on the kitchen table. They were to be skewered and taken to the charcoal broiler under the tree out back on the patio below the deck, and roasted to perfection. When talking business, Mr. McGritty spoke with a uniformity of emphasis that made his words stand out like the raised print for the blind: "The china is here, the cutlery is there, these are the spices I want you to use, but don't use these herbs," and so on and so on.

Sofia lacked a proper feel for Mr. McGritty's business talk. All too many of his sentences—the verbs, nouns, adjectives and everything—sounded to her like a lot of blah, blah, blah. But you couldn't tell that she wasn't listening. No matter what she was really thinking, her face always looked bright with interest and interrogation. In fact, Mr. McGritty, as astute a critic of human nature as he was, did not detect even the tiniest iota of rashness, folly, or ingratitude in Sofia's person.

Sofia, the cooking artist, worked by inspiration and not from detailed engineering specifications. She had her own way of doing things which had served her well up until this point in her life. That is what she would say to someone who might consider her woeful indifference to her employer's directions a huge debit in her line of work.

"Now Sofia," he said, "I must attend to some business in the city. I will be back at five. I expect our guest to arrive from the airport by taxi a little after that. Let us eat promptly at six."

"Very well, Sir," Sofia said as Mr. McGritty departed.

Sofia started by making a basting sauce using herbs and spices of her own choosing, and let the birds soak in it for an hour or so. As she strolled about the house observing various beautiful and rare *objets d'art*, she drifted into a rosy zone of contemplation. She pondered the differences between her lifestyle and Mr. McGritty's. She thought about her childhood, about her seven brothers and six sisters, about her mother, the waitress, and about her father, the security guard. How sweet and reasonable the pale images of those who smile from some dim corner of our memories! How could she have expected her parents to have saved enough money to put her through some fancy college? On the other hand, as far as Mr. McGritty was concerned, she concluded that as a child, he had been all too selfishly pampered by overabundance.

To keep in her mind some kind of prince and pauper comparison, she had to passionately exaggerate the menacing shadows of hunger and poverty in her own upbringing. With that came the notions that her matchless character had been molded by the random and austere hand of adversity, and her career as some kind of important person had been sacrificed to a futile sort of treadmill. She hugged the thought of her own unknown and unapplauded integrity.

She returned to the soaking birds and thought about them for a while. They, too, like humans, were subject to the vicissitudes of fortune. Then she skewered them and placed them on the spit and commenced to roast them over a low fire.

As five o'clock neared, the birds began to brown, and were nearly done. Sofia went to the front door and looked out. The sun had set behind the pine trees up the lane. In a sky stained with purple, the moon slowly rose. But the two expected diners were nowhere to be seen.

"If Mr. McGritty and his guest don't hurry up and get here," Sofia said to herself, "I'll have to take the birds away from the fire. It's a pity and a shame not to eat them now, just when they are done to a turn."

Sofia returned to the patio and took the fowls from before the fire. "I've been standing here for so long in front of the fire," she said, "and now I am hot and thirsty. Who knows when they will come! In the meantime, I'll pour a bit of Mr McGritty's wine over some ice and have a drink." So she took up a mug, filled with ice and Rosé d'Anjou, and saying, "Here's to me!" took a most generous swig.

"One good drink deserves another," she said, "and it should not be cut short." If Sofia had any blind spots, they were her insensibility to moral perspective and proportion, and her numbness to injustice—so far as her appetite was concerned. So she took another hearty swig. Then she went and put the fowls down to the fire again, and, basting them with her butter sauce, she turned the spit briskly around. And they began to smell so good that Sofia saying, "I must find out if they really are all right," licked her fingers, and then cried, "Well, I never. I've outdone myself again! These birds are good; it's a sin and a shame that no one is here to eat them!" She felt a gripping twinge in her belly that she found impossible to resist acknowledging.

She ran through the house to the window to see if Mr. McGritty or his guest was coming; but since she could see nobody, she went back to her fowls. She found the tardiness of the two gentlemen exasperating to the nth degree. "Why, one of the wings is burning!" she cried, "I had better eat it and get it out of the way." So she cut it off and ate it up, and it tasted good, and then with uncommon prudence and discernment, she thought, "I had better cut off the other too, in case Mr. McGritty or his guest should miss anything." And when both wings had been disposed of, she again went and looked for Mr. McGritty or his guest, but still they did not come.

"Who knows," said she, "whether they are coming or not. They may have met and stopped at a restaurant somewhere." She realized that inclinations building inside of her ran counter to all established customs, but after a moment she said, "I might as well make myself happy. First I will make sure of a good drink and then of a good meal, and when I am finished, I'll feel wonderful."

What others might consider insolent and riotous excess, Sofia often saw as the natural and inevitable course of events. So she ran for more ice and more wine for her mug and, although those who had aged and bottled this particular vintage intended it as a kind of nectar to be delicately sipped at leisure, Sofia sloshed it down in two great gulps. Then she ate up one of the fowls with great relish. When that was done, and still neither Mr. McGritty nor his guest had come, Sofia eyed the other fowl, saying, "What one is the other must be also, things equal to the same thing are equal to each other, it is only fair that they should be treated alike. Perhaps when I have had another drink, I shall be able to manage it."

So she permitted herself the liberty of another hearty drink. Should she, or should she not? Sofia was not one to become lost in a labyrinth of conjecture. She was not one to fight against the overpowering forces of circumstance and necessity. And most certainly she was not one to be paralyzed by infirmity of purpose. So the second fowl went the way of the first.

Oh, she felt good. She now savored a spacious sense of the amplitude of life's possibilities. Where once she was plagued to a small degree by nagging doubts about the ethics of giving complete license to her desires, she now embraced the soothing view that what she had done was justifiable—given the particular urgency of the situation. Availing herself of this pragmatic intellectual conception, she poured herself yet another drink, and proceeded to minutely expose the illogic of any remaining qualms to merited ridicule. Giving credence to any of her misgivings after the fact, she knew from experience, led only to morbid and subjective brooding.

Not long after she finished eating the second goose and had worked her thinking into an ironclad dogma, Mr. Samuel McGritty came back.

"Oh, I'm sorry I'm late, Sofia. That darn beltway traffic! But hurry up," he implored, "I saw my guest back there at the traffic light in a taxi. He'll be here any minute!"

Despite feeling a little jaded from her gastronomical exertions, Sofia managed to maintain an optimistic after-dinner mood. "Yes, sir, Mr. McGritty," she answered, "the geese are ready. I have them warming in the oven."

In a frenzy of apprehension, Mr. McGritty went to see that the table was properly laid out, and, taking the great carving knife with which he meant to carve the fowls, he stepped out back on the deck and began to sharpen it with great pitch.

Sofia heard the taxi pull into the driveway. Presently came the guest knocking very genteelly at the front door. Sofia went to meet him, and although under other circumstances she might find herself responding to the pull of this short and handsome stranger's masculinity, this situation called for her to make one of life's many ironical adjustments. When the guest caught sight of her, she put her finger on her lips saying, "Shh! Get out of here as fast as you can. If that psycho catches you, he's going to cut you. He's invited you to supper, but he really means to lop off your ears! Listen to him sharpening the knife!"

The guest, having no reason to disbelieve her, and hearing the noise of the sharpening, became infused with an unwholesome terror and bolted down the steps and away from the house.

(It is necessary here to point out a few things about the would-be guest lest those readers who are thinking only of the stranger's brief appearance at the door and Sofia's possible affection for him, tend to idealize his personality. Let me assure you that this man's good looks and unimpeachable correctness of demeanor are sadly counterbalanced by numerous faults. We could now criticize him with unsparing vigor, but that would only disturb our own sanity and quietness of soul. Briefly, it is the stranger's wont to espouse, however politely, theories rooted in immeasurable miscalculation and falsity. He believes that Socrates was the wisest man who ever lived and, more significantly, he is a foe of immoderation and excess. He and Sofia could never have made a pair).

Immediately upon the guest's precipitous departure, Sofia ran screaming to Mr. McGritty, "What an awful man you have asked to the house!" she cried.

"What do you mean," he demanded.

"Why, he has gone and run away with my pair of fowls I had just dished up."

This unexpected information did insufferable violence to Mr. McGritty's emotions. He felt an iciness, a sinking, a sickening of the heart. His hurrying thoughts clamored for utterance.

"Such despicable conduct!" he said, feeling very sorry about the fowls. "That rat might at least have left me one so that I could have something to eat." Mr. McGritty, now suddenly infected with a feverish kind of dissatisfaction, and throwing a ton's weight of resolve upon his muscles, ran out the door after him, chasing him down the lane in the moonlight, hollering for him to stop. But the guest made out like he didn't even hear him.

Nevertheless, Mr. McGritty, the knife still in his hand, kept running after him, crying out, "Only one! Only one!" meaning that the guest should let him have at least one of the fowls and not take both. But the guest, reading so much lately about madmen such as this, thought he meant to have only one of his ears, and so he ran much faster that he might get away with both of them safe.

It is a common error among ignorant people to think that C students from working class backgrounds must suffer in their economic intercourse with polished society. When Mr. McGritty, disheveled and distraught, returned from his unsuccessful pursuit of one of two imaginary fowls carried by a real but estranged ex-potential client, he felt so guilty about involving Sofia in such an embarrassment that he was moved to unaccustomed tears. Overwhelmed with self-reproach, he gave her twice again the amount of money he had given her to begin with —as a token of thanks for what he believed she had endured on his behalf.

Although he never managed to seat a guest in her presence or taste her cooking, on many occasions since, he has been proud to recommend Sofia to his friends on Broad Neck as a chef *par excellence*. ◆

Waiter, There's a Dead Fly in My Wine. I THOUGHT YOU LIKED WINE WITH A LITTLE BODY IN IT.

COMPLETE TREE & SHRUB CARE

RICHARD'S
Tree Care
410 - 757 - 5793
www.richardstreecare.com

richardstreecare@aol.com

47 YEARS SERVING BROADNECK

Cabling

Pruning, Take-Down and Removal

Pre-Construction Consultation

Deep-Root Fertilization

Lightning Protection

15-Yard Roll-Off Dumpsters

Disease Control Programs

Monitoring Programs

Licensed Tree Expert No. 534
MDA License No. 24222

Member
Maryland Arborist Association
Tree Care Industry Association
Arbor Day Foundation

FREE ESTIMATES

Quality Care Automotive, Inc.

- Engine Installation • Customizing
- Maintenance • General Repairs
- Shocks • Struts • Brakes
- Tune-Ups

- ASE Certified • Full Maintenance & Diagnostics for Cars and Trucks
- All Major Credit Cards
- Accounts Welcome

410 - 757 - 9000

Conveniently Located at the End of the Cape Shopping Center
Hours: 8 a.m. to 5 p.m.
Monday - Friday
Opened Jan. 3, 2000
Rusty Rucks Owner/Operator.
Broadneck Resident 46 Years

SERVICE YOU CAN TRUST

What Do You Call an Extremely Obese Psychic? A FOUR CHIN TELLER.